A SHORT HISTORY OF SPANISH LITERATURE
REVISED AND UPDATED EDITION

THE GOTHAM LIBRARY
OF THE NEW YORK UNIVERSITY PRESS

The Gotham Library is a series of original works and critical studies published in paperback primarily for student use. The Gotham hardcover edition is primarily for use by libraries and the general reader. Devoted to significant works and major authors and to literary topics of enduring importance, Gotham Library texts offer the best in literature and criticism.

Comparative Literature and Foreign Language Literature: Robert J. Clements, Editor
Comparative and English Language Literature: James W. Tuttleton, Editor

A SHORT HISTORY OF SPANISH LITERATURE

REVISED AND UPDATED EDITION

James R. Stamm

NEW YORK · NEW YORK UNIVERSITY PRESS

COPYRIGHT © 1979 BY NEW YORK UNIVERSITY PRESS
PRINTED IN THE UNITED STATES OF AMERICA

Library of Congress Cataloging in Publication Data

Stamm, James R
   A short history of Spanish literature

   (The Gotham library)
   Bibliography: p.
   Includes index
   1.   Spanish literature—History and criticism.
I. Title.
PQ6033.S7   1979   860'.9   79-16467
ISBN 0-8147-7791-0
ISBN 0-8147-7792-9 pkb.

PREFACE

Spain as a country and a culture has always had its detractors, its apologists, and its enthusiasts. The diffusion of Spanish culture has been considerably inhibited by the operation of the *leyenda negra,* the "black legend," a phrase which expresses, perhaps exaggeratedly, the low opinion in which Spanish culture has been held by other European nations since the beginning of the Reformation. The Spanish sometimes explain the existence of the *leyenda negra* by the envy which other nations feel for Spain's enormous accomplishments in many areas of human endeavor. The Protestant countries seem to have felt that Spanish culture was aborted by the choking obscurantism of the Inquisition; the Mediterranean countries, by the physical and social isolation of the peninsula; the industrial nations, by the inability or unwillingness of Spain to overcome its feudalism and to keep up with the progress of science and the industrial revolution, with their attendant social reforms. Some of these charges may contain a grain or so of truth; others are easily refuted by the historian. The censorship and control of Spain's cultural life under the Inquisition, which was not a Spanish invention, comes off comparatively well against similar attempts in England and France during the same period, and very well indeed in comparison with events in Germany and Russia in this century. Nor can much of a case be made for Spanish isolationism when we bear in mind that, almost from the unification of Spain, Hapsburgs and Bourbons occupied the throne. Nor can a necessary link be shown to exist between technological development, democratic political institutions, and the creation of great works of art. Certainly the phenomenon is complex, and none of these reasons is adequate to explain why a major and innovating national literature has been so little known and appreciated beyond its own geographical and linguistic frontiers.

While there is hardly a widely read and broadly educated person in the world today who is totally unfamiliar with the *Poema de mío Cid, Don Quijote,* the theater of Lope de Vega and García Lorca, and the novels and essays of Unamuno, the number among that group who have read any significant part of these works in the original language is probably quite small. Modern and good translations of major Spanish works appear in increasing numbers, and we may hope that the same road that leads most contemporary readers to Homer, Dante, Goethe, Molière, Ibsen, and the Russian novel will bring increasing numbers to the masterpieces of Spanish creativity. The old saw, *traduttore, traditore*—translator, traitor—points out the limitations (and hints at the difficulties) of the art. Still, we must admit that it is the rare person who reads in more than two or three languages with comfort and full understanding. The complexity of our pluralistic society demands that much of our knowledge of literary achievements outside our native language be acquired through translations and résumés.

As more good translations of important Spanish works appear, it is more and more possible to acquire familiarity with isolated works and authors without reading Spanish. It is more difficult to acquire a meaningful, panoramic orientation with this handicap. Histories of Spanish literature have been available in English since the middle of the nineteenth century. The work of Ticknor, Longfellow, Washington Irving, and others identified the fecundity of the literature for the American reading public, although perhaps these early Hispanists overstressed its exotic aspect. Since their time, important studies of all periods, of specific authors and genres, and of the overall development of the literature have been made by American and British Hispanists, and there are numerous professional journals which deal in whole or in part with Spanish literary themes. Unfortunately, most of the histories of Spanish literature in English are either out of date or out of print. Recent works, excellent though they are within their frames of reference, seem to be either too sketchy to give a comprehensive view of the literature and its relationship to Western traditions, or they are so massive and detailed as to overpower the reader with a welter of names, dates, and titles of minor works and writers.

A Short History of Spanish Literature has tried to fill a vacant middle place between the skeletal outline and the overfleshed compendium of all who wrote in the language, by giving a meaningful idea of the most important writers, movements, ideas, and works which have had resonance and progeny in Spain and abroad. It was inevitable that many writers in a given school or tradition should be excluded, some of these being figures of considerable interest to the specialist. A selected bibliography of more extensive and more specialized studies in English is included for the use of those who may want to pursue the subject. I have presupposed a general familiarity with the main traditions and currents of Western literature. The summaries at the end of each chapter are given to aid the reader to clarify his understanding of major periods and general lines of development in Spanish literature.

I have limited the scope of this study to the literature of Spain itself for reasons of economy and clarity. The Hispanic literature of the New World, both in the colonial period and following the movements of American independence, is closely related to that of peninsular Spain, and certainly there have been both influence and feedback. To present the total picture would require a much more extensive treatment than the present *Short History* is intended to provide. The one notable exception is an inevitable one. The impact of the Nicaraguan poet Rubén Darío has been so massive that his name and work could not be omitted without doing violence to the whole course of modern Spanish poetry. Portuguese and Catalan literature have been excluded for the same reasons of brevity and focus.

All translations are mine. They are limited except in a few cases to poetry. Prose passages, however well chosen, usually do not give an adequate idea of an author's style and personality unless they are lengthy samples, and I felt that this was to be avoided. Spanish poetry, while certainly harder to translate effectively, can often give in a few lines a faithful and exact reflection of styles, movements, and concepts within the national literature. Thus, poetry, especially lyric poetry, has been cited extensively, not only by reason of its intrinsic value, but also as providing significant and concise clues to the spirit and temperament of a given age.

James R. Stamm

PREFACE TO THE REVISED AND UPDATED EDITION

A dozen years have passed since the first edition of this *Short History* was published. The original Preface still defines the concept and limitations of the book. The major alterations that have been made are an updating of the content. Much has happened in Spain and in Spanish literature since 1966. Tastes have changed, writers who showed promise then have either emerged into full creative maturity or have not done so, and new criticism and scholarship have made it necessary to recast some judgments which seemed quite sound and solid at that earlier time. The gradual relaxing of political and moral censorship has made it possible to use themes and settings which were well beyond the pale in the early sixties. The death of Francisco Franco and the establishment of a constitutional monarchy, although very recent events at this writing, are already having a profound effect on the quality and substance of Spanish literature, especially in the theater and the novel. A new measure of economic prosperity has markedly changed the tone of Spanish society in many ways. All of these factors are reflected in current Spanish writing, and so a new edition of this guide seems warranted.

Again, the commitment to brevity has been a painful but necessary consideration. As before, the interested reader is encouraged to use this book as a starting point for his own literary adventure, and an expanded, but by no means complete, bibliography of works in English is provided for that purpose.

James R. Stamm

CONTENTS

Preface	v
Preface to the Revised and Updated Edition	ix
Chapter 1. Introduction	1
2. The Emergence of a National Literature	31
3. The Fifteenth Century	52
4. The Golden Age	73
5. The Age of Reason	113
6. The Nineteenth Century	128
7. The Generation of 1898 and "Modernismo"	162
8. Spain in the Twentieth Century	201
Bibliography	263
Index	271

A SHORT HISTORY OF SPANISH LITERATURE
REVISED AND UPDATED EDITION

CHAPTER 1

INTRODUCTION

A Historical Sketch of Spain

Spain is located in the Iberian Peninsula, which lies to the extreme southwest of continental Europe, between the western extreme of the Mediterranean Sea and the Atlantic Ocean. Spain occupies the western boundaries of the "known world" of classical times, and so it was the last Mediterranean area to feel the cultural impact of the early civilizations whose movement was roughly westward, from Asia Minor through Greece to Rome. Therefore, when one considers the growth of Spanish literature, one must take into account many different factors—of geography, history, the migrations of primitive tribes, early maritime contacts, indigenous languages.

Little is known with any real certainty of the early inhabitants of Spain. The accounts of Greek and Phoenician travelers give a fairly good idea of the extent of coastal settlements and indicate that the land was inhabited by relatively primitive peoples. These seafarers did not penetrate far inland and at best give only incidental descriptions of the inland groups with whom they did come into contact. Archaeological investigation, particularly within the last century, has confirmed that the Iberian Peninsula was the scene of many early settlements, populated by primitive peoples coming from both Africa and Europe.

The earliest inhabitants undoubtedly came into the

peninsula by land, either from North Africa or from Central or Western Europe. These were Stone Age peoples who left abundant evidence of their presence in tombs, artifacts, cave and shelter paintings, and stone fortifications. The magnificent drawings found in the caves of Altamira, on the northern coast of Spain, rank among the most remarkable primitive artistic expressions of Europe. The cave art of northern Spain has been dated as "flowering" at about 16,000 B.C. Where these early settlers began their migrations and whether or not the Basques, who have conserved a non-Romance language and a degree of cultural unity through the millenniums of recorded history, represent a remnant of those people are questions which have not been conclusively answered.

It is known, however, that Celtic migrations brought a new racial and linguistic stock to the peninsula possibly as early as the tenth century B.C., and that successive waves of migration increased this Indo-European element in the population down to Roman times. In some sparsely settled areas they seem to have dominated and retained some aspects of their culture while in other areas, particularly in central Spain, they fused with Iberian tribes to form a Celtiberian culture. Neither civilization was highly advanced in terms of art and architecture, and so relatively few remains are to be found. There are, however, tombs, trinkets, pots, statuary, and inscriptions which tell something of their life.

The earliest contact with the more advanced cultures of the Near East came when Phoenician sea traders established ports of call and trading posts in southern Spain. Just how early that contact took place is not known with any certainty; most historians put the initiation of this contact in the twelfth century B.C. or earlier. The Phoenicians established an empire of sorts, or at least permanent trading centers, some of which were fortified. They dominated the southern coast of Spain, with centers in Málaga, Algeciras, Cádiz, Sexi, and Adra, penetrated into the interior to Seville, and controlled the island of Ibiza. Many of the place names of the southern and eastern coasts have a Phoenician origin, and the name for the whole region, *Hispania*, is probably from a Phoenician source, meaning either "hidden," "remote," or "country of rabbits." Along with elements of their language, the Phoenician traders introduced metal coinage, forms of ceramic and stoneware, statuary for funerary and religious purposes, and some industrial and mining techniques.

The Phoenicians had established a more important and permanent center in the Western Mediterranean, the city of Carthage, on the coast of North Africa, probably founded in the ninth century B.C. The importance of Carthage increased in proportion to the decline of the Phoenician homeland and its sea power, owing to repeated attacks on the major eastern city of Tyre by the Assyrians and Chaldeans. By the middle of the sixth century Carthage dominated trade in the area and was sending colonists and labor forces into Spain, supported by well-organized military outposts.

A second cultural influence was the contact with Greek traders and colonists. It is impossible to date the earliest contacts with any certainty, but it is likely that some relations had been established by the end of the seventh century. Establishing a center at Marseilles, the Greeks eventually came to dominate the central part of the east coast. Their major cities were Emporion (literally "market place"), now Ampurias, Hemeroskopion, farther south, Dianium (Denia), and Lucentum (Alicante). There is archaeological evidence to indicate that the Greeks penetrated into the interior of Spain both by land and by sea. Greek artifacts have been found in many parts of the east and south of Spain and along the coast of Portugal, Galicia, and Asturias in the west and north. The cultural impact of the Greeks was important, as well as the commercial. Legend has it that the Greeks introduced the cultivation of olives and wine grapes to the peninsula, and there is a clear influence in architecture, ceramics, mosaics, glassware, and coinage in several parts of the peninsula. The Greeks may have introduced the theater to the peninsula and certainly established schools and academies. This land was known to the Greeks as either Hesperus or Iberia. The development of Greek influence was considerably inhibited by the presence of the stronger and more firmly entrenched heirs of the Phoenician Empire, the Carthaginians, whose interest it was, if not to drive the Greeks out of the Western Mediterranean, at least to limit their expansion in territory which the Carthaginians claimed as their own.

A third force, the Roman Republic, had begun to flourish in this area since the eighth century, and by the third century B.C. had come into violent contact with the Carthaginians in a dispute over colonies on the island of Sicily. This territorial conflict led to the first of the Punic Wars. The Carthaginians (or *Poeni*, as the Phoenicians called themselves) sought with the aid of native troops to hold their settlements against the expansion of the Romans. They were defeated in 242 B.C. and lost their colonies in Sicily. They began immediately to intensify their activities in Spain as a base and source of supply for anticipated future conflict with the Romans. The Carthaginian leader, Hamilcar, tried to subdue the Celtic and Iberian tribes of the peninsula and to conscript them in his wars against Rome. Hamilcar and his successor, Hasdrubal, were successful to a large extent in establishing and consolidating a major military force on the peninsula, and it was this force which came under the command of the young general Hannibal when Hasdrubal was assassinated. Hannibal hoped to avenge the previous defeat of Carthage by the Romans and to re-establish the domination of his people in the Western Mediterranean. In 218 B.C. Hannibal began his long march with a large force of infantry, cavalry, war machines, and the famous elephants. Marching north from Cartagena to cross the Pyrenees, he encountered opposition from Iberian settlements and Greek colonists. Nevertheless Hannibal was able to lead his force across both Pyrenees and Alps to penetrate the Italian Peninsula, where he met his defeat.

With the end of the Second Punic War (ended 201 B.C.) Spain became legitimate spoil for the Romans. The conquerors immediately occupied the more urbanized areas of the east and south. The complete domination of Spain was a slow process, impeded by the primitive tribes of the central and western areas who had never been subjugated by more advanced Mediterranean peoples; Roman legions battled with indigenous forces for fully a century more to subjugate the major areas of the peninsula. Local uprisings and pockets of Iberian and Celtic resistance persisted to the end of the pre-Christian era. Romanization was of course easiest in the urban centers of Andalusia, long accustomed to commercial, political, and cultural domination by foreigners, and Roman colonists were encouraged to settle in the pacified areas. In these cities, particularly, the process of acculturation in all its aspects—of language, law, political organization, dress, and architecture—was rapid. It is from this period that the history of the peninsula can be traced with some accuracy through the accounts of Roman historians, and it was under the civilizing and orderly influence of the Pax Romana that a literature began to develop. The earlier contact with Phoenicians, Carthaginians, and Greeks had certainly brought significant cultural influences to the peninsula, but these contacts had been haphazard and limited to commercial or military objectives. Never before had an organized and diversified attempt been made to bring the whole peninsula under the systematic domination of a superior culture.

By the time of Augustus Caesar and the Roman Empire, Spain had become an important part of the Roman world. Roads had been built to establish major routes linking the important cities of the east and south with centers in the west, such as Mérida and Braga. Military roads and local systems made it possible, though probably not very easy, to travel to almost any part of the peninsula. In the first and second centuries of the Christian era truly monumental building programs provided bridges, aqueducts, arenas and theaters, baths and forums. In A.D. 98 Spain provided Rome with an emperor, Trajan. His successor, the illustrious Hadrian, was also born, though of Italian parents, in Spain.

Romanized Spain proved to be a fertile land for Christian proselytizers. Although there is no record of when Christianity was introduced into the peninsula, St. Paul announced his intention to take his evangelical mission to Spain: "Whensoever I take my journey into Spain, I will come to you: for I trust to see you in my journey, and to be brought on my way thitherward by you, if first I be somewhat filled with your company. . . . When therefore I have performed this, and have sealed to them this fruit, I will come by you into Spain" (Romans 15:24, 28). By the end of the second century, Tertullian tells us, Spain was generally Christian, and in the third century Christians suffered persecution and martyrdom in several parts of the peninsula. Catholic tradition accepts the journey of St. James to Galicia, and the tomb of Santiago (St. James) de Compostela became one of the most important shrines of the Middle Ages, visited by pilgrims from all parts of the Christian world.

The fate which Rome suffered from the barbarians in the fifth century was shared by Spain in a series of invasions in the first half of that century. In the vast migrations of Germanic tribes, overrunning Gaul, Italy, and Spain, the movement was chaotic and the occupation of territories was generally impermanent. The migrant barbarians invaded, sacked, plundered, settled down as long as they could hold a given area, fought among themselves and with other tribes, and moved along whenever the grass appeared greener elsewhere. The Vandals occupied southern Spain for a time before moving on across the strait into Africa; they gave their name to the region we know as Andalusia (Portu Wandalu). In the second half of the fifth century the Visigoths entered Spain. These people, also Germanic in origin, had been in contact for a long period with Roman civilization, had served the Romans as mercenary soldiers, had come to know the fruits of Roman order and discipline, and became Christianized, although they belonged to the heretical Arian sect. Although small in numbers, their superior level of culture made it possible for them to dominate the peninsula and to set up a Visigothic kingdom with its center in Toledo. This kingdom did not comprise all of the peninsula. The Byzantine Empire of the East held portions of Andalusia. The Suevi, another Germanic tribe, held much of Galicia, and the Franks were a constant threat at the Pyrenees. The Arian Visigoths were, however, able to maintain a court, promulgate laws based on their customs and traditions, and in general bring order to the area they controlled. The greatest problems facing the Visigothic reign were: the religious conflict between Arianism and the orthodox Catholicism of both the Byzantine south and the Suevian north; and the difficulty of accommodating the loose tribal association and warlike psychology of the Visigoths to the demands of stable and ordered sovereignty. The history of their reign is one of assassination, revolt, betrayal, broken vows, and interrupted dynasties.

The Visigothic domination lasted, with all its ups and downs, for about two hundred and fifty years. The transition from Roman to Visigothic Spain was a relatively easy one. The invaders had, in their long contact with Rome, come to accept the language, many of the institutions, and a form of Christianity. Certainly the change of leadership and cultural orientation was not as abrupt, radical, or as far-reaching in terms of over-all culture as the period which lay ahead would be.

Under the proselytizing force of the Mohammedan religion a tremendously explosive and dynamic religious and military movement swept across North Africa in the latter half of the seventh century. In the first decade of the eighth century, an impressive military force made up of Arabs, converted Berbers, and other African peoples who had been swept along in the tide of Muslim movements, occupied almost the whole of North Africa and began to look across the strait to Spain. The invasion took place in the spring of A.D. 711 at a time when the Visigothic king Roderic was fighting in the north. As soon as the first invaders were established in the south, reinforcements were sent from Africa and the northward movement began. The forces of Roderic were routed in July of that year and the way was clear for the Moorish occupation of the peninsula. All of the major cities were taken and placed either under Moorish rulers or left in the hands of Visigothic nobles willing to accept the position of tributaries. In some cases the Spanish Christians were converted to Islam and quickly became a part of the new order. Those who would neither convert nor accept Moorish domination were forced to flee to the mountainous northern coast. There they formed pockets of resistance which consolidated into a force which would be the nucleus of the reconquest, a crusade which would take almost eight hundred years to be complete. The attempt of the Moors to push on to France was defeated by Charles Martel and the invaders, contained in the peninsula, began to settle there.

The largest segment of the invading Muslims was the semicivilized Berbers, who crossed into Spain from their settlements in North Africa. They were given land by the Arab elite in northwestern and central Spain, which was well suited to their pastoral background. The Arabs reserved to themselves the cities, towns, and fertile plains of lower Andalusia. Three great cities served as cultural and administrative capitals in Arabic Spain: Seville, Córdoba, and Granada. In the ninth and tenth centuries the luster and learning of the East were represented here in an abundant trade in luxury items such as jewels, fabrics, leather goods, books, slaves, spices, and every sort of *objet d'art*. Libraries were established, music and poetry were cultivated, schools and academies flourished. The sciences, particularly astronomy, botany, and medicine, along with mathematics, philosophy and theology, were cultivated to an extent that made the Dark Ages of medieval Europe seem all the darker. Particularly in the Caliphate of Córdoba under a succession of three strong leaders in the tenth century, Abdu'r-Rahman III, Al-Hakam II, and al-Mansur, the brilliant culture of this city reached a level that no other city of Europe would attain for half a millennium.

This splendor was, however, soon to pale. Dissent among various factions in the Muslim hierarchy in Spain, religious quarrels, the jealousy which the African converts felt toward the Arab rulers, the absence of any clear-cut and accepted principle of transmission of authority among the polygamous Muslim, and rivalries among the ruling families of various parts of the peninsula and Africa made the internal situation extremely unstable. In 1009 there was a revolution in Córdoba and in 1031 the caliphate itself came to an end as the ruling families chose to constitute the city and its dependencies a republic.

Another factor contributing to the dissolution of Arabic

control was the very real threat of the embattled Christians of the north, who had never ceased to resist the conquest of their land, and who pressed constantly against the Moorish settlements. From the battle of Covadonga—where in 722 the Asturian leader Pelayo beat off a Muslim expedition into the mountains of the northern coast—to the final conquest of Granada, in 1492, the constantly increasing society of Christian warriors constituted a menace to the stability of Moorish Spain. By the middle of the tenth century Christian kings held approximately half of Portugal, Salamanca, Avila, Segovia, the whole of the northern coast and Pyrenees, and Catalonia to a point south of Barcelona. The ups and downs of frontier warfare make it impossible to give a single coherent picture of the gains of the Christians; at a given moment the situation depended on the conquests of individual leaders, temporary alliances and dependencies between Muslim and Christian leaders, and the intervention of peripheral powers such as the Christian Franks at the Pyrenees and Catalan borders and the Muslim forces in North Africa. With the fall of the Caliphate of Córdoba in the eleventh century, Muslim Spain had degenerated into a group of city-states, the *taifas*, which at one point numbered as many as twenty-six separate "kingdoms," though the innate weakness of such a system led inevitably to take-overs of the smaller and weaker units by their larger and more powerful neighbors, such as Seville, Granada, and Córdoba. Against this picture of disintegration in the Muslim world, the general pattern among the Christians was one of consolidation and the establishment of central government. Under Ferdinand I, Castile and León were united into a political and military force whose aim was consciously that of reconquest and whose dedication was the expansion of the Christian area and resettlement of Christians in the land won through warfare or political domination. The siege of

Toledo and its capitulation in 1085 restored the ancient Visigothic capital to Christian Spaniards and placed the balance of territorial power in their hands. Against the growing threat of a unified and implacable Christian force, the much-weakened *taifas* looked to Africa for military aid. Reform movements in the Muslim world had generally been as much military as doctrinal, and in the latter part of the eleventh century the Almorávides, "men of religion," a fanatical fundamentalist Berber sect under the leadership of Yusuf ben Texufin, had taken over North Africa from what is now Senegal to Algiers. With some reluctance his aid was sought by the rulers of Badajoz, Seville, Granada, and Córdoba, and in 1086 Yusuf crossed into Spain with a large army. He met the forces of Alfonso VI at Zalaca and defeated the Christians completely, with enormous losses on Alfonso's side. To the gratified surprise of the Spanish Muslims, Yusuf then returned to Africa leaving a small garrison of his Almorávides at Seville. The success of Yusuf fired the ambitions of the Andalusian princes: they attempted to take the fort of Aledo near Murcia, a particularly strong Christian outpost which had long served as a center for raids on the Moorish-held countryside. The attempt failed, and once again Yusuf was called upon for aid. This time, although he was unable to take the fort with his force of Almorávides, he inflicted such damage upon it that it was no longer defensible by the Christians and had to be abandoned. The Andalusians were not so fortunate this time. Seduced by the richness of the land and scandalized by the religious laxness of the *taifa* kings, Yusuf embarked on a reform movement which had as its first object the dethronement of the *taifa* rulers and the complete domination of Andalusia. This was accomplished with little difficulty, given the decadent state of the *taifas,* and under Yusuf, Andalusia was united as a part of the Almorávide empire. The successors of Yusuf lacked both his zeal and energy and within half a century the movement had declined into one more luxurious decadence. The Almorávides lacked the administrative ability to maintain a prosperous state. Commerce declined notably, prices rose, land fell into disuse with resulting shortages, and civil disorder was rampant.

The result of these conditions was still another reform movement in African Islam led by the Almohades, "Unitarians" from the Atlas Mountains of Morocco. Unrest in the peninsula under the Almoravide empire made the Andalusians as anxious now to throw off the heirs of Yusuf as they had previously been to unseat the *taifa* rulers and unite under a strong leadership. Local governors in the Algarve of Portugal, in Murcia, Córdoba, and Valencia had, with the support of Christian rulers, set up independent governments in what amounted to a second period of *taifa* states. To resolve this situation, the Almohades came to the rescue from Africa in the latter part of the twelfth century. They had already demolished the Almorávide empire there and had little difficulty taking over the reins of power in Andalusia, with their capital in Seville.

The Almohades, however, represented essentially more of the same in so far as any real leadership or program was concerned. Another wave of fundamentalist zeal, prosecution of the frontier wars against the Christian forces, and an attempt to unify the cities of Andalusia against the infidel had, as before, temporary success but made no permanent headway. The Almohade occupation, like that of the Almorávides, had one notable effect, and that was to lessen still further the prestige and influence of the Arab families, the original lords of Andalusia. From the middle of the twelfth century until the capitulation of Granada in 1492 the power, prestige, and extent of the Muslim world in Spain continually lessened in proportion to the growth, unification, cohesiveness, and gradual cultural maturing of the Christian forces under the leadership of the kings of Castile and León. It is with the capitulation of Granada in that fateful year for the Spanish destiny, 1492, that Spain enters its modern period, and from which we can begin to speak of it as a nation.

Language

The prehistory and prenational history of Spain are reflected to some extent in the formation of the Spanish language; not only is linguistic archaeology possible through the examination of the remains of early cultures in the languages of the peninsula, but in fact a study of these materials has aided considerably in providing a knowledge of early contacts and movements of peoples in the peninsula. Through the evidence of place names, the early contacts of the Phoenicians, Carthaginians, and Greeks can be established as certainly as through the examination of burial sites, fortresses, and temples. Rather more difficult is the linguistic documentation of the earliest settlers for two reasons: the absence of written records or inscriptions, since these were preliterate cultures, and the natural tendency of the more advanced Mediterranean cultures to implant their own language in the areas where contact was frequent. Thus an attempt to establish any findings concerning the early Iberian tongue or tongues proceeds from negative assumptions: words, place names, prefixes, or suffixes which show no relation to the known tongues of Europe, the Near East, or Africa may be at least tentatively considered to be survivals of the Iberian substratum. Many philologists have considered the Basque language, spoken in many dialectical forms in the valleys of the Pyrenees in both France and Spain, to be a survival of the earliest tongue spoken on the peninsula, and in the sixteenth and seventeenth centuries there were not lacking enthusiasts who held that Basque was the language spoken by Adam and Eve in the Garden of Eden and by Noah on board ship! The origin of the language certainly offers problems. In structure it shows similarities to languages of the Caucasian Mountains, but the vocabulary offers no apparent connection; in vocabulary it has some elements in common with the Hamitic tongues of the Libyan area, but differs greatly in structure. There is no written record of Basque before the tenth century A.D., and by that time a great deal of Latin vocabulary and, most likely, some distortion of structure and phonology, had made their appearance to confuse further the problem of tracing its origins. It is fairly certain that, as the Greek geographer Strabo affirms, the peninsula did not have anything approaching linguistic unity in his time, the Augustan period. The words of probable Iberian origin, including Basque, which have remained in modern Spanish are few and relate to very specific ideas. Among the most common: *izquierda*, "left"; *barro*, "mud"; *perro*, "dog"; *conejo*, "rabbit."

The Celtic migrations also had their effect on the Spanish vocabulary. Many Spanish place names show a Celtic origin: Coimbra (Conimbriga), Segovia, Coruña, and the names of half a hundred smaller towns and villages. Much Celtic vocabulary, however, came into Latin through the contact which the legions had with Celtic mercenaries and from Celtic settlements which came under Roman jurisdiction, and thus passed into the peninsula as an adopted element of the Latin language. Articles of apparel, such as the *camisa*, "shirt," and *bragas*, "trousers," of the Celts, their favorite beverage, *cerveza*, "beer," their mode of transportation, *carro*, "wagon," their skill as *carpinteros*, "carpenters," their offensive weapon, *lanza*, "lance," all came to enrich the peninsular vocabulary.

The early contact with Phoenicians, Carthaginians, and Greeks gave rise, as has been seen, to a number of place names for cities and trading and shipping centers, but left no significant mark on the vocabulary of Spanish. The extremely high state of Hellenic culture, as compared to Roman culture of the republic and the empire, gave enormous prestige to Greek philosophy, literature, architecture, and science in general. The Greek language was much studied and came to play an important part in the formation of an aesthetic and philosophic vocabulary previously lacking in Latin. Thus the Latin which became the standard language of the areas conquered and held by the Romans carried with it a large number of Greek terms. These are generally terms related to the more cultural elements of Greek life, and have come into English as well: idea, fantasy, philosophy, music, poetry, mathematics, tragedy, comedy, chorus, ode, rhetoric, athlete, and scholar; all are Greek terms and concepts which passed by way of Latin into both English and the Romance tongues. The total list of Greek derivations would be a very long one. Generally the words adopted reflected the advanced state of Greek civilization, expanding rather than replacing elements of the more concrete, workaday Latin vocabulary. The proportion of learned Greek vocabulary in Spanish is about equivalent to that in English.

The great base of modern Spanish is, of course, Latin. The Roman Empire established the Latin language as the official tongue for all dealings, commercial, administrative, and military, with the provinces, and in most parts of the Roman world it soon came to replace the local languages in all public activities, in the home, and in the streets. This was the Vulgar Latin of verbal communication among persons of various levels of culture, not the "classical" or literary Latin of the poets and orators. Most records were kept in classical Latin, the language of the speeches, poems, plays, and philosophical essays whose literary value assured their survival. The reconstruction of Vulgar Latin, the everyday, spoken language, must depend upon the occasional slips of writers, the occasional use of a slangy term by a playwright, treatises of grammarians—such as the *Appendix Probi*, which lists a number of popular errors, giving the "correct" form alongside, and some few writings of less well educated people—the travel diary of a nun who visited a number of civil monuments and religious shrines, a veterinary treatise on how to cure sick mules, a number of legal and religious documents of various periods whose particular value lies in the errors they contain or in their departures from the classical norms.

Of course there is no one Vulgar Latin. Speech varied very considerably at different times and in different places. A Roman historian records that a speech given by the Spanish-born Quaestor—later Emperor—Hadrian was delivered in such strongly accented Latin that the entire Senate broke into laughter. Following the barbarian invasions and the fall of the empire in the fifth century the provinces were further isolated and the growth of dialects and local divergences became ever more marked. Thus the Latin spoken in Marseilles came to differ in sound and form from the Latin spoken in Zaragoza, and both differed from that of Genoa. As these differences and divergences multiplied, the speech became mutually unintelligible, particularly after the centralizing forces of Roman administration diminished in power. At the point where differences became sufficiently acute, we may begin to speak of the existence of a great family of Romance languages, comprising French, Italian, Portuguese, Spanish, Catalan, Rumanian, and a number of minor tongues, such as Sardinian. Scholars dis-

INTRODUCTION 17

agree as to the point at which the dialects of Vulgar Latin may properly be called distinct and separate Romance languages; some place the determining point at the restoration of the Roman Empire under Charlemagne at the beginning of the ninth century, which established clerical Latin as the language of the Church and thus gave a certain freedom to the vernacular tongues to go their own ways. Others, holding rather extreme views, set the period as early as the sixth century, and at least one renowned scholar maintains that we are still dealing with dialects of one multiformed Romance speech. For practical purposes we may date Spanish as a distinct language at the period when its first great literary document was composed, the *Poem of El Cid*, about the middle of the twelfth century.

Before the language was to assume the characteristics apparent in that great epic, two more linguistic stocks had made their appearance in the peninsula and left their mark upon the nascent tongue. The barbarian invaders, particularly the Visigoths, whose influence was greatest, were already to a large extent Romanized at the time of their entry into Spain. Latin remained the language of their court and of their contact with peninsular peoples, and such new linguistic elements as they introduced were primarily terms of warfare and products and customs related principally to their way of life. Many of these have cognates in the Germanic origins of English. Thus *jabón* from *saipo*, "soap"; *guerra* from *werra*, "war"; *robar* from *raubon*, "to rob"; *estribo* from *streup*, "stirrup"; *yelmo* from *helm*, "helmet"; *arpa* from *harpa*, "harp."

The second important non-Latin influence is Arabic. Brought into Spain with the invasion in A.D. 711, the language of the conquerors of Spain had no elements in common with the Latin of the peninsula. For a period of nearly nine hundred years these languages, peninsular

Romance (Spanish, Catalan, and Portuguese in various stages of development) and Arabic, with various admixtures of Berber and other tongues of North Africa, coexisted and to some extent interpenetrated. Bilingualism was not uncommon, certainly, especially among the Mozárabes, Christians living in Muslim-dominated areas. The Arabic culture of this period was at a much higher level of development than that of the Visigothic Christians, and so it was natural enough that Arabic learning, poetry, and the innumerable elegances of Arabic life should dominate in the cities of the south, and that the ruder culture of the Romance-speaking Christians, with no appreciable literature and no centers of learning, should succumb to the invader. By the middle of the ninth century the acculturation of the Mozárabes had become so advanced that the Christian Bishop of Córdoba complained that his flock read the literature of the Arabs and studied the writings of the Mohammedan Koran and the Muslim theologians to the total exclusion of Christian Scriptures and the Latin commentaries. Young Christians of ability, he tells us, have forgotten their own language and, while unable to write even so much as a letter in proper Latin, compose exquisitely in Arabic and even exceed the Arabs themselves in poetic skill.

Yet spoken Romance remained alive among those who lived under the Arabs, even though the study of Latin for any use other than the needs of the Church languished. The Mozárabe dialects are extremely hard to document because so little that was written endures. Some *aljamiado* manuscripts, Romance texts written in Arabic or Hebrew characters, have survived, but these give only a partial and unsatisfactory idea of the state of the spoken language. The best testimony of the liveliness of the vernacular is the relatively recent discovery of a verse-form called *jarchya*. The *jarchyas* are short popular refrains added to Arabic lyrical poetry, written usually in a mixture of Arabic and Romance. While their poetic value is minimal, they are of enormous value to the study of the development of the Romance dialects.

Mió sidi Ibrahim	My Lord Ibrahim
ya nuemne dolye,	oh sweet name,
vente mib de nojte.	come to me by night.
In non, si non queris,	If not, if you don't want to,
iréme tib:	I will go to you:
garme a ob legarte.	tell me where I may find you.
Venid la Pasca, ay, aún sin ellu,	Easter is coming, ah, still without him,
laçrando meu corayún por ellu.	rending my heart for him.

As a result of the presence of the Moors in Spain for the better part of a millennium, something over four thousand words and derivations of Arabic origin entered the vocabulary of Spanish. Not all remained current, of course, but still Arabic sources constitute, after Latin, the largest element of the language. Those which were conserved were mostly from the categories of military terms, agriculture and botany, weights and measures, mathematics and science.

Bilingualism was perhaps less frequent in the Christian north, although certainly in the frontier areas there is evidence that it was not uncommon. The Romance tongue of course prevailed in these areas and became official in territories which the reconquest recovered from the Moors. This was not a homogenous tongue, but rather a wide spread of Romance dialects, including Castilian, Leonese, Aragonese, Catalan, Valencian, and Galician Portuguese. The consolidation of these dialects, or rather the establishment of a standard speech, was a by-product of the reconquest and the unification of Spain. Even today the traveler in Spain who knows Spanish is aware of innumerable variations and colorings in the local speech as he moves from one area to another. A major project has been under way for some years to prepare a linguistic atlas of the peninsula, showing variations in the pronunciation of vowels and consonants, modifications of words from one area to another, and contrasts in vocabulary.

Following the unification of Spain under King Ferdinand and Queen Isabella, the language continued to evolve, but at a more stable rate and without the violent introduction of foreign elements by way of conquest and occupation. The domination of Castilian over the other Spanish dialects is a phenomenon that is explained by the historical role of Castile in the gradual unification of the Christian territories. The centralization of political control shifted the hub ever more from northwestern (Leonese) territories to the central plateau as the reconquest pushed south. Thus Burgos, Valladolid, Toledo, and finally Madrid came to dominate politically and to serve also as standards for linguistic unity.

The enormous cultural impact of the Italian Renaissance introduced a sizable new literary vocabulary into Spain in the fifteenth and sixteenth centuries, some part of which took permanent root. Since the Renaissance was basically a revival of Greek and Latin learning, its manifestation in Spain was an imitation of classical syntax as well as the adoption of an ornate and sophisticated vocabulary. Similarly the neoclassicism of the eighteenth century brought the influence of French thought and literature to Spain and the accommodation of a considerable amount of French vocabulary. At present English is exerting a linguistic influence on Spanish in Spain, Spanish America, and among Spanish-speaking populations in the United States. Terms from sports (*fútbol, béisbol, yate* ["yacht"]), politics (*mitin, líder, repórter*), cuisine (*rosbif, bistec, bacon, sandwich*), and miscellaneous expressions from sciences, industry, and technology make themselves useful in the absence of legitimate Spanish expressions.

"Occupied" Literature

Before the first manifestations of a "national" literature —a literature of artistic importance which might represent the conscious awareness of a culture which was in its broad outlines Hispanic—Spain underwent a period of some twelve hundred years of intellectual and political domination by invading and occupying forces whose cultural endowment was essentially foreign to the Iberian Peninsula. It may of course be said that, after a dozen generations in Córdoba, the Arabic-speaking Muslim was as much a Spaniard as his Romance-speaking Christian counterpart in Burgos, whose ancestors entered Spain in the Visigothic invasions of the fifth century. In terms of their literature and general cultural endowment, both carried on traditions which had been implanted from without. However much adaptation to the new environment had been made, the basic characteristics of Roman, Visigothic, and Arabic literatures did not spring from the realities of Spanish life but sought rather to imitate forms elaborated by the master cultures. It is convenient, therefore, to think in terms of a pre-Romance literary period beginning about the middle of the first century B.C. and ending with the composition of the *Poema de mío Cid* in the middle of the twelfth century A.D. In terms of this division, three major cultural influences can be distinguished.

(1) *The Roman World*

Following the defeat of Carthage in the Second Punic War, the Romanization of Spain assumed the practical aspects of colonization, government, extension of Roman military domination to the more remote areas, and the establishment of schools through which a process of acculturation might be accomplished. The literary fruits of this often haphazard program began to appear in the period of the empire which coincides with the "silver age" of Latin literature.

The major figure of this period is the Stoic philosopher and dramatist Lucius Annaeus Seneca, born in Córdoba about 4 B.C., the son of a wealthy and influential Spanish family which produced other writers of distinction as well. Seneca's father wrote a number of treatises on rhetoric and debating, and his nephew, Lucan, was the author of the second great Latin epic, the *Pharsalia*. Seneca pursued a political career in Rome as lawyer, orator, statesman, and teacher, in spite of a lifetime of poor health. As a result of his pre-eminence in the public and intellectual life of Rome, he was named tutor to the emperor-to-be, Nero. The more enlightened aspects of the first five years of Nero's reign are often attributed to the influence of Seneca, but as the true character of the emperor began to assert itself in a figure whom history has generally branded as a matricide, fratricide, arsonist, and mass murderer, relations grew ever more strained. Finally in A.D. 65 Nero ordered the philosopher to take his own life. Seneca did so with a fortitude which followed the best tenets of the Stoic philosophy of equanimity in the face of bad fortune. The circumstances of his death resemble the last hours of Socrates. Assembling a group of friends and family, the Stoic addressed them at length on the moral rewards of virtue and the good life, and then calmly severed the arteries of his arms and died.

Seneca's fame rests on nine verse dramas and a body of philosophic writings in the tradition of Roman Stoicism. The dramas take their themes from Greek tragedy, but

Seneca shows considerable originality in his treatment of the ancient myths and legends. He amplifies both action and language in terms of a highly polished rhetoric and the psychological examination of intense passion. These tragedies reflect the demands of an urban and sophisticated Roman public, accustomed to scenes of luxury and splendor in triumphal celebrations, and to the display of overwhelming violence and cruelty in the arena. Most notable are his *Medea, Phaedra,* and *Hercules Mad.* In the form of dialogues and epistles his works of philosophy generally present the world view of Roman Stoicism, which sought to attain an imperviousness to the vagaries of fortune through the pursuit of inner fortitude and tranquillity.

Marcus Annaeus Lucan (A.D. 39–65) had a career very similar to that of his paternal uncle Seneca. Also born in Córdoba, Lucan too was educated in Rome and achieved early political success. He managed to antagonize the despot Nero, possibly by writing a satire against the emperor. In any event, whatever the cause, Lucan fell into disfavor and was implicated in a plot against Nero's life. The emperor again utilized his favorite form of indirect assassination and in the same year Seneca died, Lucan was ordered to take his own life. The younger man did not show his uncle's Stoic fortitude in the matter; he indulged in a number of abject pleas for his life, offering to implicate his own mother in the abortive plot in order to save himself. But Nero remained adamant and the poet died by the same means that his uncle had taken, in the same year. It is likely that much of Lucan's work has been lost. What remains is a long historical poem, the *Pharsalia,* which details events of the civil war between Caesar and Pompey.

Marcus Fabius Quintillian (A.D. 35–96) born near Calahorra and educated in Rome, was a master of rhetoric and oratory: indeed he was the first man of the Roman world to make a profession of rhetoric by receiving a salary from the state. One work, *On the Causes of the Decadence of Oratory,* has been lost, but twelve books of the *Institutes of Oratory* have been preserved. Quintillian enjoyed great prestige in classical times and his writings came into prominence again in the Renaissance, but he is not much read today.

A fourth figure of importance is Marcus Valerius Martial (A.D. 42–104) born near the Spanish city of Calatayud. His epigrams stand as an enduring embodiment of Latin wit and satire. These concise and highly polished comments on the foibles of Roman society have survived to delight their readers through periods when more lofty works have been neglected, largely because they are a supremely human commentary on social pretentiousness in all its forms. Some of the victims of his satire are: Tongilius, who pretends to be ill so that his friends will send him the best wines and most delicate foods to hasten his recovery; Selius, who runs all over town looking for friends who will invite him to dinner; a physician who has become an undertaker, which is not strange, says Martial, because he is merely following the same profession in another form; and another physician who brings so many students along on his house calls that, after they all finish poking and prodding and putting their cold hands on the patient, he's sicker than before.

(2) *Visigothic Spain*

The Gothic tribes which began to enter Spain in the early part of the fifth century brought with them no recorded literary tradition, although it is likely that a verbally transmitted form of epic poetry, celebrating victories and the deeds of their heroes, was current among them. The level and form of their society, a loose confederation of tribes with elected leaders or "kings" did not provide a durable social basis to foster a national literature, and Roman literary forms did not survive the fall of the empire. The sole literary tradition which remained alive was that of the Church. While the Visigoths struggled among themselves to establish dynasties and hierarchies in northern and central Spain, the cities of the south came under the influence of the expanding Byzantine Empire. This contact sustained and nurtured classical learning and scholarship in a period in which it had all but disappeared elsewhere in Western Europe. The writers were churchmen and their language was a learned, pedantic Latin kept alive only in Church circles. The dominant figure of this period is St. Isidor of Seville (570–636), whose erudition was truly encyclopedic. His major work is the *Etymologies,* which was later divided into twenty books, or parts. In this immense collection, written in Latin, St. Isidor deals with the trivium and quadrivium of the liberal arts; with medicine, law, theology, language (hence the title of his work); anatomy, zoology, geography, architecture, mineralogy, agriculture—in short, with the whole range of human knowledge, belief, and experience of his time. This monumental work had an enormous influence throughout the whole of the Middle Ages and played a major part in the shaping of European thought and education. There is nothing original in the work of St. Isidor; it is purely a work of conservation and transmission of a great body of accumulated learning from one society to another. Yet the reorganization and reshaping of this knowledge gave to it a new form and a new relevance to the society for which it was intended. The work of St. Isidor was carried on by a number of erudite disciples in a series of chronicles, discourses, and compilations of similar character. Thus the literary product of the Visigothic period really represents nothing Gothic at all. It may be characterized as serious, didactic, and Christian, and represents a modification of classical learning.

(3) *Arabic Spain*

This third period of cultural influence, the Arabic, or Moorish, brought a totally new orientation to peninsular thought. The areas in which the Arabic tradition excelled were philosophy and lyric poetry, and these forms were cultivated in the peninsula as Arabic culture began to take root in the cities of the south. The flowering came late, however, for the same reasons that all Eastern contact was delayed: Spain was always the journey's end of these movements across the Mediterranean world. Other factors contributed as well, such as the hostile reception of Islam by Spanish Christians, the political disorganization and factionalism of many sorts among the conquerors, and the lack of an established literary tradition, as it existed in Persia and other Eastern cultures, on which to build. The masterworks and classical forms of Arabic poetry were of course brought in with the invaders and prized among them.

Two new poetical forms were invented by Spanish Moors in the period of the brilliant court of Abdu'r-Rahman III in Córdoba, the *muwashshah* and the *zéjel*. These forms are very similar in their structure and were originally popular folk poetry with no pretensions to rivalry with the older classic forms. They caught on, however, and soon came to achieve real literary stature as reputable forms of lyric poetry. The themes are festive, amorous, witty, and occasionally bawdy. The major difference between the *muwashshah* and the *zéjel* is that the former was generally written in classical Arabic and was limited to five or six strophes, while the latter was written in vulgar Arabic with no formal limitation on the number of strophes. The *jarchyas,* mentioned above, were short final verses in vulgar Arabic or Romance appended to the *muwashshah.* The device of writing lyric poetry in short, regular stanzas was new to Arabic literature and seems to be a native Spanish product of the intermingling of the two cultures. The *zejél,* equally adaptable to Romance and to Arabic, remained popular in both the Islamic and Christian communities. Beautiful examples appear in the *Cantigas* of King Alfonso the Wise in the thirteenth century and as late as the middle of the fourteenth century in the *Book of Good Love* of Juan Ruiz. An example from the *Cantigas* illustrates one variation of the typical verse form and its adaptation to the Christian frame of reference. The poem is written not in Castilian but in Galician Portuguese, favored over the harsher central speech for the composition of lyric poetry.

ESTA PRIMEIRA É DAS MAYAS

Ben vennas, Mayo, et con alegría;
poren roguemos a Santa María
que a seu Fillo rogue todavía
que él nos guarde d'err'e de folía.
　Ben vennas, Mayo, et con alegría . . .

Ben vennas, Mayo, con toda saúde,
porque loemos a de gran vertude
que a Deus rogue que nos sempr'aiude
contra o dem' e de si nos escude.
　Ben vennas, Mayo, et con alegría . . .

THIS IS THE FIRST OF MAY-DAYS

Welcome, May, and with joy;
for this we pray to Holy Mary
that she pray always to her Son
that He guard us from error and folly.
Welcome, May, and with joy . . .

Welcome, May, in good health;
for we give praise to her of great virtue
that she may pray God always to help us
against the Demon, and to shelter us.
Welcome, May, and with joy . . .

The basic form of the *zejél* is a refrain established in the first verse—here "Welcome, May, and with joy"—followed by three or four monorhymed lines, and a repetition of, or variation on, the refrain. Many variations on this pattern were used, employing couplets, quatrains, and longer or shorter lines of verse.

Traditional Arabic forms were cultivated with much success. One of the outstanding figures of the eleventh century was Ibn Hazm (994–1064) of Córdoba. His delicate and lyrical anatomy of chivalrous love, *The Dove's Necklace,* deserves a place in universal literature and may well have played a role in the later development of the conventions of courtly love. Ibn Hazm also wrote extensively on religious, philosophical, and historical themes, but few of these treatises have survived. Among those we have is one of the earliest works on comparative religion, *The Book of Religious and Philosophical Sects.* It was typical of the Arabic tradition that theologians should write love poetry, that poets should also write historical chronicles; in short, that the man of learning and letters should turn his hand to many forms.

Perhaps most valuable and influential in the Western tradition was the work of the Muslim philosophers, not so much in terms of the originality of their work as for the fact that these scholars had preserved a body of the works of Aristotle and through their commentaries preserved and communicated the method and content of Aristotelian thought, which had been lost to Christian Europe. The philosopher Averroës (1126–98) conserved and annotated the bulk of Aristotelian philosophy, including the *Physics,* the *Metaphysics,* the *Organon,* and the *Nicomachean Ethics*. Averroës' original works were important, as well, and concerned primarily the resolution of conflicts between reason and faith. His work foreshadowed and contributed to the great synthesis of St. Thomas Aquinas in the thirteenth century.

In the Arabic world of southern Spain, a numerous and flourishing Jewish community, in a liberal and stimulating intellectual atmosphere, made brilliant contributions in philosophy, literature, science, and theology. The poet and philosopher Avicebrón (1021–70) had considerable influence on the scholastic philosophers Duns Scotus and Bruno. Avicebrón, like other philosophers whose work contributed to the flowering of Jewish culture in Spain during the tenth through the twelfth centuries, preserves and reinterprets the Neoplatonism of the Hellenistic Near East, which was to emerge to prominence again in the Renaissance. Avicebrón's work pales somewhat beside the light of his great successor, Maimonides (1135–1204). He was educated in the liberal atmosphere of Córdoba, but Maimonides' family was forced to flee before the invasion of the Almohades. He traveled through various parts of Spain and at some point apparently made at least a token conversion to Islam. His works were of importance in three fields: medicine, theology, and philosophy. His *Morah Nebukin* (Guide of the Perplexed) is a compendium of Jewish thought which contributed to the attempt of Albertus Magnus and other Scholastics to resolve the conflict between reason and faith in Christian terms.

Summary

The location of the Iberian Peninsula at the western extreme of the Mediterranean Sea delayed contact with the earlier civilizations whose commercial, colonizing, and cultural expansion was generally a movement from east to west (Phoenicia, Greece, and Rome). As a result also of the maritime distances involved, such centers as Cádiz, Córdoba, and Cartagena remained primarily trading posts and did not experience a great diffusion of the culture of the more advanced peoples. Following the fall of Carthage in the Second Punic War, Spain was intensively Romanized and began to contribute to Latin literature with the works of Seneca, Lucan, Quintillian, and Martial.

With the decline of Rome in the fifth century, Spain, already largely Christianized, was conquered and occupied by the invading Visigoths. The conquest was simplified by the fact that the Romanized barbarians had for the most part adopted both Christianity and the Latin language; therefore, no serious cultural barriers had to be overcome. Visigothic literature flourished in Spain during the seventh century. Most of it shows the influence of St. Isidor, and is serious, didactic, and profoundly Christian.

The Romano-Gothic synthesis was violently interrupted by the Moorish conquest of Spain in A.D. 711. There were incessant frontier wars, and both Christians who resisted the conquest and those who lived under the Moors existed in primitive conditions which did not promote literary activity. The Arabic-Hebrew culture of southern Spain reached its highest point in the tenth through the twelfth centuries with the development of lyric poetry, philosophy, and theology. The Caliphate of Córdoba was without doubt the most brilliant cultural center of Europe in the Middle Ages. The influence of Averroës and Maimonides had a significant place in medieval scholastic thought and in the intellectual currents of the Renaissance.

CHAPTER 2

THE EMERGENCE OF A NATIONAL LITERATURE

A "national" literature begins in Spain with the composition of *cantares de gesta,* "songs of great deeds." There has been much critical disagreement about the origins and primitive form of these *cantares:* Did they begin as short episodic works, recounting a battle here, a duel there, the sacking of a city, the celebration of a marriage; episodes which were later stitched together to form one long poem about a central figure or event? Or were they, in their earliest form, complete narrations which were later expanded with detail and description? Was the form brought into Spain by the Visigoths, taking root in a Spanish warrior tradition, or are they merely "Spanifications" and imitations of the French *chansons de geste?* Was there an Arabic influence in the most primitive *cantares?* Was each epic poem the work of one minstrel, or do they represent a gradual accretion over decades, a sort of group effort? The evidence for any of the theories of their origin and early form is slim because so few examples are extant in poetic form. Prose versions, published in later chronicles and histories of Spain, attest to the flowering of epic poetry in Spain between the tenth and thirteenth centuries, but since the tradition was an oral one, presumably few copies were made, and whatever did exist in written form has for the most part been lost. Only in the present century has a concerted attempt been made to reconstruct some of these *cantares* from prose accounts—which occasionally fall into patterns of spoken verse typical of the epics—and later short *romances* which echo the themes and episodes of the earlier poems. The themes are all Spanish and are based more or less solidly in historical events: the loss of Spain to the Moors, the struggle for the independence of Castile from León, dynastic intrigues, assassinations, and delayed vengeance. In the later stages, approaching the decadence of the folk epic, a French influence is apparent in the treatment of Charlemagne's campaign into Spain and the death of the Frankish hero Roland. The Spanish *cantares* were composed in assonant verse, the lines varying from ten to eighteen syllables with no attempt at regularity. The most typical aspects of the epics are realism, the paucity of miraculous or fantastic events, strong emotion portrayed with great simplicity, and a pervading sense of moral rectitude.

Of the original large number of *cantares de gesta* only the *Poema de mío Cid* and a fragment of a Spanish version of *Roncesvalles*, the theme of the *Song of Roland*, are extant. The *Poema de mío Cid* is the earliest existing literary work in a Romance language in Spain. It was composed probably between 1140 and 1200 near Medinaceli and comes to us in a single manuscript made in 1307 by one Per Abbat. The opening verses are lost but have been reconstructed from later chronicles. The poem is made up of three major parts, *cantares*, which are closely and chronologically related. The first *cantar* tells of the banishment of the Cid (an Arabic title equivalent to "Lord") by Alfonso VI when he is falsely accused by enemies at court of having withheld tribute money which he had collected for Alfonso from the Moors of Andalusia. The Cid, with a small band of followers, departs from his homeland and proceeds to lay waste Moorish holdings in eastern Spain. The opening lines capture strongly and simply the emotions of the falsely accused

THE EMERGENCE OF A NATIONAL LITERATURE

warrior as he departs from his village to undertake a totally unpredictable destiny.

De los sos ojos tan fuertemientre llorando,
tornava la cabeça i estávalos catando.
Vío puertas abiertas e uços sin cañados,
alcándaras vázias sin pielles e sin mantos
e sin falcones e sin adtores mudados.
Sospiró mio Çid, ca mucho avié grandes cuidados.
Fabló mio Çid bien e tan mesurado:
"Grado a tí, señor padre, que estás en alto!
"Esto me an buolto mios enemigos malos."

From his eyes bitter tears were streaming;
he turned his head and remained a moment looking back.
He saw open doors and doors without locks,
empty racks without clothing of fur or wool,
perches without falcons or the young molted birds.
My lord sighed for the great pain he felt.
My lord spoke then, well and with gravity:
"This be the will of God, who is on high!
This is what my evil enemies have brought upon me."

This brief passage is typical of the direct simplicity of the poem, which in a few details is able to communicate the awful sense of desolation and injustice which the Cid feels, along with a firm faith in his destiny and the will of God. The Cid goes forth with his vassals, a small band facing the uncertainty of exile in a harsh and embattled land. In a series of field engagements with the Moors of central and eastern Spain, the Cid begins to build his troops, his fortune, and his personal reputation as a warrior. Finally he is prepared to move against the seaport of Valencia, a major holding of the Moors.

The second *cantar* concerns the marriage of the Cid's two daughters. Having established himself in the important coastal city of Valencia, the Cid sends his lieutenant, Alvar Fáñez, back to King Alfonso with a gift of one hundred horses and the request that the Cid's wife and two daughters be allowed to join him in Valencia. Peace is restored between the Cid and King Alfonso, who then requests the Cid's daughters as wives for two young nobles of his court, the Princes of Carrión. The Cid reluctantly yields to Alfonso's wishes despite his personal dislike for the future sons-in-law. The double wedding is performed in Valencia.

In the third *cantar* the Princes of Carrión show themselves to be cowards and are ridiculed by the Cid's nobility in Valencia. They ask permission to return with their wives to Carrión, to which the Cid agrees. No sooner are they back in Castile than they take their vengeance on their brides by maltreating, stripping, and abandoning the girls in the forest of Corpes. When the Cid learns of this, he asks justice of the king. A hearing is held in Toledo in which the Cid reclaims the dowery and the marriages are annulled. Messengers from the Princes of Aragon and Navarre arrive to ask for the daughters in marriage. All agree to this, but the affair is carried further by three of the Cid's warriors, who accuse the Princes of Carrión of cowardice and treachery. A series of duels is fought in which the honor of the Cid's family is restored.

The general outlines of the story and many of the events are based solidly in history. The Cid, Rodrigo Díaz de Vivar (1040?-99), married Doña Jimena, a cousin of Alfonso VI, and was banished from Castile in 1081. After a long career of local warfare, sometimes fighting on the side of the Moors and sometimes against them, he conquered Valencia in 1094. One daughter, Cristina, married the Prince of Navarre. Aside from its basic fidelity to history, the geography is exact and there is a forceful quality of realism about the work. The language is blunt and clear, the events are of sustained interest, and the characterization of the central figures is strongly developed in terms of personality and human motivation. In comparison with the other great epic of this period of Romance literature, the French *Chanson de Roland*, the poem of the Cid displays greater realism, the characters are more flexible and alive, are less modeled on an impossibly heroic scale, and elements of humor are developed.

The movement of the poem is generally as swift as the language is terse. In many scenes of warfare we are given direct and bloody accounts which fully communicate the savage joy of battle.

*A Mynaya Albar Fáñez   bien l'anda el cavallo,
daquestos moros   mató treínta e quatro;
espada tajador,   sangriento trae el braço,
por el cobdo ayuso   la sangre destellando.
Dize Minaya: "agora so pagado,
"que a Castiella   irán buenos mandados,
"que mio Çid Roy Díaz   lid campal a arrancado."
Tantos moros yazen muertos   que pocos bivos a dexados.*

For our brother Albar Fáñez the horse runs well,
of those Moors he killed thirty-four;
the slicing sword, his arm flowing enemy blood,
from the elbow the blood dripping down.
Our brother says: "Now I am content,
that to Castile will go good news,
that my lord Ruy Díaz has won a battle on the field."
So many Moors lie dead that very few are left alive.

In some episodes, short stanzas of set verses with consonant rhyme and more regular meter are used. These appear to be stock series which the reciter could use interchangeably. Neither characters nor place are mentioned, and so they would fit any battle sequence anywhere.

*Enbraçan los escudos   delant los coraçones,
abaxan las lanças   abueltas de los pendones,
enclinaron las caras   de suso de los arzones,
ívanlos ferir   de fuertes coraçones.*

> They raise their shields before their hearts,
> they lower their lances adorned with pennants
> they lower their faces to their saddle trees,
> they went forth to kill with strong hearts.

There are three primary reasons why so small a part of the robust and virile epic literature survived, while earlier and less interesting documents were preserved. The first, this popular poetry, usually recited by professional entertainers for small groups, was rarely written down, but rather committed—often imperfectly and with variations and omissions—to memory. The second, the unsettled times of the period, with frequent if not constant warfare both between Christian and Moor and within these camps themselves. Under such circumstances works could not easily be accumulated and preserved save in the relatively stable atmosphere of monasteries and the larger churches. The third, when copies of the poems did reach the learned monks of the monasteries, they were often looked down upon as vulgar and worthless. The churchmen were accustomed to the literary Latin of the Scriptures, the Church fathers, Roman classics, and the erudite works of St. Isidor and his followers. They could generally see little of value in these poems, written to amuse a semiliterate audience in a language which they regarded as a barbarous perversion of the ancient tongue preserved by monastics. It was not until the eighteenth century that a true and unbiased estimate of their worth could be formed and scholars could resurrect and re-evaluate these products of a crude but vigorous society of warriors and heroes.

The fact that a copy of the poem of the Cid was made by a clergyman in the early fourteenth century, however, indicates a growing interest among the educated in the popular works and in the national history of Spain. More important, the *eruditos,* the learned and literate, were not only becoming interested in conserving creative documents of the recent past, but by the middle of the thirteenth century were themselves writing poetry in the popular tongue. These poems, called *mester de clerecía*, as distinct from the popular epics of the people and professional entertainers, are written by a single author who brings to his work greater regularity of meter and style, a classical and historical background, and language more elevated and more varied than that of the *cantares de gesta*. The form of this poetry is *cuaderna vía*, which consists of stanzas of four monorhymed Alexandrines, or lines of fourteen syllables, each divided into hemistichs of seven syllables. There is an apparent similarity in this form to the rhymed series in the *Poema de mío Cid* last quoted. The *Poema de Fernán González*, written between 1250 and 1271, is a learned version or rewriting of an earlier *cantar de gesta*, in the measured and polished style of the *clerecía*. It begins with a preamble which narrates the history of Spain from the appearance of Christianity to the conquest of the Visigothic kingdoms by the Moors and outlines some events of the reconquest. Fernán González, who gains the independence of Castile from León and Navarre through both shrewdness and military ability, emerges as a national hero in battles which are more feudal and political than religious.

The earliest Spanish poet known to us by name is Gonzalo de Berceo (late twelfth century through 1264), probably a clergyman in the Benedictine monastery of San Millán de la Cogolla. Berceo's extensive work is religious in subject matter. Three poems are dedicated to the lives of saints, three more are dedicated to the Virgin Mary. The most important of these is the *Milagros de nuestra señora* (*Miracles of Our Lady*), a collection of twenty-five popular legends recounting miracles attributed to the intercession of the Virgin. These legends were widely circulated in the Middle Ages, and so the subject matter comes to Berceo ready-made. The originality of his work lies in the grace and charm of his verse, the skill with which he retells these legends in the language of his time, and the light touch which he usually retains in introducing learned elements and language into his work.

Two elements that are most outstanding in his poetry are his personalism, his awareness of his own creative role in the composition of his verse, and his lyrical awareness of the world about him. These qualities stand in direct contrast to the *cantar de gesta,* which was anonymous and cumulative, the product of a whole tradition, in which there is little awareness of landscape or the setting in which events occur. We see at once in the opening stanzas of the *Milagros* that a totally different idea of man in the world is being presented.

> *Yo maestro Gonzalvo de Berceo nombrado*
> *yendo en romería caecí en un prado*
> *verde e bien sencido, de flores bien poblado,*
> *lugar cobdiciaduero para hombre cansado.*
>
> *Daban olor sobejo las flores bien olientes,*
> *refrescaban en hombre las caras e las mientes,*
> *manaban cada canto fuentes claras corrientes,*
> *en verano bien frías, en invierno calientes.*
>
> *La verdura del prado, la olor de las flores,*
> *las sombras de los árboles, de templados sabores*
> *refrescáronme todo, e perdí los sudores:*
> *podría vivir el hombre con aquellos olores.*

I, Master Gonzalvo de Berceo by name
going on a pilgrimage, happened on a meadow,
green and uncut, abundant with flowers,
a delightful place for a weary man.
The fragrant flowers gave delightful odors,
refreshing a man in body and mind,
from every rock there flowed fresh, running fountains,
in the summer cool, in the winter, warm.

> The green plants of the field, the smell of the flowers,
> the shade of the trees, a soothing delight,
> they all refreshed me, and I lost my hot sweat:
> a man could live on those smells alone.

The poet goes on to describe fruits, birds, stones, and fountains in strongly personal, sensual language, and then interprets each of the images as metaphors of the Christian religion. The green and spotless meadow is the symbol of the Virgin; the four fountains are the four Gospels, the trees are the miracles of the Virgin. The work is thus translated into medieval allegory, but the quality of the verse which describes the first level of visual and sensual response to the world of nature is undeniably the tone of a new direction in poetry. This is the voice of man in the world, in close and immediate contact with the joys of nature, and the first poetic awareness in Spanish of the external world as a realm of aesthetic meaning and beauty.

Under the leadership and direction of King Alfonso X (1221–84), known with good reason as Alfonso the Wise, there flourished in Castile a renaissance of lyric poetry, legal theory and reform, and a recapitulation of national history and the natural sciences. It cannot be determined to what extent Alfonso X took a hand in the writings which issued from his court, but certainly the direction, commission, and completion of these projects show him to have been a superbly gifted and intelligent patron of arts which, in the Middle Ages, had been little appreciated or cultivated. The *Cantigas* is a collection of over four hundred lyric poems, written in *gallego,* a dialect of northwestern Spain related to Portuguese. *Gallego* was at that time considered a more "literary" dialect than Castilian Spanish, probably owing to a more firmly established tradition of lyric poetry. The *cantigas* are poems in praise of the Virgin, and are generally believed to be the work of Alfonso himself. An example of one of the *cantigas* is given on page 27. Of the poems, forty express deep and sometimes exaggerated religious sentiment. The remainder are narrative, dealing with popular legends and accounts of miracles attributed to the Virgin. A number of these coincide with Berceo's *Milagros*, and it is clear that both collections make use of widely diffused tales popular throughout Spain and most of Europe in the Middle Ages.

The first *Crónica general* is a compilation of peninsular history which was begun under the direction of Alfonso X and finished, after his death, in the reign of Sancho IV. The first part of the *Crónica* traces the early history of the peninsula through the Roman colonization and through the Gothic period up to the time of the Moorish invasion. In linking the history of the peninsula with the Roman and earlier populations, Alfonso expresses a nascent nationalism which will achieve its full development some two centuries later with the unification of Spain under Ferdinand and Isabella. The second part of the *Crónica* is rather more interesting from a literary point of view; it contains prose versions of many of the earlier epic poems, through which it is possible to reconstruct, to some extent, their content and form. This realistic fusion of epic and historical elements is unique in European literature.

The *Siete partidas*, earlier entitled the *Book of the Laws*, is a compendium of legal theory and codes of practice which represents the work of many jurists under the guidance of Alfonso. These, like Alfonso's works on astronomy and chess, are of scant literary interest, although they are of some importance in the related field of philology, in providing examples of Spanish as it was written and spoken in the thirteenth century. Perhaps the greatest accomplishment of this literary court is the stabilization of the language and the provision of norms for a standard speech. The prose is recognizably Castilian and can be pretty well understood in its general outlines by anyone familiar with contemporary Spanish. *Calila y Dimna*, a book of fables which Alfonso ordered translated from Arabic to Spanish, has been very influential in Spanish, indeed in world literature. The source of *Calila y Dimna* is an ancient Sanskrit collection of fables, the *Panchatantra*, which provided the material of many collections familiar to the Western world. They reached Europe first in the Arabic version and were later translated into Latin, Greek, Hebrew, and Spanish.

The fourteenth century in general presents itself as a period of recompilation, imitation, uninspired continuation of earlier forms, and the recording of trivial events. The forms which had developed earlier are continued with little verve or originality. The popular epic form is represented in the *Mocedades de Rodrigo*, a contrived and fantastic account of the early exploits of the Cid which lacks the historicity and directness which the older poem has. The *mester de clerecía* also declines in this period. Two examples, the *Vida de San Ildefonso* and the *Proverbios del sabio Salomón* (*Proverbs of Solomon the Wise*) lack Berceo's grace of language and poetic skill. Historical chronicles are numerous, many of them consisting of rehashed material from the first *Crónica general* of Alfonso X. One figure, however, stands forth in this century as a literary giant, to take his place among the outstanding creative poets of Western literature. This is Juan Ruiz, Archpriest of Hita, author of the *Libro de buen amor* (*Book of Good Love*). Very little is known of Juan Ruiz beyond his name, his position, and the fact that he lived and wrote in or near Alcalá de Henares, a town a few kilometers outside Madrid, which was later to become the seat of a great Spanish university and was the birthplace of Cervantes. Ruiz probably wrote considerably more than we have extant; what remains of his work is a long poem—1728 strophes, much of it in *cuaderna vía*, the four-line, monorhymed stanza employed in the *mester de clerecía*. The poem comes to us without a specific title but has come to be known as the *Libro de buen amor*, as Juan Ruiz himself repeatedly calls it.

The title refers to the main theme of the work, a distinction between the ordinary love for the things of this world, and the love of the divine, which is "buen amor." So grand a theme obviously gives the author ample room to explore the love of food and wine, of women, of money, of self, and to contrast these passions with the love of the divine. Large and diverse as it is, the book is not an encyclopedia or compendium. It is, rather, episodic: the author alternates amorous adventures with "examples" or moral points made through apologues, fables, and anecdotes; autobiography with songs in praise of the Virgin; complex allegory with the most realistic sketches of his servants, his go-between, and his ladies. Juan Ruiz shows himself to be entirely familiar with the earthier side of human frailty and, although clearly a religious man, he is the product of a society which took neither itself nor its professed moralities too seriously. He was a man who lived his times to the full, and with the genius of a major poet shows us a witty, charming, and robust picture of Castilian life in the fourteenth century. There is nothing in Romance literature to match the *Libro de buen amor* for its spirit, charm, and originality until, almost two centuries later, Rabelais gave the world his *Gargantua* and *Pantagruel*. The spirit of the works is similar in many ways, but the satire and humor of Juan Ruiz does not depend upon the fantasy and exaggeration, the overblown rhetoric, and scatological detail for which Rabelais is known. The *Libro de buen amor* is a magnificent example of the economy of style, precision of language, and compression of meaning which typifies the genius of Spanish literature.

The poem is made up of many parts and many influences. The author was a man of good though not extraordinary education for his times, who brought to his work not only all that he knew but all that he had observed and lived. For convenience, it is possible to divide the work into two basic elements, one narrative and the other lyrical. The narrative line appears, disappears, and reappears throughout the poem and is concerned mainly with the archpriest's various loves and amorous adventures. This aspect of the work has been considered by some critics as a forerunner of the picaresque novel. Interrupted from time to time by the lyrical portions, fables, allegories, and satire, it reappears always to detail the archpriest's struggle with a new passion and his frustrations in the pursuit of Moorish girls, mountain girls, city girls, a nun.

Typical of his biting satire is a long section subtitled "On the Properties of Money."

Mucho faz' el dinero, mucho es de amar:
Al torpe faze bueno é ome de prestar,
Ffaze correr al coxo é al mudo fablar,
El que non tiene manos, dyneros quier' tomar.

Sea un ome nesçio é rudo labrador,
Los dyneros le fazen fidalgo é sabydor,
Quanto más algo tiene, tanto es de más valor;
El que non há dineros, non es de sy señor.

Sy tovyeres dyneros, avrás consolaçión,
Plazer é alegría é del papa ración,
Conprarás parayso, ganarás salvaçión:
Do son muchos dineros, es mucha bendiçión.

Yo vy allá en Roma, do es la santidat,
Que todos al dinero fazíanl' omilidat,
Grand onrra le fazían con grand solenidat:
Todos a él se omillan como a la magestat.

Ffazíe muchos priores, obispos é abbades,
Arçobispos, dotores, patriarcas, potestades,
A muchos clérigos nesçios dávales denidades.
Fazíe verdat mentiras é mentiras verdades.

Money does great things, it is greatly to be loved:
It makes the dull man good and worthy,
It makes the lame to run and the mute to speak,
Even the man with no hands tries to grab it.

If a man be a foolish and simple laborer,
Money makes him noble and wise,
The more he has, the more he's worth;
He who does not have money is not even lord of himself.

If you have money you shall have consolation,
Pleasure and joy, and from the Pope, benefits,
You will purchase Paradise, you will earn salvation;
Where there is plenty of money, there are many blessings.

I saw there in Rome, where holiness dwells,
That all gave obeisance to money,
They gave it great honor with great solemnity;
All bow down before it as they would to royalty.

It has created many priors, bishops, and abbots,
Archbishops, doctors of the church, patriarchs, potentates,
It has given high dignities to many foolish priests,
It has made truth of lies and lies of truth.

This anticlericalism is a part of the traditional criticism of the clergy which is one manifestation of the most devout qualities of Spanish Catholicism. The Spaniard has always been quick to denounce any deviation from the high ideals which he expects the clergy to embody. Thus these lines, written by an archpriest a century and a half before the first stirrings of Protestantism in Europe, do not represent a rejection of the established Church, but rather a typical excoriation of worldly abuses in a period of considerable clerical license. He is equally quick to commend true religious devotion and self-sacrifice when he encounters it.

The personalism which first began to emerge in Berceo is fully developed in Juan Ruiz. We see his reaction to all aspects of the life of his period, and for the first time in Spanish literature we have a self-portrait of the author, given by his go-between to ensure objectivity:

"Señora," diz' la vieja: "yo le veo a menudo:
"El cuerpo á muy grant, mienbros largos, trefudo,
"La cabeça non chica, velloso, pescuçudo,
"El cuello non muy luengo, cabel' prieto, orejudo.

"Las çejas apartadas, prietas como carbón,
"El su andar infiesto, bien como de pavón,
"El paso segurado é de buena rasón,
"La su nariz es luenga, esto le desconpón'.

"Las ençías bermejas é la fabla tunbal,
"La boca non pequena, labros al comunal,
"Más gordos que delgados, bermejos como coral,
"Las espaldas byen grandes, las muñecas atal.

"Los ojos há pequeños, es un poquillo baço,
"Los pechos delanteros, bien trefudo el braço,
"Bien cunplidas las piernas; el pie, chico pedaço;
"Señora, dél non vy más: por su amor vos abraço.

"Es ligero, valiente, byen mançebo de días,
"Sabe los estrumentos é todas juglarías,
"Doñeador alegre, ¡por las çapatas mías!
"Tal ome qual yo digo non es en todas erías."

"Madame," says the old lady, "I see him often:
He's large-bodied, long-limbed, spirited,
His head not small, shaggy, thick-necked,
The neck not very long, dark hair, flap-eared,

The eyebrows well separated, black as coal,
His walk is pompous, rather like a peacock,
His step is sure and determined,
His nose is long; this bothers him.

His gums bright red and his voice cavernous,
His mouth is not small, his lips so-so,
More thick than thin, and red as coral,
His shoulders quite large, his wrists likewise.

He has small eyes, he is rather dark,
Deep-chested, thick-armed,
Well-developed legs, small-footed;
Madame, that's all I've seen of him: in the name of his love
                              I greet you.

He is graceful, valiant, young but mature,
He plays several instruments and knows songs,
A gallant, by the shoes I'm wearing!
Such a man as I describe is not found on every corner."

The archpriest's unfortunate and inconclusive love life is treated with wit and irony and a wry knowledge of the ways and wiles of women. He gives lusty literary embodiment to the figure of the *trotaconventos*, the elderly female go-between in love affairs, entrusted to carry messages and to arrange meetings. The type of the cynical, mercenary old woman who, for a price, manages to overcome all the social barriers and safeguards, is found again and again in Spanish literature, but her character and role are first developed in the work of Juan Ruiz. The biographical element is certainly to some extent fictionalized, but there are undoubtable touches of realism in the work. Other portions of the narrative are straightforward compositions, with elements from classical sources, such as episodes derived from Ovid and retold fables from Aesop and other collections. An important component is allegorical material derived from medieval folk sources. The lyrical poetry provides us with a very rich collection of religious and profane verse. A number of *cantigas* or praises of the Virgin follow the tradition of Berceo and Alfonso the Wise. A collection of mountain songs, student songs, and the rhymes that blind beggars chanted provides us with a knowledge of the popular verse of the period. Juan Ruiz tells us that he composed many of these on demand and he includes a few examples of his skill in the *Libro de buen amor*. A fine example of the goliardic tradition, in which student singing groups went from tavern to tavern performing for the guests and requesting payment in coins or a glass of wine, is the following *zéjel:*

Señores, dat al escolar,	Gentlemen, give to the student,
Que vos viene demandar.	Who comes to beg of you.
Dat lymosna é rraçión:	Give a coin and a tidbit:
Faré por vos oraçión,	I'll pray for you,
Que Dios vos dé salvaçión;	That God save you:
Quered por Dios a mí dar.	For His sake be generous.
Quando a Dios diéredes cuenta	When to God you must give account
De los algos é de la renta,	Of how you used your goods and income,
Escusarvos ha de afruenta,	It will help to ease your shame,
La lymosna por Dios far.	The charity given in God's name.
Por una raçión que dedes,	For a little tidbit you may give me,
Vos çiento de Dios tomedes;	From God you'll receive a hundred;
E en parayso entredes:	And into Paradise you'll go:
¡Así lo quiera él mandar!	May God have it so!

The immense literary value of the *Libro de buen amor* derives primarily from the personality and sheer literary genius of the author: the economy of language, the vivid descriptiveness of certain passages balanced against rapidity of action in others, the choice and arrangement of episodes to give movement and variety to the narrative, the creation in a few simple lines of characters who come instantly to life, the amused and tolerant view of a society which could itself integrate a deep and sincere religious devotion with a full acceptance of all the pleasures the world offers. While it would not be correct to say that the *Libro de buen amor* is a work of the Renaissance—at least as the term specifically encompasses the works of Petrarch and Boccaccio in Italy—a new vigor, an interest in popular traditions, and a new feeling for the popular language as an articulate and powerful poetic vehicle, so typical of the early Renaissance, are surely present. In addition to this, the fusion of popular and religious material with an all-encompassing wit and an intense personalism provides us with a major work as distinctively Spanish as the *Cantar de mío Cid* before, or the masterpiece of Cervantes which was yet to come.

Another figure of talent and originality is Pero López de Ayala (1332-1407). A man of unusual intelligence and abilities, López de Ayala had a brilliant political career as ambassador to France, mayor of Toledo, and chancellor of Castile. His *Crónicas*, which deal with the history of his period, the second half of the fourteenth century, are detailed, dramatic, and judicious. The delineation of personalities and the interpretation of events in a turbulent and violent period show the author to have been gifted with detachment and insight, and are still quite enjoyable reading. Ayala is also the author of an extensive poetic work, the *Rimado de Palacio*, one of the last examples of the *mester de clerecía*. It is made up of various themes and poetic forms; the content of the *Rimado* is almost as varied as that of the *Libro de buen amor*. Like the *Libro*, the only central unity is the personality of the author himself. The tone of the poem, however, is quite different. It is primarily didactic and moralistic, with long sections devoted to various aspects of virtue and vice, to the examination of questions of theology, to political philosophy, and to social satire of the atmosphere of the royal court and of its innumerable hangers-on. As in Juan Ruiz's work, lyrical sections are scattered throughout. They are mostly of a devotional nature similar to the songs dedicated to the Virgin which the archpriest wrote. The touch of universal genius, the enormous creative talent, the ability to create character and infuse life into words, which Juan Ruiz so abundantly possessed, is lacking in Ayala. He was unable to rise above the complexity of his material or to integrate it into a meaningful statement of his own experience. In short, it lacks in theme the exuberance to lift it to the highest level of creative literature.

The third figure of major importance in the fourteenth century is Don Juan Manuel (1282–1349?), a member of the royal family and grandson of St. Ferdinand. His major work, *El Conde Lucanor o el libro de Patronio* (*Count Lucanor or the Book of Patronius*), is a collection of fifty apologues or short stories loosely strung together by a central motif. In each case, the young Count Lucanor brings a question of moral or social relations to his mentor and counselor, the sage Patronio. In each case, Patronio resolves the problem by means of a tale which is ended with a rhymed couplet, giving the "moral" of the story. The sources are to be found in Aesop's fables, in the oriental collections brought to Spain by the Arabs (*Calila y Dimna, Sendebar*), in the Bible, in classical sources, and in earlier Spanish chronicles. The importance of Don Juan Manuel's work lies primarily in his ability to bring these diverse tales and fables together in a coherent structure and to give them expression in clear Castilian prose, retaining at all times his vision of a unified work of art. *El Conde Lucanor* was completed in 1335—antedating Boccaccio's *Decameron* by thirteen years. While it lacks the zest and raciness of the Italian masterwork, it provides one of the early sources of the novel in Western literature. Many of the apologues are familiar to us from other sources: such fables as the story of the milkmaid who is taking her pitcher of milk to market, the story of the fox and the crow, a version of the story from which Shakespeare wrote *The Taming of the Shrew,* and a source of Andersen's *The Emperor's New Clothes.*

Summary

The earliest literary work in Spanish which has survived to the present time is the *Cantar de mío Cid.* It is clear evidence of a virile tradition of folk poetry in which contemporary history, wars, weddings, and conquests were recounted. Evidence that this work was not an isolated phenomenon is found in fragments of other poems and in later prose chronicles which retell the stories which the earlier epics celebrated in verse. A century later, a more learned and sophisticated form of literature had developed. By the middle of the thirteenth century the *mester de clerecía,* poetic narratives written by educated monks in the popular language, shows itself in a highly developed form in the work of Gonzalo de Berceo. These narratives drew primarily on Church history, anecdotes from the lives of saints, and popular tradition or legends based on miracles attributed to the Virgin. The differences in these two types of work are numerous. The *mester de clerecía* employs a freer and more sophisticated form of language; the demands of rhyme and meter are strictly observed; the content is most frequently of a religious or historical nature.

In addition to these forms, there was in the northwestern part of the peninsula a growing tradition of lyric poetry written in a dialect intermediate between Spanish and Portuguese, called *gallego.* So popular and influential was this tradition that, when Castilian poets undertook to write lyric poetry, they imitated works in *gallego* in both form and language. For this reason, Alfonso X wrote his *Cantigas* in the dialect of the northwest. The works of history, law, and science begun at the behest of Alfonso X represent a major attempt in the great tradition of St. Isidor to bring together in one great body of knowledge all of the learning and traditions of the Roman, Visigothic, and Arabic periods of Spain's multicolored history. In the translation of *Calila y Dimna,* King Alfonso transmits in some part the tales and folklore of the very ancient Aryan past.

The fourteenth century in Spanish literature is a period in which earlier forms, particularly the epic and the *mester de clerecía* continued to be written with diminishing artistic success. Two of the outstanding writings of the period, Juan Ruiz's *Libro de buen amor* and Pero López de Ayala's *Rimado de Palacio,* are technically examples of the *mester de clerecía*—long, carefully polished poems which elaborate on religious, didactic, or historical themes—but in both tone and material these works exceed the limitations of the earlier *mester* and point the way to a literature which is more subjective, more immediate, and more varied. With the *Conde Lucanor,* of Don Juan Manuel, a venerable type of literature which had its prehistoric origins in the Eastern world is given a new look, an organic integration, and a Castilian voice. The influence of the work has been wide, and in it we see the beginnings of a literary form which will grow in interest, sophistication, and significance in European literature—the novel.

CHAPTER 3
THE FIFTEENTH CENTURY

As the Moorish states in all parts of Spain fell into progressive political, military, and literary decadence, the atmosphere of the established Christian centers became increasingly more favorable to an intensive and varied literary development. The growth of cities had produced a comparatively urban and cultured population with sufficient leisure and security to find time for literary entertainment. The growth of commerce had brought Spaniards into contact with other societies that had developed original and stimulating literary traditions. The growth of a recognized and responsible central government, following the definitive unification of Castile and León under Ferdinand III early in the thirteenth century, had provided a court or central cultural focus toward which men of literary ability could gravitate. The growing self-awareness of the writer as a unique creative personality, from the anonymity of the *cantares de gesta* to the tentative identification we see in the poetry of Berceo, to intense and affirmative individualism of the later *mester de clerecía* in Juan Ruiz and López de Ayala, demands an ever broader field in which to realize and fulfill itself. In obedience to this sort of aesthetic need and nurtured on the expanding possibilities of a settled and prospering society, the fifteenth century represents a period of great fecundity in the development and widening of literary genres.

The medieval *cantar de gesta*, which had so magnificently served the needs of a society of embattled warriors, undergoes a major change, possibly through the influence of the *mester de clerecía*. In the new society there was neither time, place, nor public for the recitation of the long and usually complex epic poems, but the great deeds, the great heroes still held their magic for the general public. These survive in a new poetic form, the *romances*. The anonymous *romances* are short poems of regular meter and assonance which capture an intense and dramatic moment—of sorrow, of defeat, of parting, of return—in simple and direct language. They are generally fragmentary, combining lyricism and narration taken from the dramatic high points of the epics. Some critics have thought that the oldest *romances* represent a survival of the raw material from which the long *cantares* grew, but the more generally accepted opinion is that they represent the opposite process; as the old *cantares* fell into oblivion, the best moments and the most stirring passages were conserved and polished and given new life.

Supporting this view is the fact that the earliest *romances* go back only to the middle of the fourteenth century, a time in which the *cantares* were in a period of final decadence and the oldest epic poems already forgotten. They share the realism and directness of the *cantares*, and also the greater polish and lyricism of the *mester de clerecía*. Some thousands of them have been collected and not all relate to the material of the Spanish epics. A number of them present dramatic moments of the conflict between Moors and Christians in frontier encounters (*fronterizo* ballads), while others deal with the legends of King Arthur and the Knights of the Round Table and the expedition of Charlemagne into Spain. Among the most interesting are those dealing with the history of Spain, which are close to the national consciousness, and with which the unknown poets who composed or adapted them felt an immediate identification.

One of the *romances* tells the story of the last Gothic King, Don Rodrigo, and the fall of Spain to the Moors in the year 711. Don Rodrigo, a brash and violent man, defies local tradition and all warnings by entering the enchanted Cave of Hercules in Toledo. There he sees a tapestry peopled with Arabic figures, and reads an inscription which tells him that, when the first person enters the cave and sees the tapestry, Spain will be conquered by the nation represented. Don Rodrigo falls in love with a girl who is present at the court, called La Cava, the daughter of Count Julián.

Don Rodrigo takes the girl by force: instantly she loses her beauty, turning hideous in his arms. She then sends a message to her father, asking vengeance. Count Julián secretly allows the Moors to enter Spain and they not only dethrone Rodrigo but overrun the whole land. Rodrigo, a penitent fugitive, takes refuge in the mountains. There he meets a hermit who tells him that, to save his soul, he must seal himself in a cave with a two-headed serpent which will devour him alive. Rodrigo does so, and as he dies, the church bells ring out miraculously, announcing his salvation. The *romance* of Don Rodrigo is one of the later poems of this group, probably dating from the early sixteenth century. It serves as an example of the thematic material typical of these poems: legend, superstition, religion, and national history. We see elements of the earlier epic tradition as they are conserved and refined in the *romances:* the themes of heroism and tragedy, the extremely terse and compact language, and the uniquely Spanish verse form of a sixteen-syllable line divided into equal parts of eight syllables each. This form is seen in the lament of Don Rodrigo:

Ayer era Rey de España,—hoy no lo soy de una villa;
ayer villas y castillos,—hoy ninguno poseía;
ayer tenía criados,—hoy ninguno me servía;
hoy no tengo una almena—que pueda decir que es mía . . .

Yesterday I was King of Spain—today I rule not a town;
Yesterday towns and castles—today I possess not a one;
Yesterday I had servants—today no one serves me;
Today I haven't a battlement—that I can say is mine . . .

In addition to the *romances*, two important collections of lyric poetry date from the fifteenth century. The *Cancionero* (Songbook) *of Baena* (named for Juan Alfonso de Baena, who compiled the work) is a major collection of lyric verse by many poets from the latter part of the fourteenth century and the early part of the fifteenth, much influenced by Galician and Italian poetry. The *Cancionero of Stuñiga* (named for Lope de Stuñiga, whose work appears first in the collection) is an omnibus of verse produced in the highly sophisticated and humanistic Spanish court of Naples.

Perhaps the most "complete" literary man of the period was the Marqués de Santillana (1398–1458). A man of great intelligence and culture, Santillana knew the Latin classics well and was particularly well read in the French and Italian humanists. He was also interested in literary criticism, and his *Letter to the Count of Portugal* is the earliest work of reasoned literary opinion in the language. In the *Comedieta de Ponza*, a historical poem on the defeat of the Spanish ruler of Naples by the Genoese, and in the *Dialogue of Bias against Fortune*, a didactic poem of 180 stanzas, Santillana brings into play his almost excessive erudition with the use of allegory, classical and biblical allusion, and frequent reference to Dante and Boccaccio. His *Sonnets in the Italian Style* show the influence of Petrarch and frequently imitate the Italian writer directly. Santillana's work, at worst, is an imitation of the more overblown, elegant, and precious elements of Italian poetry of the Renaissance. Certainly he is a writer and intellectual who was most effective in introducing the Italian forms in Spain to the detriment, some critics feel, of Spanish verse traditions. At best, Santillana wrote with grace and a sensitive feeling for the Castilian language, as may be seen particularly in his ten *serranillas,* poems about the mountain girls who guided travelers through difficult mountain passes.

A poet of similar tastes and influence was Juan de Mena (1411–56). An imitator of Dante and translator of Homer, Mena's outstanding work is the *Laberinto de Fortuna,* known also as the *Trescientas* for the fact that it has nearly three hundred stanzas. This long poem is a sustained allegory, strongly influenced by Dante's *Divine Comedy,* by Lucan, and by Virgil. Of particular importance are the episodes from Spain's history, in which the poet shows an elevated patriotism and sense of Spanish national unity. His language is generally high-flown and complex, employing many expressions adopted from Latin and Italian, but occasionally Mena displays the touch of the real poet. Guided by Prudence, the poet is shown the "world machine"—the three wheels of past, present, and future, and the rewards for virtuous action, as exemplified in the lives of distinguished figures of classical and peninsular history. Mena reflects thoroughly Renaissance attitudes in his choice of language, his numerous allusions to classical myth and history, and his frequent reference to the totally inexplicable caprices of Fortune.

The greatest single poetic work of the century is the *Coplas por la muerte de su padre* (*Verses on the Death of His Father*), by Jorge Manrique (1440?–79). While other compositions of Manrique are little more than mediocre, this work of some forty stanzas achieves an appeal and a perfection which have been universally recognized. The American poet Longfellow translated the *Coplas* into English with marked success. Three major themes dominate the work: the evanescence of worldly goods (the classical *ubi sunt* of François Villon's "where are the snows of yesteryear?"); the importance, nonetheless, of gaining a name for rectitude and honor in this world; and finally the need for securing eternal life. Thus the poem offers an organic progression. The Stoic values are established, in which the world's illusions of pomp and wealth are devalued and the true worth of personal merit and integrity are proclaimed. Finally salvation as man's ultimate destiny is revealed.

These ideas are certainly not original; the civic virtues are announced clearly by the Roman Stoics, the total view is present in the *Poema de mío Cid,* and may be detected in every step of the evolution of Romance literature that follows. What is outstanding in the *Coplas* is the adequacy of poetic expression in a moment of great personal involvement with human sorrow. Rarely has Spanish verse so beautifully and effectively stated the Stoic acceptance of the inevitable, the human regard for personal integrity, and the divine hope for the salvation of the soul.

Recuerde el alma dormida, avive el seso y despierte contemplando cómo se pasa la vida, cómo se viene la muerte tan callando; cuán presto se va el placer, cómo, después de acordado da dolor, cómo a nuestro parecer cualquiera tiempo pasado fué mejor. . . .	Let the sleeping soul awaken, arouse and enliven the mind, contemplating how life passes, how death comes so silently; how quickly pleasure goes, how pleasure remembered gives pain, how it always seems to us that any moment of the past was better. . . .
Nuestras vidas son los ríos que van a dar en la mar, que es el morir; allí van los señoríos derechos a se acabar y consumir;	Our lives are the rivers that are flowing into the sea which is death; the lofty titles flow straight to extinction and oblivion;

allí los ríos caudales, / there the great rivers,
allí los otros, medianos / there the others, middling
y más chicos; / size, and the smallest;
allegados, son iguales / once arrived, all are equal,
los que viven por sus manos / those who live by their hands
y los ricos. . . . / and the rich. . . .

Ved de cuán poco valor / See of how little value
son las cosas tras que andamos / are the things we run after
y corremos; / and pursue;
que, en este mundo traidor, / for in this deceptive world,
aun primero que muramos / even before we die
las perdemos: / we lose them:
de ellas deshace la edad, / Some are decayed by age,
de ellas casos desastrados / some by disasters
que acaecen, / that occur,
de ellas, por su calidad, / some, by their very nature,
en los más altos estados / in their finest moment
desfallecen. / fade away.

A rich vein of satire is uncovered in the fifteenth century which will prove to be one of the most viable and productive forms of Spanish literature. Certainly satirical elements had appeared earlier; they are strongly present in some sections of the *Libro de buen amor*. In the *Danza de la muerte* (*Dance of Death*) satire becomes a major element of the work, although there is a didactic religious tone present as well. This anonymous poem of the early part of the century elaborates a theme that was widely used in European poetry and painting, as in the German *Totentanz* and the French *Danse macabre*. The figure of Death appears, calling to all classes, high and low, to come, join the dance. The macabre master calls all in turn: emperor, pope, king, cardinal, duke, merchant, beggar. Each tries to flee or postpone his hour, but in vain. The lesson is a democratic as well as religious one: that the grave yawns alike for high and low, that rank, wealth, and power are essentially meaningless in the face of man's common fate. The satiric elements and the grim humor of the remarks which Death addresses to each figure present a wry commentary on a highly structured society of privilege and prerogative and, not infrequently, abuses.

DICE LA MUERTE:

> *Yo soy la muerte cierta a todas criaturas*
> *que son y serán en el mundo durante;*
> *demando y digo: "¡Oh, hombre!, ¿por qué curas*
> *de vida tan breve en punto pasante?*
> *Pues non hay tan fuerte nin recio gigante*
> *que desde mi arco se puede amparar,*
> *conviene que mueras cuando lo tirar*
> *con esta mi flecha cruel traspasante . . ."*

DICE EL EMPERADOR:

> *¿Qué cosa es ésta que a tan sin pavor*
> *me lleva a su danza a fuerza sin grado?*
> *Creo que es la muerte que non ha dolor*
> *de hombre que grande o cuitado.*
> *¿Non hay ningún rey nin duque esforzado*
> *que de ella me pueda ahora defender?*
> *¡Acorredme todos! Mas non puede ser,*
> *que ya tengo de ella todo el seso turbado.*

DICE LA MUERTE:

> *Emperador muy grande, en el mundo potente,*
> *non vos cuitedes, ca non es tiempo tal,*
> *que librar vos pueda imperio nin gente,*
> *oro nin plata, nin otro metal.*
> *Aquí perderedes el vuestro caudal,*
> *que atesorasteis con gran tiranía,*
> *faciendo batallas de noche e de día:*
> *morid, non curedes; venga el cardenal.*

DEATH SAYS:

    I am the certain death of all creatures
that are or will be while the world lasts;
I ask and I say: "Oh, mortal! Why so much care
for a life so brief and fleeting?
Since there is no giant so strong or so powerful
who can defend himself from my bow,
thou too must die when I loose
my cruel, transfixing arrow. . . .

THE EMPEROR SAYS:

    What is this that so fearlessly
drags me off to dance against my will?
I think it is Death, which has no pity
on any man, however high or lowly.
Is there no king or brave duke
who can defend me against it?
Help me, all of you! But it may not be,
for already it has my brains reeling.

DEATH SAYS:

    Great Emperor, power in the world,
don't bother, for this is not the moment
when your realm or your vassals can help you,
or gold or silver, or any other metal.
Here you will lose your treasure
which you stored up by tyranny,
fighting battles night and day:
Die; don't struggle. Let the cardinal come.

The cardinal joins the dance too; his weaknesses and shams are exposed and he meets the same implacable fate.

The turbulent times of the reign of Henry IV gave rise to a number of political satires, the most venomous being *Coplas del Provinciano* (*The Provincial's Songs*) in which the court of Henry IV is seen as a monastery which the provincial, a church official, comes to inspect.

Every sort of vice and chicanery is uncovered with specific allusions to the courtiers involved. Needless to say, these *Coplas* are anonymous, and every effort was made to suppress them, but still they circulated from hand to hand and often in very imperfect copies. The *Coplas de Mingo Revulgo*, of the same period, assume a more modified tone. The treatment of the theme is allegorical, in the form of a pastoral dialogue between Mingo Revulgo (*revulgo* means "ordinary" or "common"), who represents the *pueblo* or villagers of Spain, and a prophetic shepherd who inquires after the present state of the flock and then foresees social turbulence, wars, and famine.

The major work of social satire of the fifteenth century is the *Corbacho* or *Reproval of Earthly Love*, of Alfonso Martínez de Toledo, Archpriest of Talavera. (1398?–1470?). Little is known of his life or background beyond his title, some church offices which he held, and his literary product. The *Corbacho* resembles the *Libro de buen amor* in many ways, and it is clear that the author had that work before him if not as a model at least as an inspiration. He satirizes the follies and vanities of both men and women, nobles, ecclesiastics, and commoners. Like Juan Ruiz, his eye misses nothing and the realism of his work is refreshing. The *Corbacho* is a prose work and it marks a great advance in the creation of a direct and vivid style which is completely adequate to its theme. Two opposed currents of language are blended together, the humanistic, Latinate tendencies of the Renaissance and the vivid and direct realism of everyday Castilian speech. His satire is more caustic and his attitude more didactic and moralistic than that of Ruiz, but the two archpriests, who wrote a century apart, have in common an eye for detail, an ear for popular language, and an ability to characterize sharply and precisely.

There is much historical writing in this period which gives a fascinating account of a decadent and unsettled society, but it is of scant literary interest. There is, however, a biographer of the era whose work is both absorbing and enlightening. Fernán Pérez de Guzmán (1370?–1460), through his *Generaciones y semblanzas* (*Generations and Sketches*), may be ranked as the first writer of modern biography in the peninsula. His style is clear and precise, his treatment of the major figures of his time exact, detailed, and piquant. His model is Plutarch, and, like the classical biographer, he demonstrates an unusual ability to portray the outstanding and interesting personages of his period with insight, understanding, and objectivity. His work is a compendium of absorbing studies which continues to be a model for contemporary Spanish biography.

The development of the novel of chivalry was of great importance in this period. These long, complex novels were of immense popularity, read by all who could read, often read aloud to those who could not. Among the more avid Spanish readers were St. Ignatius, St. Teresa, the Humanist Juan de Valdés, and the Emperor Charles V. In terms of the might and loyalty of the heroes, the purity of the maidens, the capacity for evil of the villains, and the fantastic quality of the adventures, these novels may in some aspects be compared to the comic books of today. The sources of the genre may be found in the medieval epic, in the legends of King Arthur and the Knights of the Round Table and other Breton elements and in the traditions of courtly love. The plots are complex, the characterizations are generally rudimentary, the ideals of courtly love and religious piety are monumental, and the whole atmosphere of conflict is developed in an unrealistic never-never land, with enchanted islands, magical swords, super-horses as well as supermen, hulking giants, long-bearded wizards, and an overwhelming sense of divinely guided destiny. The novel of chivalry brings to Spanish prose a sense of the marvelous, the miraculous, the divinely oriented, and the fantastically imaginative.

These long works were cliff-hangers probably meant to be read aloud during a long winter. The earliest Spanish novel of chivalry is the *Caballero Cifar*, which, despite its derivation from traditional Eastern sources, has obvious Spanish elements. Although the earliest edition of the work was published in Seville in 1512, its origin can be placed in the early years of the fourteenth century. The caballero's squire Ribaldo is derived from life, similar in some respects to the astute lieutenants of el Cid, to Don Furón, whom the Archpriest of Hita hires as his go-between when Trotaconventos dies, to Sancho Panza, and to the later heroes of the picaresque novel. But the most popular of the novels of chivalry was *Amadís de Gaula*. We do not know the date of composition, the identity of the author, the country of origin, or even the language in which the original was written. It has been attributed to Spain, Portugal, and France without decisive proof. The earliest mention of the novel places it, in some primitive form, before 1325. The extant version is a highly polished refurbishment, put together with many changes in style, plot, and language, by Garci Ordóñez de Montalvo and published in 1508. Fragments of a version of about 1420 have recently come to light which give an idea of the extent of later changes.

All is fantasy here—from the birth of Amadís, a foundling who, like Moses, is set adrift in a basket along with cryptic but identifying trinkets, through his training and career as a knight, his much-interrupted courting of Princess Oriana, to his ultimate cataclysmic victories and the birth of their son, Esplendián. The hero moves always in a world of magic and adventure, battles and spells, misunderstandings and separations.

Soon the novel of chivalry began to proliferate and, like the contemporary soap opera, was carried on through generations. There are a dozen *Books of Amadís* in all, by various continuators of varying talent. Other knights-errant were created too; Cervantes tells us that Don Quijote had more than a hundred novels of chivalry on his bookshelves.

The resurgence of theater is a development of major importance in fifteenth-century Spain. With the fall of the Roman Empire and the decline of an urban civilization the theater, both as popular entertainment and as an artistic medium, had all but disappeared. A primitive form of drama had remained alive in the Church in tableaux celebrating central themes of biblical history, such as the Adoration of the Magi and the representations of Holy Week. This liturgical drama has survived in many European literatures; in Spain it is best represented in the *Auto de los Reyes Magos,* a fragment of a verse-play of 147 lines probably of the early thirteenth century, which represents the three wise men, each following the star, meeting, agreeing to journey together, arriving at the court of King Herod, and asking Herod where they may find the newborn King. It ends with Herod's plot to slaughter the newborn infants. In these opening lines, King Gaspar sees the star and resolves to follow it.

GASPAR, SOLO

Dios criador; ¡cuál maravilla!
¡No sé cuál es aquesta estrella!
Agora primas la he veída,
poco tiempo ha que es nacida.
¿Nacido es el Criador
que es de las gentes señor?
Non es verdad, non sé qué digo,
todo esto non vale un figo;
otra noche me lo cataré,
si es verdad, bien lo sabré.

> *¿Bien es verdad lo que yo digo?*
> *En todo, en todo lo prohío.*
> *¿Non puede ser otra señal?*
> *Aquesto es y non es al;*
> *nacido es Dios, por ver, de fembra*
> *en aqueste mes de diciembre.*
> *Allá iré o que fuere, adorarlo he,*
> *por Dios de todos lo tendré.*

GASPAR, ALONE

> God the Creator; how marvelous!
> I don't know what star that is!
> Now for the first time I've seen it,
> It was born just a while ago.
> Is the Creator born
> Who is Lord of all men?
> It can't be true, I don't know what I'm saying,
> All of this is meaningless;
> I'll watch for it another night
> If it is true, I'll know it then.
> Can what I say be true?
> I believe all of it, all of it.
> Can it be some other sign?
> That's what it is and nothing else
> God is born, truly, of woman
> In this month of December
> I shall go there, wherever it be, I will adore him.
> I shall take him for the God of all.

The form of the work is dialogued verse of very irregular scansion and uneven alliteration. There is no doubt that a religious theater of this sort was very popular both in the Church and in lay representations. More difficult to document is the existence of a secular theater, although it is likely that some primitive popular representational tradition had persisted.

Late in the fifteenth century a writer of great talent began to compose short dramatic works for the entertainment of the aristocratic guests of the Duke of Alba.

Juan del Encina (1469–1529) has been called the "patriarch of Spanish theater" for the fact that he is the first to compose dramatic works whose purpose was to amuse and whose plots had themes other than biblical. His works are strongly influenced by the classical eclogues of Virgil; indeed, he translated into Castilian and paraphrased several of Virgil's eclogues. The form of the eclogue presupposes a light and delicate fiction which shortly was to become very much the vogue in all forms of Spanish literature; a fiction which idealizes the life and loves of shepherds and shepherdesses, setting for its scene the green fields and tinkling brooks of the countryside and having as its action little more than meetings and conversations, usually on the theme of love, of those who tend the sheep. The *serranillas* of the Marqués de Santillana, as well as the older *autos* or religious dramas, which often represented the adoration of the shepherds, are influences on this artificial and often coy form. Juan del Encina is able, however, to inject strong comic and even tragic overtones into his work. In the *Auto del Repelón* two shepherds narrate in dialogue the mistreatment and boorish practical jokes which some university students inflict on them, and in the eclogue *Fileno, Zambardo y Cardonio* Fileno tells his friends of his love for the shepherd girl Cefira, who will have nothing to do with him. When his friends are unable to help or console him, Fileno kills himself.

The theater which follows Juan del Encina takes on aspects of the Italian influence then apparent in all genres of this period. Bartolomé de Torres Naharro (?–1531?) is the first writer to provide a reasoned theory of the nascent drama in his *Propalladia*, the general title under which he published his theater and poetry sometime around 1517. In a *Prohemio*, or statement of critical standards, he establishes the drama of five acts and limits the number of speaking parts, allowing not more than a dozen, but requiring at least enough to provide some activity on the stage. Torres Naharro also conceives of two types of dramatic possibility, real-life events or fantasies, which would include any historical situation in the one case and any theatrical invention or made-up plot in the other. Thus there is implicit in his theory of dramatic genres the whole range of subject matter later elaborated in the drama of the Golden Age. The plays of Torres Naharro embody these amplified ideas of theatrical possibility with a number of *comedias* in both genres. They bring a liberal realism to the literature of the time which will have its full fruition later in the plays of Lope de Vega, Calderón, and Tirso de Molina. The new amplitude of concept, in terms of character, milieu, and action, is to a large extent the result of Italian influences. The plots are light and trivial, but the characters and language often reflect very trenchant realities of the times, paricularly in picturing the lower classes of the period.

The intermingling of Renaissance influences, primarily Italian and French, with the more firmly rooted native realism and satire, produced a hybrid that was not in all cases viable. The foreign influences stressed a new poetic vocabulary and elements of complex allegory and classical allusion. The native Spanish currents stressed characterization and realism, "calling bread bread and wine wine." It is not surprising, therefore, that a certain dichotomy should exist, that literary production should occur on both levels, and that a resolution should be possible in which these currents would mix and find a common denominator.

The media which best facilitates this resolution is the novel. The growth of towns and established municipal governments in the fourteenth century had increased the degree of literacy enormously, and some elementary education was generally available to townsmen. Some basic literacy, at least, was within the reach of most who lived in provincial capitals, and in the absence of other diversion, the reading of entertaining fictions became popular. As in most societies, the most popular theme was love and its frustrations. In the last half of the fifteenth century, a number of sentimental novels appeared which grew out of the European tradition to achieve a new form. They incorporated much that had gone before: adventures and knight-errantry from the novels of chivalry; introspective psychological analysis from the tradition of Arabic, medieval, and Renaissance poetry; moralistic and didactic qualities from Latin and Visigothic sources; and occasionally the native realism of the Hispanic turn of mind. These sentimental novels reflect the ideals of courtly love as well as an almost savage insistence on sexual morality, where a penurious and exacting code allows for no dalliance on either side, a dalliance which, if discovered, would result in death for either or both partners.

The best of the sentimental novels is *La Carcel de amor* (*The Prison of Love*), of Diego de San Pedro. Written in the last decade of the fifteenth century, this novel employs allegory, an exotic locale, the passions of the highborn, and all the apparatus of courtly love, to detail the highly exaggerated frustration of a perfectly possible romance. Leriano, son of the Duke of Macedonia, loves Laureola, daughter of the king. The author first meets Leriano as he is being dragged into allegorical captivity by a savage wildman who represents Desire. Psychologically imprisoned by his emotions and frustrations, the prisoner employs the author as an emissary to carry letters to Laureola. Much of the novel consists of the correspondence between the suffering lover and the disdainful princess, whose sole concern is what people might think should she yield to a moment of tenderness. Envious courtiers learn of Leriano's love and denounce the two to the king, falsely declaring that they have been seen together under suspicious circumstances. The mere suspicion of an illicit love is enough to make the king condemn his daughter to death. Leriano liberates the princess and kills the chief rumor-monger in a duel. The princess rejects her suitor even more emphatically and so he pines away of love and hunger. In the final scene, Leriano's mother comes to persuade him to desist from his avowed death by hunger, but all that Leriano will take for nourishment is a final cup containing the fragments of a letter from Laureola.

Courtly and chivalrous elements appear in these novels along with the fascination for exotic locales and a pristine sexual morality which allows for no reasonable compromise. Any possibility of a happy ending is avoided even when the solution to the presumptive dilemma is overwhelmingly evident. There is no conceivable impediment to the marriage of Leriano and Laureola; the problem is purely a literary and conventional one. The form is clearly as idealized as the novel of chivalry or the Byzantine novel, and the outcome is prescribed with no regard for real and normal relationships. The whole atmosphere is "long ago and far away." The structure of the novel is monolithic and suggests the fabulous architecture of Giotto and other early Renaissance painters. The epistolary style and a sense of urgency and excitement in the battle scenes as Leriano liberates Laureola bring realism to the narrative that enhances the theatricality and dramatic immediacy of this transitional novelistic form.

The great masterpiece of the fifteenth century appears at the very end of the period. It is a prose drama which really defies classification into any of the molds which had existed earlier in European literature. The *Tragicomedia de Calisto y Melibea,* later known simply as the *Celestina,* was published, in its earliest known form, in

1499. Considerable mystery surrounds the authorship of the work. The only claimant to authorship is a Jewish convert, Fernando de Rojas, who held a law degree from the University of Salamanca. In the prologue to a later edition of the *Celestina*, Rojas—or someone speaking for him—tells us that he came across a manuscript of the first act of a prose drama which interested him, and that in a two-week vacation from his studies at Salamanca he added fifteen acts to the original. Very shortly thereafter a new version of twenty-one acts appeared. This mystery would be of very minor interest if it were not that the *Celestina*, in any of the various versions, is one of the greatest literary creations of all time.

The plot is extremely simple. Calisto, a young nobleman, chases a hunting falcon into the garden of Melibea, a girl of equally noble lineage. He falls in love with her, apparently at first sight, and declares his devotion. She rejects him as a presumptive madman and dismisses him. Calisto suffers a period of intense love-sickness until a conniving servant suggests that he hire a renowned go-between, an old woman who has wide experience in cases of this sort, and whose life is spent reducing virgins to docility and repairing the consequences. Calisto agrees immediately to accept any aid he can get and employs Celestina as his intermediary. She undertakes her work and soon reduces all of the principals to her desires, collecting fees and gifts for her services as she goes along. She brings Calisto and Melibea together, but inspires the greed of Calisto's servants. When she refuses to share her take with them, they stab her and flee through the window. They are soon apprehended and summarily beheaded. This matters little to Calisto, whose only concern is to meet Melibea that night. He climbs the wall of her estate with a ladder, but after a brief meeting with the love-stricken maiden, he flees over the wall, loses his footing, and falls to his death. On learning this, Melibea goes alone to a tower and, in hysterical grief, shouts the whole story of her love and the loss of her virginity to her father, and plunges to her death.

The aspects which most notably contribute to the artistic perfection of the *Celestina* are the subtlety of language and the intense and dramatic characterization of the figures in the work. The language is Castilian prose at its spare, economical best, with little of the overblown, Italianate, sententious adornment of Santillana or Juan de Mena. There are, however, enormous and subtle contrasts of tone in the language. When the old procuress chats with her covey of prostitutes, her use of language is adequate to the mentality, background, and interests of the company. When the servant Sempronio lectures to his young master on the anatomy of love, his tongue drips Aristotle, Seneca, and Petrarch. When Calisto woos Melibea, he uses the speech of the sentimental novel and the tradition of courtly love.

Calisto and Melibea are basically unformed youths caught up in a passion which neither contemporary morality nor good sense can control, but Celestina herself emerges as one of the great literary creations of all time; grasping, flattering, cajoling, miserly, capitalizing on all the frailties of human character. There is not a human weakness or desire that she does not understand and exploit for some small gain. It is no wonder that the book is best known by her name. The minor characters, too, are perfect pictures of petty greed, vanity, and opportunism. The sources of the *Celestina* are many. Rojas was a well-read man, and his literary background is shown in the wide variety of materials upon which he draws for the *Celestina*. For Celestina herself, there are prototypes in Trotaconventos of the *Libro de buen amor* and in Latin literature, particularly in the plays of Terence and Plautus and the poetry of Ovid. But other influences—Aristotle, Seneca, Virgil, the Bible, patristic literature, Petrarch, Boccaccio—have been identified. Yet whatever the influences, immediate or remote, Rojas created a work which is without equal in Spanish, or indeed, European literature.

Summary

The fifteenth century is a period of fertile innovation in both style and genres. The *mester de clerecía* gives way to the shorter, more lyrical *romances*. The Italian and French forms of the Renaissance make their appearance in the *cancioneros* of Baena and Stúñiga and in the poetry of Santillana and Juan de Mena, bringing new verse forms, a new polish, and a quantity of new vocabulary. A major prose form is the novel of chivalry, represented by the immensely popular *Amadís de Gaula*. The possibilities of prose fiction are further explored toward the end of the century in the sentimental novel.

Another major advance is seen in the drama. While not precisely "popular," since its appeal and availability was limited to aristocratic society, it was nevertheless a secular theater whose purpose was to entertain and delight on the artistic level. The themes are predominantly, though not exclusively, pastoral and the plot is developed chiefly in conversations. The content is usually amorous, although occasionally topical reference to politics and current events is found.

Satire of a political and social nature finds expression in works of anonymous popular verse. Historical chronicles are numerous and there is important contemporary biography. The great masterpiece of the century, *La Celestina*, is published in its last year. This novel in dialogue sets for all time the figure of the elderly female go-between; clever, astute, avaricious, part witch, Celestina manipulates her clients through their own weaknesses, and adds one more universal archetype to a Spanish literary gallery which includes Lazarillo, Don Juan, and Don Quijote.

CHAPTER 4

THE GOLDEN AGE

With the sixteenth century begins the Golden Age of Spanish literature, an era which, for the historians of literature, produced literary riches comparable to the vast treasures of gold and silver which Spanish conquerors were bringing in from the colonies of the New World. The period may best be understood in terms of the literary genres or types which developed, in which mention will be made of only the main literary trends and outstanding works and authors. The Italian Renaissance made a lasting and somewhat deforming impression on Spanish letters, particularly in poetry. This influence, felt in the fifteenth century, comes to dominate sixteenth-century poetry, both lyrical and narrative, as it had earlier dominated the work of Santillana and Juan de Mena. The marks of this influence are an Italianate vocabulary, rich, elaborate, and self-consciously highbrow; a type of syntax which becomes more and more contrived and intricate, to the point where the typical sparse, direct, and economical language of the *cantares* and *romances* is lost in a welter of words and complex images; and a penchant for allegory and preciosity which sharply contrasts with the terse realism of the *Libro de buen amor* or the *Celestina*.

This tradition produced two outstanding poets who gave Spanish intonation to the Italian models. The first of these is Garcilaso de la Vega (1503?–36) whose short life was one of intense activity and poetic inspiration.

Soldier, courtier, and poet, Garcilaso gave Spanish poetry an unforgettable lyricism and a treasury of imagery. He was a member of the highest nobility, a companion of the Emperor Charles V, and a soldier whose valor in battle cut short his life. His poetry was printed posthumously and, owing to his early death, is quite a small body of work. It is, however, among the most lovely and melodic in the Spanish language. In all, his work consists of two elegies, three pastoral eclogues, five odes, thirty-eight sonnets and a few minor compositions. As a poet of the Renaissance, his inspiration is largely classical, with stylistic overtones derived from the Italian poets. Typical of the setting and language of his poetry is this short passage from the *First Eclogue,* in which the poet laments the death of his beloved and develops a theme much used in the Renaissance: there is no misery more overwhelming than the contemplation of erstwhile happy times in a moment of bereavement:

> *Corrientes aguas, puras, cristalinas;*
> *árboles que os estáis mirando en ellas;*
> *verde prado de fresca sombra lleno;*
> *aves que aquí sembráis vuestras querellas;*
> *yedra que por los árboles caminas*
> *torciendo el paso por su verde seno:*
> *yo me vi tan ajeno*
> *del grave mal que siento,*
> *que de puro contento*
> *con vuestra soledad me recreaba,*
> *donde con dulce sueño reposaba,*
> *o con el pensamiento discurría*
> *por donde no hallaba*
> *sino memorias llenas de alegría.*
> *Y en este mismo valle, donde agora*
> *me entristezco y me canso, en el reposo*
> *estuve ya contento y descansado.*

> Running waters, pure, crystalline;
> trees who contemplate yourselves in them;
> green field filled with cool shade;
> birds who sow your little quarrels here;
> ivy marching up the trees
> twisting a path through their green lap:
> I saw myself so far removed
> from the grave misfortune which I feel,
> that from pure contentment
> in your stillness I was refreshed,
> where with sweet slumber I reposed
> or in my mind rambled about
> in places where I found nothing
> but memories filled with joy.
>
> And in this very valley, where now
> I am saddened and burdened, in repose
> I then was happy and without care.

A friend and mentor of Garcilaso, Juan Boscán (1487 or 1492–1542) is of interest not so much for his own literary production as for his primary role in introducing the poetic forms of the Italian Renaissance into Spain and for his influence on Garcilaso. His sonnets, tercets, and *octavas* are of very uneven quality but served to establish a vogue for the eleven-syllable line, a type of poetic language which abounds in contradiction and exaggeration, and the poetic examination of states of mind in a pastoral setting. The poet typically expresses his amorous sufferings and erotic anxieties against a background of flower-spotted green fields, murmuring streams, and crystalline fountains. One of Boscán's most important contributions to Spanish letters is his translation of Castiglioni's *The Courtier,* a work which established the tone of polite and aristocratic manners and which exercised a strong influence on generations of Spanish writers.

The scholarly aspects of the Renaissance, such as studies in the Greek and Roman classics, in the philology of the vernacular languages, and stylistic criticism of literary works, had developed in Italy along with the flowering of lyrical poetry and other creative literary forms. This intellectual component of the new attitudes was introduced into Spain primarily through the work of Antonio Nebrija (1444–1533). Nebrija was an outstanding Latinist who studied the teaching methods used in Bologna and returned to apply those techniques at the University of Salamanca. In effect, he revolutionized the study of the liberal arts in Spain and introduced the movement which came to be known as Humanism. His bilingual dictionaries served as basic texts for at least half a century. More important yet was his *Gramática castellana* (*Spanish Grammar*), the first grammar of a modern European language, published in 1492. The *Gramática* established the rules of acceptable Spanish speech and prose and added to the dignity of the language both at home and abroad. Nebrija was called upon by Cardinal Cisneros to participate in editing the Polyglot Bible of Alcalá de Henares, the first of its kind, with texts in Latin, Greek, Hebrew, and Chaldean, along with textual criticism. Typifying the Humanistic currents of the period, Nebrija wrote a number of treatises in many fields—rhetoric, botany, philosophy, and theology among them—in Latin and in Spanish.

The influence of Erasmus of Rotterdam (1466?–1536) was great in Spain. His scholarship, criticism of the more decadent aspects of the clergy, and his call for a more simplified Christianity were enthusiastically received and he was for a time a counselor of the Emperor Charles V. His theological position unfortunately became confused by many with some of the heretical doctrines of mysticism and the movements of Protestantism in Germany and the Low Countries. The predictable result was that Erasmus and his more ardent followers fell from favor, as did his doctrines. Catholicism was not yet ready for the intensive Counter Reformation whose principles would be hammered out over the years in the Council of Trent.

Among the most important followers of Erasmus in Spain were two brothers, Alfonso (1490?–1532) and Juan (?–1541) de Valdés. Alfonso lent his literary support to the Emperor Charles V in the hectic, usually violent politicking of the period, in the form of dialogues in which various theological and political positions are examined, opposed, and defended. In the "Dialogue of Mercury and Charon" there is a considerable touch of satire, reminiscent of the *Dance of Death*, as Valdés consigns various luminaries of the period to a seat in Charon's ferryboat to hell. The use of dialogue form reflects the classical tone of the period in reviving Plato's favored method of presentation.

The *Diálogo de la lengua* (*Dialogue of the Language*) of Juan de Valdés is of considerable literary interest. With excellent linguistic taste, he discusses the history of the language, its vocabulary, orthography, and standards of literary style, and gives judicious and reasoned criticism of major earlier writers and works. He defends the Spanish language as a worthy literary instrument, as effective as Latin or Greek for the expression of noble ideas and the creation of literary models. Valdés' critical judgments of Encina, Torres Naharro, the *Celestina*, and other major works and authors show a breadth of mentality and perspective that are typically Humanist.

In the novel, a wide variety of themes is developed in the sixteenth century. The novel of chivalry passes from vogue for a variety of reasons: very significant alterations in the manners and social structure of the period, boredom with uninspired continuations of the fantastic adventures of the knights-errant, and the introduction of new literary themes from Italy and France. The novel of chivalry was already dead when Miguel de Cervantes' magnificent burlesque of the form appeared in *Don*

Quijote de la Mancha. After *Don Quijote,* no reader could take seriously the jousts, penances, and enchantments which the long-suffering hero must endure. As escapist literature, the novel of chivalry is replaced in popular esteem by the pastoral novel.

This form, already foreshadowed in lyric poetry and the early theater, develops the fiction of an ideal society of shepherds and shepherdesses, innocently tending their sheep in idealized natural settings, in a realm untouched by wars, famine, greed, pestilence or economic vicissitudes, troubled only by the pangs of frustrated love. This affliction reaches endemic proportions in the pastoral novel; A loves B who loves C who loves D, but B detests A and C detests B, and so on through all the Phyllises, Strephons, and Eliseos who populate these novels. Utterly removed from reality, utterly lacking in naturalistic detail, the pastoral novel is in its way as fantastic and remote from the here-and-now as the novel of chivalry. Yet it gained tremendous popularity. The vogue was established first in Italy, with the *Arcadia* of Jacopo Sannazaro (1458–1530), but soon took root in Spain with the *Diana* of Jorge de Montemayor (1520?–61). In its early form, the genre is little more than a novelesque setting for amorous dialogue and poetry, the type of material that had been developed in other genres by Boscán, Garcilaso, and Juan del Encina. These novels proliferated in Spain and the form was cultivated by Cervantes and Lope de Vega. In the case of Cervantes, whose first novel, *La Galatea,* was a pastoral work, new dimensions of psychology and characterization are immediately apparent; the man who would later create that enormous masterpiece, *Don Quijote,* could not, even in his first attempt at the novel, be content with the empty trivialities which constituted the customary pastoral form. Thus *Galatea,* one of the last of the pastoral novels, goes far beyond the earlier works in terms of character, relationships, psychological penetration, and action.

In sharp contrast to the artificiality of the pastoral novel and the anachronism of the novel of chivalry, a new literary conception emerged in the sixteenth century—the picaresque novel. The first of these works, and, in the opinion of many, the best, is the anonymous *Lazarillo de Tormes,* which appeared in 1554. Written in deceptively simple, even vulgar language, it tells the adventures of Lazarillo, a young boy who finds himself abandoned and alone in the world and who must work as a servant to a series of masters to keep body and soul together. He is a guide for an astute and miserly blind beggar—and so famous has this episode become that the term *un lazarillo* is still applied generically to any guide of the blind—until, frequently beaten and always half starved, Lazarillo gets his revenge by placing the sightless old man in front of a stone pillar, telling him that they are standing before a large puddle of water and that he must jump for all he is worth to avoid getting wet. With this farewell salute, Lazarillo moves on to become the house servant of a penurious priest, the assistant to a fraudulent seller of papal indulgences, the servant of a young nobleman who is abundantly prideful but so penniless that Lazarillo himself must beg bread to feed the two of them. Finally at the end of the book Lazarillo finds himself "at the peak of good fortune" with a job as town crier, which he gets as a reward for marrying the mistress of a lecherous archpriest.

Cynical, wry, unillusioned, this book opens a whole new world to the novelist—the world of the lower margins of society, where hunger and poverty are the hero's frequent companions, and in which the novelistic problem is no longer that of frustrated love or of knightly quests, but the sheer necessity of surviving in a world of hard knocks by any means, including occasional petty criminality. It is difficult to say, however, that *Lazarillo de Tormes* is a "realistic" novel. Critics have shown that the work derives many of its episodes from medieval folklore and various literary sources. It is fairly certain that the book is not autobiography, as it appears to be from its first-person narration. Neither is it social criticism of an objective sort, aimed at improving conditions of the poor and unprotected. Anticlerical without hatred, antisocial without real malice, the book owes much to the *Libro de buen amor* and to the *Celestina*: to the former for its subjectivity and unblushing candor; to the latter for its themes of cupidity and survival in a harsh, unmagnanimous society.

The terms *pícaro* and *picaresque* are of debatable origin. Some critics have held that *pícaro* is a corruption of the word *Picard*, designating the mercenary soldiers from southern France who were employed by the Spanish and, often unpaid, showed great aptitude for surviving by their wits at the expense of the local population. Others have sought the source in the verb *picar*, to sting or prick, and still others have looked for an Arabic source, since a literature based on the entertaining but unscrupulous escapades of a rogue-hero did exist in the Islamic world. It cannot be said for certain which, if any, of these sources provided the term. The word appears in the sixteenth century, first used to designate a serving boy, often kitchen help, and then the adventurous hero of these novels, who by opportunism, theft, or petty swindles manages to survive. *Lazarillo de Tormes* was immensely popular from the moment of its publication. Attempts to suppress the book by the Inquisition—primarily because of its anticlericalism and its general tone of social nihilism—failed, as did later attempts to circulate a censored version which eliminated passages which satirized the clergy most bitingly. Yet the book continued to delight readers throughout the Spanish-speaking world and to influence other writers, both Spanish and foreign. Shakespeare refers to the novel, and it played a part in the literary formation of Fielding and Defoe.

A gulf of almost fifty years separates *Lazarillo* from the next important picaresque novel. The first part of *Guzmán de Alfarache,* by Mateo Alemán (1547–1615?), appears in 1599, and the second part in 1604. Alemán incorporated three shorter *novellas* as well as a number of stories, anecdotes, proverbs, allegories, moralistic digressions, jokes, and even sermons into his long novel. It is as intricate and complex as *Lazarillo* is terse and economical. Alemán put into the work, subtitled "Watchtower of Human Life," everything he had seen, heard, read, or encountered. The novel begins with the adventures of a boy who, for rather tragic reasons, finds himself on his own with neither money, family, nor the background to earn his own way in life. Guzmán quickly drifts into petty vices and not-so-petty thefts and swindles. From this point on, the story is largely about the adventures of an adult criminal. It is told from the point of view of a repented felon, condemned for his crimes to row in the galleys. In this way, it differs from *Lazarillo,* in which the orientation is never criminal, although on occasions, when he is literally starving, Lazarillo does steal food from his miserly masters.

With its immense variety of interpolated materials, *Guzmán de Alfarache* is a showcase for the author's literary talents and his considerable knowledge of the culture of his time. Heavily loaded with didactic and moralistic material, it is also a work of the Counter Reformation—the attempt of a devout Catholic to reaffirm traditional Spanish beliefs and values against the tide of reform that was sweeping Europe at the time. Despite the recurrent theme of hunger which the two novels share, first-person or autobiographic narration, an essentially episodic structure through which the various adventures are joined only by the identity of the *pícaro* or antihero who experiences them, and the orientation of a young boy to a world which is essentially a cold and alien "school of hard knocks," the two novels are very different and reflect the different times in which they were written. *Lazarillo de Tormes* is a product of the Renaissance, ebullient, joyful, witty, and essentially optimistic. Even when he is starved, beaten, and neglected, Lazarillo retains a wholesome and cheerful resilience which sends him on to new masters all the wiser for his past rebuffs. He achieves the peak of his material wellbeing, finally incorporating himself into the lower levels of respectable society by compromising his honor as a husband. But he seems to say with a shrug, That's the way of the world and there is nothing to be done about it. Mateo Alemán conceives his novel essentially in moral and religious terms. The world is a corrupt and senseless place in which Man is isolated by his own corruption from the one good, which is God. The more his *pícaro* experiences of life, the more bitter and disillusioned he becomes until finally, purging his guilt in the galleys, he comes to a spiritual awakening, a conversion, and a new orientation toward the salvation of his soul. Thus the two novels end on a "peak"; both have an essentially happy ending, as Lazarillo finds a materialistic solution to his basic problems of survival, and Mateo Alemán's Guzmán finds a spiritual solution to his own perverse inclinations.

The history of the picaresque novel after *Guzmán de Alfarache* is a history of literary decadence. Two phases or components which Alemán had kept in careful artistic balance tend to separate in later picaresque novels. The moral and didactic aspect, in which the excesses of the *pícaros* are developed as examples of wrong conduct to the accompaniment of more or less integrated sermons and moral deliberations, dominate in Alcalá Yáñez, *El donado hablador* and Vicente Espinel, *Marcos de Obregón*. Another group of novels exploits the freedom and irresponsibility of the life of the *pícaro* for the sake of novelistic amusement and adventures; the moralistic element is essentially lacking or is treated in burlesque fashion in the novels of Castillo Solórzano, *Teresa de Manzanares, Las harpías en Madrid, La garduña de Sevilla,* and in the presumably autobiographical *Life of Estebanillo González*.

An interesting development of the picaresque genre is the introduction of feminine protagonists. The first of these is *La pícara Justina,* of doubtful authorship. It is a long, rambling, occasionally incoherent novel, which has been called by one critic a "monument of bad taste." The role of the *pícara* is later expanded and refined, particularly in the novels of Castillo Solórzano. These are essentially frivolous novels, showcases for the author's ingenuity and urbanity, which lack any real contact with the world of Lazarillo and Guzmán. The adventures of the antiheroines are generally chaste and occasionally ascend to the level of elegance. The continuing Castilian standards of austerity generally preclude any descent into accounts of prostitution or real immorality. In one case, however, the reverse is true, and we find one picaresque novel which almost satisfies the canons of Zola's naturalism. *La hija de Celestina* (*The Daughter of Celestina*), of Salas Barbadillo (1581–1635), harks back to Rojas' classic to describe a milieu of prostitution, illicit cohabitation, theft, swindles, and finally murder. Many of its scenes are stark and moving, but there is generally an absence of prurience even in recounting the most debased elements of human experience. In its intensity and shocking criminality it goes rather beyond the established bounds of the picaresque novel into an area that will not be seen again in European literature until the advent of French and Russian naturalism of the nineteenth century.

Only one picaresque novel of the seventeenth century captured something of the original charm, spirit, spontaneity, language, and characterization of the original *Lazarillo de Tormes*. This is the life of Pablos, *El Buscón*, by Francisco de Queveda y Villegas (1580–1645). The novel follows the usual formula of the picaresque, beginning with the early years of the *picaro* and progressing through a series of episodes to his adult life. The tone of the work is humorous and satirical and the style depends heavily on puns and other verbal humor, grotesque situations, and exaggeration. Pablos' father is a barber who specializes in picking his customers' pockets as he shaves them. His mother is a witch who collects such ornaments as necklaces of dead men's teeth and uses hangman's rope to support her mattress. Pablos goes to the school of Master Cabra, where he and his fellow pupils suffer near-starvation. Describing the first meal, Pablos says, "they brought in a broth in little wooden bowls, so clear and limpid that if Narcissus were to eat from one of them he would be in more danger than in the fountain. . . . Then came an adventurous turnip and the Maestro said, 'we have turnips? For me there is no pheasant that can equal them; eat up, for I enjoy seeing people eat.' Then he served each of us such a tiny bit of lamb that, between what stuck under our fingernails and what lodged between our teeth it was all gone, leaving the belly excommunicated from participation."

Pablos and his classmate are taken out of the school when one of the pupils dies of starvation. He then attends the university until his uncle, the hangman of Segovia, informs him of the death of his father in a letter. "Your father died a week ago with the greatest show of valor that any man has ever shown in dying; I say this as the man who hanged him. . . . He marched through the streets with a fine air, looking in the windows and bowing to those who stopped their work to watch him. . . . He took the rope in his hands and adjusted it around his neck, and, seeing that the priest wanted to give his sermon, he turned to him and said, 'Father, let's have a little of the Credo and get on with it; I don't want to appear to drag things out.' He took his tumble without drawing his legs up or flailing his arms about. . . . I quartered him and gave him the crossroads for a tomb; God knows how it bothers me to see him there providing public board for the jackdaws . . ."

This type of humor—and indeed the whole tone is burlesque, gruesome, and irreverent—is typical of Quevedo's style. His view of the world has been compared to that of Goya's *Caprichos* with good reason; both present the world in an artistic deformation that exaggerates the morbid and the whimsical, that makes a *memento mori* of a frill, and in general elaborates the dark tones of life. In the conclusion of the work Pablos, completely disenchanted with the falsity of the world around him and with his own pretensions, makes plans to go off to the New World. The reader is fully aware that he is taking his old problems and inadequacies with him; that for Pablos there is no new world and no new life. Quevedo was, for his wit, brilliance, imaginative literary gifts, and command of language, the outstanding man of letters of seventeenth-century Spain. In addition to *El Buscón,* one of the sharpest, most entertaining and best-written of the picaresque genre, Quevedo wrote lives of St. Paul and St. Thomas of Villanueva, and translated the Epistles of Seneca. He wrote a number of satirical works, among them the most mordant social criticism of the century. In a group of dramatic essays called *Sueños* (*Dreams*), Quevedo satirizes personages, fads, and the abuses of his time in a series of fantastic dreams or visions of Hell and the Last Judgment. These works are all satire and malicious wit; there is no theological aspect to his consignment of the foolish and vain to the nether regions. Quevedo also excelled as a poet, although his verse is usually more clever and intellectual than lyrical, more biting than beautiful. As a literary critic Quevedo was more spiteful than constructive, although his attacks on one literary movement of the period, *culteranismo*, had abundant justification.

Toward the end of his life, Quevedo achieved an almost stoic resignation and tranquillity. One particularly beautiful sonnet of this period deserves attention for precisely those qualities.

Miré los muros de la patria mía,
si un tiempo fuertes, ya desmoronados,
de la carrera de la edad cansados,
por quien caduca ya su valentía.

Salíme al campo, vi que el Sol bebía
los arroyos del yelo desatados,
y del monte quejosos los ganados,
que con sombras hurtó su luz al día.

Entré en mi casa; vi que, amancillada,
de anciana habitación era despojos;
mi báculo, más corvo y menos fuerte.

Vencida de la edad sentí mi espada,
y no hallé cosa en que poner los ojos
que no fuese recuerdo de la muerte.

I looked on the walls of my homeland
once so strong, now all decayed,
wearied by the passage of time,
which is already sapping their strength.

I went out to the country, I saw that the sun was drinking
the streams which the ice released,
and the cattle were complaining of the forest,
that its shadows stole their light of day.

> I went into my house, I saw that, tarnished,
> it was but the ruin of an ancient dwelling;
> my staff, more bent and less strong.
>
> I felt my sword was conquered by age
> and I found nothing I might look upon
> that was not a reminder of death.

The prose of Baltasar Gracián (1601–58) offers certain similarities to that of Quevedo. The baroque style of *conceptismo* is displayed clearly in Gracián's work with all its virtues and vices: conciseness of expression, originality of thought, the aptness of literary style to content, frequency of aphorisms, a style so meaty that it must be pondered and dissected to be understood; at the same time his work is filled with puns, allegories, grotesque comparisons and insistent repetitions. Gracián's importance as a writer has fluctuated greatly. His work has experienced periods of considerable vogue and of almost complete obscurity. He was widely read throughout Europe in the seventeenth century. The Enlightenment buried his works along with most of the Spanish Baroque. German scholarship restored Gracián to prominence in the nineteenth century and he had an influence on Schopenhauer and Goethe. Nietzsche had some acquaintance with his thought, but the two had little in common. In this century Gracián has not been popular, but his worth has been generally recognized and an impressive volume of scholarship has been devoted to his ideas. The body of his work consists of four political treatises, a work of aesthetics and criticism, a philosophical novel, and a religious treatise.

The political works are of a Machiavellian tinge but are effectively modified with Christian teachings; Gracián was a Jesuit who could not see the state as completely devoid of moral purpose. He predicates the necessity for control of the state by the hero, the man who is in all ways a man of excellence: intelligent, resolute, wise, and virtuous. One of these treatises, the *Oráculo manual* (*The Portable Oracle*) is a collection of three hundred short aphorisms on the qualities of the hero, a sort of guidebook to excellence. His study of literary style, *Agudeza y arte de ingenio*, is a rhetoric of *conceptismo* which analyzes the style of a large number of writers in terms of the conceits, metaphors, and various other turns of speech with which they achieve artistic effect. Gracián comes very close to the textual analysis of the new stylistics and may certainly be considered one of the most perspicacious analysts of style that critical literature has produced.

Gracián is best known for his philosophic novel, *El Criticón* (*The Hypercritic*). The novel is a long and complex allegory. Critilo is shipwrecked on an island while searching for his wife, Felisinda. He is saved by a young savage who has grown to manhood alone on the island and thus is totally lacking in knowledge of the world. Critilo teaches him to speak and gives him the name Andrenio. They set out on an allegorical pilgrimage in search of Felisinda, who represents happiness. They visit the Fountain of Deceits and the Inn of the World, where each vice has its booth; Andrenio falls victim of the enchantments of the temptress Falsirena, giving Gracián motive for an invective against women in general. They pass through the Desert of Hypocrisy, the Court of Fame and the House of Madmen, where the whole human race is represented. They finally encounter Felisinda, visit the Cave of Death, and arrive at the Isle of Immortality. There is a strong current of baroque pessimism to the novel. Most of life, as Gracián sees it, is folly, sham, pretense, and disappointment. The Stoic currents are strong; on every page there are distillations of Cicero and Seneca, as well as of other sources from the classical period, from the Renaissance, and from contemporary writers. The qualities that have been most praised in the novel, aside from the soundness of the moralisms and the broad learning which Gracián displays, are the harmonious structure which the work is given and the general excellence of its literary style. It is a perfect monument of baroque imagery and conceptual development.

Culteranismo was a movement in poetry which had its vogue in the first quarter of the seventeenth century, and as its high priest Luis de Góngora (1561–1627). His important major poems, *Polifemo* and *Soledades,* exemplify the style which has come to be known as *gongorismo.* Partly as a result of the revival of interest in Latin poetry, partly in response to the Italian forms which had earlier influenced Santillana and Mena, this poetry was written for the *cultos,* the highly educated literary avant-garde, as distinct from the common people, who were often referred to disdainfully as the *vulgo. Culteranismo* employed a strained and high-flown vocabulary, a curiously twisted syntax which sought to imitate classical Latin, farfetched and extravagant metaphors, and allusions to the most remote and unfamiliar elements of classical mythology, geography, and history. The poetry of Góngora was long scorned as mannered, effete, and unreadable, until a generation of Spanish critics in this century undertook a revaluation of his work and found a real treasury of delicate imagery, poetic insight, and a heightened awareness of the descriptive capacities of the Spanish language. Góngora emerges, under the critical analysis of a group of the most sensitive poets and analytical critics of present day Spain, as a poet of enormous visionary and linguistic power. He was a major influence in the most representative voices of the Generation of 1927, discussed in Chapter 8. Despite this refurbishing of a major but inordinately complex poet, Góngora still remains difficult to read and enjoy, impossible to translate, and enigmatic even to those who have made the closest approach to his peculiar aesthetic.

Quevedo declared literary war on the movement and initiated violent attacks. Góngora and his numerous followers, imitators, and apologists were subjected to a barrage of satire from the most vitriolic pen of the period in *La culta latiniparla* (*Cultured Latin-Talk*) and *Aguja de navegar cultos* (*Compass to Steer the "cultos"*). One happy result of the battle was the publication by Quevedo of the poetry of Fray (Brother) Luis de León as an example of the finest traditions in Castilian verse. Such was the heat of the dispute in literary circles that a whole body of Góngora's poetry was almost overlooked. Not all of his verse was typical of the movement; much was simple and clear, direct and lovely. Such is the contrast between his sonnets and the *Soledades*, for example, that critics have written of "the two Góngoras," one "prince of light" who wrote with economy and beauty; the other, "prince of darkness," whose verse is obscure, affected, and so unintelligible as to merit a recent prose adaptation in Spanish. Quevedo fell victim to *conceptismo*, which avoided the excessive erudition and pedantry of the Gongorists, but in its turn relied upon puns and elaborate—sometimes ridiculous—comparisons and conceits often carried too far for good sense or good literary taste.

Apart from the rivalries and polemics that affected the literary court in Madrid, two provincial schools of poetry had developed more or less independently of the contending movements. The school of Seville had its great leader in Fernando de Herrera (1534–97). Continuator of the Renaissance brilliance and Italianate eloquence of Garcilaso, master of the erudition of his time, completely dominating the poetic diction of both the heroic odes and laments of love which were the topics of his period, Herrera represents the epitome of the late Renaissance in Spain. Perfection of form, elegance of language, and exquisite poetic taste bring to his poetry a lacquered finish which makes it seem cold, astute, and overly urbane. Yet Herrera has, for all his academic suavity, some beautiful lines, some real insight, and an elevated concept of lyrical composition. He was the outstanding member of the Sevillian school, a group of poets whose most salient characteristic was their refined scholarship and their attempt to revive the classical models of Greek and Roman poetry.

In the same period another "school" formed in the university town of Salamanca dominated by the figure of Fray Luis de León (1527–91), an Augustinian monk who taught in various fields related to theology. One of the outstanding biblical and classical scholars of his time, Fray Luis also translated important Italian, Latin, and Greek works into Spanish. The envy of his colleagues brought about his imprisonment by the Inquisition for four years, though he was eventually cleared of charges of heresy. A popular anecdote has it that, following his release, the monk returned to his lecture hall at the university, where his students awaited him, and began his lecture imperturbably with the words, "As we were saying yesterday . . ."

The poetry of Fray Luis is freer and more flexible than that of the Sevillian school. His themes are both religious and secular, stressing the life of tranquillity and retirement, the intellectual pleasures of music and poetry, and the mystical joys of religious devotion. There is generally a feeling of simplicity and even ingenuousness to his poetry, but this is deceptive; it is really the result of meticulous pruning and a sophisticated search for the simplest and most direct poetic communication.

AL SALIR DE LA CÁRCEL

Aquí la envidia y mentira
me tuvieron encerrado.
Dichoso el humilde estado
del sabio que se retira
de aqueste mundo malvado,
y con pobre mesa y casa
en el campo deleitoso,
con sólo Dios se compasa,
y a solas su vida pasa,
ni envidiado ni envidioso.

ON LEAVING PRISON

Here envy and lies
kept me imprisoned.
Happy is the humble state
of the wise man who retires
from the miserable world out
there,
and with poor table and
house
in the delightful countryside
with only God as his measure,
passes his life by himself
neither envied nor envious.

Writing on religious topics, from Visigothic times through the reconquest, the Renaissance, and the baroque period, had been represented by glosses, theological treatises, various poetic forms, *autos,* and lives of saints. Quevedo, for example, for all his wry and pungent wit, his satire and cynicism, wrote excellent lives of St. Paul and St. Thomas of Villanova, and translated an inspirational work of St. Francis of Sales. In addition to these traditional forms, a tremendous new impulse is given to devotional literature with the resurgence in Spain of mystical theology. In both poetry and prose, some of the most magnificent and glowing passages that Spain has given to world literature are to be found in the works of the mystics and ascetics of the Golden Age.

The currents of protest which surged throughout Europe in acrid and violent reaction to clerical abuses of popular faith and to the overinstitutionalization of the Church manifested themselves in the northern countries in the theological criticism and reform waves of Erasmus and Luther. In Spain, where anticlericalism had traditionally become a habit of mind based upon an extremely demanding expectation of exemplary conduct among churchmen, a few superbly gifted reformers devoted themselves to opening new areas of spiritual experience within Catholic orthodoxy. These writers seek primarily a quickening of the experience of religious renovation; a mystic union with the Divine which is mediated neither by the intellect nor by outward formalism. This movement represents a response of the Counter Reformation to internalize the religious experience and, through prayer, meditation, and ascetic discipline, to achieve a direct and transcendant union with God.

In Spain, greatest literary importance among the mystics must be accorded St. Teresa of Jesus and St. John of the Cross. St. Teresa (1515–82) was a woman of unusual energy and dedication, of administrative ability as great as her literary talents. She founded a number of convents of the Carmelite order against very considerable difficulties and opposition, and much of her writing had as its immediate purpose the spiritual instruction of her charges. Her most important works are *El libro de su vida,* an autobiography which concerns itself as much with an account of her beatific visions and spiritual progress as with objective events, and *El castillo interior o las moradas* (*The Interior Castle or the Mansions*), which details a spiritual vision of the beneficent effect of prayer, asceticism, and spiritual purity. The spiritual life is seen as a crystalline castle with seven rooms or "mansions." Each represents a stage of purification or release from the things of the world and the self. Finally, in the last of the seven mansions, the completely purged soul achieves ineffable union with the divine essence.

El camino de perfección (*The Way of Perfection*) is a practical guide to spiritual progress which stresses the ideals of poverty, humility, self-mortification, prayer, contemplation, and Christian love. St. Teresa also wrote poetry, but there is some doubt of the authenticity of much that had earlier been attributed to her. The verse that is known to be hers has the directness, facility of expression, and religious fervor which are found also in her prose.

The life of St. John of the Cross (1542–91) is closely linked with that of St. Teresa. They were natives of the same province, Avila, and St. John came into contact with St. Teresa and was caught up in her movement to reform the Carmelites. St. John, too, encountered strong opposition and was imprisoned for a period by the antireform element of his order. He explored much the same path of spiritual exercises and leaves a magnificent poetic testament of his religious experience. His work was not published until almost three decades after his death, as a collection of *Obras espirituales* (*Spiritual Works*), which included *Subida al Monte Carmelo* (*The Ascent of Mount Carmel*), *Noche oscura del alma* (*The Dark Night of the Soul*), and *Llama de amor viva* (*The Living Flame of Love*). The *Cántico espiritual* (poetry and commentary based on the *Song of Solomon*) was published still later.

The basic structure of St. John's work is essentially the same in all of these: he develops the theme of the soul, anguished, deprived, and alone, seeking the absent Beloved, in fragile, exquisitely worded poetry. The imagery is then minutely analyzed in prose to develop orthodox mystical doctrine. Thus poetry and prose are so closely united and interdependent as to be thematically inseparable, although certainly, perhaps owing to the intuitive and quintessential nature of the mystic experience, the poetry is of far greater literary interest. St. John, as a poet, is strongly influenced by Renaissance forms. Most of his major verse is composed in the *lira,* a verse form introduced from Italy by Garcilaso.

¿A dónde te escondiste,	Where hast thou hidden,
Amado, y me dejaste con gemido?	Beloved, and left me to wail?
Como el ciervo huiste	Like the deer you fled

habiéndome herido;	having wounded me;
salí tras ti clamando y eras ido.	I followed after you crying aloud, and you were gone.
Pastores los que fuerdes allá por las majadas al otero, si por ventura vierdes Aquel que yo más quiero, decidle que adolezco, peno y muero.	Shepherds, you who may be there with the flock on the hill if by chance you should see the one whom I most love, tell him that I sicken, I suffer, and die.

The similarity to bucolic poetry of the Renaissance is readily evident, but the accompanying commentary makes the allegorical nature of the verses abundantly clear. The soul, injured and suffering for love of God, cries out for spiritual alleviation. Thus wounded, the soul must go forth, leaving the things of the world and even self-love, to seek the only spiritual healing possible: union with God. The shepherds represent the pain and anguish, the desire which the soul feels, which in themselves may serve as messengers to God. The flock represents the hierarchy of angels, and the hill, God, who is the summit of divine being.

The appearance of simplicity in St. John's poetry is highly deceptive. Alternate versions of the *Cántico espiritual* show his poetry to be painstakingly worked over and rewritten, and the complex structure of verse-plus-commentary reveals the conceptual grandeur of a major theologian. The reduction of the verse to a total economy of stylistic means makes it almost impossible to translate some of the most effective passages, but in describing the ultimate union of the soul with God, St. John achieves a very close approach to a verbal expression of the ineffable:

> *Quedéme y olvidéme,*
> *el rostro recliné sobre el Amado,*
> *cesó todo y dejéme,*

*dejando mi cuidado
entre las azucenas olvidado.*

I withdrew myself and forgot myself,
I lay my face against the Beloved,
everything ceased and I left myself,
leaving my anguish
among the lilies of the field, forgotten.

It was perhaps inevitable that so fervent, individualistic, and experimental a movement should eventually terminate in heresy. St. Teresa and St. John remain well within the bounds of orthodoxy, but when mystical doctrine is extended to its extremes, the result is some form of quietistic movement which ends in a denial of the need for institutional mediation between man and God. Such is the case with the *Guía espiritual* of Miguel de Molinos (published in Rome, 1675). The extremes of this movement had few repercussions in Spain, but French quietism, incorporating the work of Molinos, became the subject of a religious polemic in which Bossuet played a significant part. The major legacy of the Spanish mystics is not theological quarrel, but rather some of the most glowing poetry and inspirational prose of the Golden Age.

If one were to choose a single, brief example of Spanish religious poetry of this period, expressing its fervent, at the same time Stoic, qualities of devotion and spiritual resignation, it might well be the anonymous *Soneto a Cristo crucificado* (*Sonnet to the Crucified Christ*):

*No me mueve, mi Dios, para quererte,
el cielo que me tienes prometido,
ni me mueve el infierno tan temido
para dejar por eso de ofenderte.
¡Tú me mueves, Señor! ¡Muéveme el verte
clavado en una cruz y escarnecido!
Muéveme el ver tu cuerpo tan herido,
muévenme tus afrentas y tu muerte.*

Muéveme, en fin, tu amor en tal manera,
que aunque no hubiera cielo yo te amara,
y aunque no hubiera infierno te temiera.
No tienes que me dar porque te quiera;
porque, aunque cuanto espero no esperara,
lo mesmo que te quiero te quisiera.

I am not moved, my God, to love thee
By the heaven thou hast promised for me,
Nor am I moved by the hell so greatly feared
To cease, for this, to offend thee.
I am moved by thee, Lord! It moves me to see thee
Nailed to a cross and ridiculed.
It moves me to see thy wounded body;
What moves me are the insults, and thy death.
I am so moved by thy love, in fact
That if there were no heaven I would love thee,
And if there were no hell I would fear thee.
My love does not depend on thy gifts—
For even should I despair as much as I now hope,
As I love thee now, I would love thee then.

This poem, without date or signature, was widely circulated in both Spain and the New World in the seventeenth century. It has been attributed, without conclusive proof of authorship being established, to every major religious writer and thinker of the period.

When Miguel de Cervantes Saavedra (1547–1616) referred to his contemporary Lope de Vega as "the monster of nature who usurped the whole realm of the theater" in the prologue to his *Ocho Comedias y ocho entremeses* (*Eight Plays and Eight One-Act Plays*) in 1615, he was commenting with typical good humor, not only on the immense talent and popularity of Lope, but also on his own relatively small success as a dramatist. The son of an unsuccessful surgeon, Cervantes was born in the university town of Alcalá de Henares but lived in various cities of Spain, including Madrid and Seville, as his father sought to better his practice. The details of his education are scanty, but his work shows the extent of his learning to have been very great. Cervantes' adult life was as adventurous as it was unlucky. He traveled to Rome in the service of Cardinal Aquaviva and soon enlisted as a soldier in the wars against the Turks. He was wounded in the Battle of Lepanto, losing the use of his left hand. He continued as a soldier until, on his return to Spain in 1575 he and his brother Rodrigo were captured by the Turks and taken as captives to Algiers. After Rodrigo was ransomed, he set about the difficult task of raising money to ransom his brother, for whom a high price was asked. Cervantes made numerous attempts to escape and to help others to escape, all of which were unsuccessful. After five years of captivity, Cervantes was finally ransomed and he returned to Madrid. He took a series of minor jobs and began to write—*comedias* and the pastoral novel *La Galatea*, published in 1585. It should be noted that *comedia* does not have the meaning of "comedy" in English; *comedia* designates any full-length dramatic piece and is applied equally to the lightest farce and the most serious drama. These works had little commercial success and Cervantes, recently married, found himself obliged to go to Seville in search of work. He found small jobs as a commissary or subcontractor to supply the Spanish fleet, but he showed little aptitude for the work. Through slightly shady dealings or sheer ineptitude, there were discrepancies in his accounts, and Cervantes was twice sent to debtors' prison for short periods in Seville. Later he went to Valladolid to live with his two sisters and other members of his family, and in 1605 he published the first part of the "immortal book" *Don Quijote de la Mancha.*

The book was a great success, but, owing to the very flimsy copyright laws of the time and the fact that Cervantes had sold his literary rights to the publisher for an inadequate sum, his economic plight was not much improved by the extraordinary success of the book in Spanish and in its French and English translations. In Valladolid, Cervantes found himself vexed with family problems as well as economic ones. He continued to write, however, and the last ten years of his life proved to be his most productive literary period. His *Novelas ejemplares* (*Exemplary Novels*) appeared in 1613, his *Ocho Comedias y ocho entremeses* in 1615, and the second part of *Don Quijote* in the same year. His last work, *Persiles y Sigismunda*, a long and complicated novel of adventures, was finished just four days before his death in 1616. Cervantes knew at this time that he was literally writing on his deathbed: he had already received extreme unction. In his dedication of the work to the Count of Lemos, which quotes the lines of an ancient ballad *"Puesto ya el pie en el estribo . . ."* ("With my foot already placed in the stirrup . . .") Cervantes shows to the last the serenity, calm, and good cheer with which he bore a lifetime of misfortunes.

Cervantes applied his talents to most of the types of literature popular during his times. His pastoral novel *La Galatea* suffers from the essentially vapid and sentimental material of the genre, but even so it has more action, characterization, and psychological penetration than is typical of these novels. It is certainly among the most readable. His *comedias* are generally rather cumbersome and are hopelessly outshone by the drama of Lope de Vega and Calderón. On the other hand, his short *entremeses*, quick theatrical sketches in one act of village life or the low life of the city, have brilliant sparkles of wit, irony, and characterization. His *Novelas ejemplares* is a collection of a dozen short novels, very uneven in style and theme, on a variety of subjects. Perhaps most interesting among them are those which verge on the picaresque milieu. *Rinconete y Cortadillo* is the most successful of these. Two boys, fifteen and seventeen years old, adrift in the world, meet in a tavern and decide to go together to Seville on the proceeds of their winnings in a crooked game of cards. Rinconete specializes in card-sharpery and Cortadillo in picking pockets. In Seville they become members of a large gang of thieves, thugs, prostitutes, and criminal specialists of various sorts, presided over by the genial Monipodio, who keeps order, settles disputes, bribes officials, divides up the spoils of the day, and assigns districts of the city to pickpockets and others. Cervantes writes with humor and knowledge of Seville's underworld (he was twice imprisoned there and had ample opportunity to observe and learn of the world he describes). Yet his mastery of language and his innate compassion tend to remove any taint of degradation and violence from even the most sordid episodes.

Cervantes' great work, on which his universal fame is founded, is *Don Quijote de la Mancha*. An enormously complex novel, it has been the subject, in the three and a half centuries since it was written, of literally hundreds of studies. Like all great books, it has proved intriguing to the literary scholar and delightful to readers on all levels. Unfortunately, it has suffered at the hands of translators, imitators, and continuators. The facet of the book which adds most to its brilliance is the perfection with which Cervantes has captured what is most essentially and characteristically Spanish in the life of Spain: the exact proportions and manifestations of idealism, realism, materialism, mysticism, knavery, earthiness, and refinement. Though the material is universally human, the way in which it is used is unmistakably Spanish. When the book is wrenched out of the language and form which Cervantes used, it has sometimes been reduced to a series of comic or downright silly episodes.

Don Quijote surely began as a burlesque on the novels

of chivalry, a laugh-provoking parody of an absurd and worn-out literary vogue. The figures of Don Quijote, an impoverished member of the rural nobility, driven mad by insensate reading of the novels of chivalry, and Sancho Panza, a simple-minded, materialistic peasant, lend themselves readily to burlesque treatment. But as Don Quijote and Sancho set out on their quest—Don Quijote to restore ideal justice in the world and thus triumph over the giants and sorcerers who symbolize the forces of evil, Sancho in hopes of bettering his condition and realizing some personal gain from his association with the madman—the concept deepens and begins to take on complex philosophic overtones. Don Quijote seeks an ideal of justice, truth, and beauty in a world of mule drivers, country wenches, tavernkeepers, and even condemned criminals. Sancho seeks an ideal of materialistic betterment in the largesse of an ill-equipped and fantastically obsessed madman. Don Quijote is indeed a comic figure when, riding his sway-backed farm horse, dressed in rusty armor centuries old, he attacks windmills and flocks of sheep, mistaking them for giants and sorcerers. But when he speaks beautifully and movingly to a group of shepherds, sitting around the fire and sharing their evening meal, of a golden age of truth and justice; of honor and loyalty enshrined in a noble and exacting code of struggle, dedication, and self-sacrifice against human and superhuman evil, the comic and burlesque elements are transcended. Sancho too, is a comic figure in his cowardice, his constant preoccupation with food and drink—*panza* means "belly" in Spanish—but as he rattles off his strings of local proverbs and delivers frank, common-sense judgments on his master's wilder plans and fancies, he expresses the simple wisdom and stable realistic values of Spanish village life.

Gradually the roles seem to reverse: Don Quijote, after a series of blows, defeats, and cruel jokes, comes more and more to his senses, more and more to accept the world in which he lives, while Sancho, ennobled by his contact with his master, and increasingly caught up in the vision of Don Quijote's idealism, urges his knight on to further quests. The greatness of the book lies partly in Cervantes' enormous understanding of the society of his times, partly in the grandeur of his concept of pitting an insane idealism against the crudities and vulgarities of everyday life, partly in his mastery of language and construction of the novel. *Don Quijote* contains, in addition to the basic plot, an excellent short pastoral novel, an Italianate novel of amorous intrigue, a semipastoral novel of romance, poetry and verse of many sorts, relations of current events, the beginnings of a picaresque novel, and a great deal of literary criticism. *Don Quijote* has been translated into most of the world's languages, many times into English. The impact of Don Quijote's character—only suggested by the entry of the adjective "quixotic" into English—has been immense.

The overwhelming genius of the theater in the Golden Age is Lope de Vega (1562–1635). Estimates of his total dramatic productivity run as high as two thousand plays, of which fewer than five hundred have been preserved. Fragments of plays, buried in archives and libraries of the period, are still being discovered. This vagueness about the extent of Lope's work results from theatrical usages and procedures of the time. Plays were often commissioned or purchased by traveling theatrical companies and, upon purchase, became the property of the owner or manager of the group. Scripts were frequently altered by the actors and directors, making unrecognizable the work of the original author, and sometimes scripts were simply discarded if they proved unsuccessful or if the theatrical company disbanded. It is certainly possible that we possess today no more than a fourth of Lope's total dramatic product. Twenty-five volumes of his plays were published in Madrid, and others have come to us in manuscript form or in other editions. Lope wrote with enormous facility and brought to his drama, not only a great poetic and dramatic talent, but an intelligence which made it possible for him to write convincingly of different walks of life and professions; to penetrate the mentality of the haughtiest courtier or the lowliest laborer. Considering the enormous volume of Lope's work, it is not surprising that not all of it is first-rate. The same criticism may be made of Shakespeare or Racine, but it remains that their best works provide an insight and knowledge of human experience that lesser writers have failed to achieve.

Lope wrote in every theatrical genre current in his times; *autos,* religious plays, pastoral plays, plays based on classical, foreign, and national history, plays of romantic intrigue, and plays based on novels of various sorts. His finest works deal with events of Spanish history or tradition. *Fuente Ovejuna* has been translated into English and performed with considerable frequency by amateur, student, and professional groups. In this play, the military governor of the village of Fuente Ovejuna (Sheep Fountain) has long abused and mistreated the villagers, particularly through misconduct with the village girls. Finally, after a particularly atrocious affront, the villagers storm his palace and murder him. When the authorities try to find the guilty party, the entire village takes the blame. Not even torture will bring any name but "Fuente Ovejuna."

—¿*Quién mató al Comendador?*	"Who killed the Commander?"
—*Fuente Ovejuna, señor.*	"Fuente Ovejuna, sir."
—¿*Y quién es Fuente Ovejuna?*	"And who is Fuente Ovejuna?"
—*Todos a una.*	"Each and all of us."

Finally the whole affair comes to the attention of King Ferdinand, the village is pardoned, and order is restored. Based on an event of 1476, Lope infuses into the historical fact a rough poetry and a sense of honor and justice, an air of dignity and gravity typical of his best plays.

The pervasiveness of Lope de Vega's influence was unique: his plays revolutionized the whole concept of drama in Spain and created a "national theater" by establishing a dramatic tradition which used the history of Spain, Spanish traditions and folklore, and Spanish values and attitudes as their themes. One of his finest plays, *El caballero de Olmedo* (*The Knight of Olmedo*) is based on the popular tradition of a young nobleman who rode back and forth from Olmedo to Medina to court a girl of noble family. He is warned repeatedly that an unhappy fate awaits him, in the words of an ancient ballad:

Que de noche le mataron	By night they killed him,
al caballero,	the caballero,
la gala de Medina,	the pride of Medina,
la flor de Olmedo.	the flower of Olmedo.
Sombras le avisaron	Shadows advised him
que no saliese	not to go forth
y le aconsejaron	and they warned him
que no fuese	not to go,
el caballero,	the caballero,
la gala de Medina,	the pride of Medina,
la flor de Olmedo.	the flower of Olmedo.

The caballero scoffs at the warnings and continues his trips to court his lady. He takes part in a bullfight at Medina and wins the applause of the crowd while saving his rival's life at great risk and with a magnificent show of bravery. The rival is chagrined and bitter rather than grateful, and sets an ambush on the road between Medina and Olmedo. The caballero is warned by peasants singing the old ballad and by shadows on the road.

He pays no heed to them and is slain by his rival's treachery. Lope builds a powerful and tragic inevitability into his play. It is in fact, the closest approach to tragedy in the traditional sense that we find in Golden Age drama, where right and honor are customarily vindicated by justice.

In addition to the overwhelming scope of his theatrical works, Lope was also a superb poet and a prose writer; even if we were to discount his plays, Lope would still be one of the major writers of the period for his pastoral and adventure novels, his curious prose-play *La Dorotea*—which is to a large extent autobiographical and not meant for the stage—and for a large body of lyric and narrative poetry. Of peculiar interest to the critic is *El arte nuevo de hacer comedias* (*The New Art of Writing Plays*), a short didactic poem in which Lope proclaims a no-nonsense *ars poetica*. "When I set about to write a *comedia* I lock up the traditional rules with six keys; I throw Terence and Plautus out of my study so that they won't upbraid me, for truth has a way of shouting out from mute books, and I write according to the precepts invented by those who only want the applause of the low-brows; since the low-brows buy the tickets, it is only fair to give them the junk which they enjoy." This cynical attitude, often typical of the working author when called upon to talk about what he is doing, did not keep Lope from writing plays which reached heights of intense dramatic interest and contained passages of great insight and lyrical beauty.

A follower and admirer of Lope is the second major dramatist of the Golden Age, Fray Gabriel Téllez, known to world literature by his pen name, Tirso de Molina (1584?–1648). Although he wrote in other genres, his theatrical work is by far the most significant. In *El condenado por desconfiado* (*The Man Condemned Through Lack of Faith*), Tirso examines the problem of free will versus determinism in the context of a religious life. A pious hermit is told by the devil that, as things stand at present, his reward after death will be the same as that of a notorious libertine. The hermit takes this to mean that his soul is lost anyway and so there is no point to piety. He sets out on a career of debauchery and, when he dies, is condemned to hell. The bandit, however, repents his evil life at the last moment and is saved.

Tirso is best known for his setting of the Don Juan legend in *El burlador de Sevilla y convidado de piedra* (*The Seducer of Seville and the Guest of Stone*). The young Don Juan Tenorio lives a life of irresponsible debauchery, resisting the attempts of his friends and family to bring him to his senses. He is discovered in the attempted seduction of Doña Ana and, trying to escape from her apartment, kills the girl's father, the *Comendador* of Ulloa. He returns to Seville after a judicious absence to find that he is still being sought for the long list of seductions he has accomplished and for the murder of the *Comendador*. He seeks refuge in the very church where the murdered man is buried. Cynical and irreverent, Don Juan invites the funerary statue of the *Comendador* to dine with him. At the appointed hour the statue appears and they dine. The statue extracts a promise from Don Juan to be his guest for dinner the following night. Don Juan is terrified but his pride and disdain force him to keep the appointment:

¡Válgame Dios!, todo el cuerpo	God help me! My whole body
se ha bañado de un sudor,	is bathed in sweat,
y dentro de las entrañas	and within me
se me hiela el corazón.	my heart is freezing.
Cuando me tomó la mano,	When he took my hand,
de suerte me la apretó,	he gripped it so
que un infierno parecía:	that it felt like an inferno:
jamás vide tal calor.	never have I felt such heat.

Un aliento respiraba,
organizando la voz,
tan frío, que parecía
infernal respiración.
Pero todas son ideas
que da la imaginación:
el temor y temer muertos
es más villano temor;
que si un cuerpo noble, vivo,
con potencias y razón
y con alma, no se teme,
¿quién cuerpos muertos temió?
Mañana iré a la capilla
donde convidado soy,
porque se admire y espante
Sevilla de mi valor.

The breath that he breathed, carrying his voice, was so cold that it seemed a breath from hell itself. But all these are mere ideas which imagination produces: fear, and to fear dead men is the most ignoble fear; for if a noble body, alive with all its faculties and reason, and with soul, is not to be feared, who would fear dead bodies? Tomorrow I shall go to the chapel to which I am invited, so that I shall be admired and feared by all Seville for my valor.

When Don Juan arrives at the appointed hour he is given a plate of scorpions and vipers, and the wine is bitter gall and vinegar. The statue then takes his hand, and Don Juan screams, "I am burning! I am roasting!" He begs to be allowed a moment for confession and absolution of his sins, but the statue tells him he has thought of his soul too late, his time has run out. Don Juan, screaming in the pain of the fires of hell, falls dead. The underlying theme of the drama is related to that of *El condenado por desconfiado* (*Condemned for Faithlessness*): Don Juan believes that he can continue his career of seduction, murder, and home-breaking indefinitely—his motto is "*¡Qué largo me lo fiáis!*" (May the reckoning be a long time coming!)—and there will always be time for last-minute repentance and salvation, thus hoodwinking divine retribution. The statue of the *Comendador* represents inexorable justice—"*Quien tal hace, que tal pague*"

(He who sins must pay in the same measure). The figure of Don Juan, the heartless and insatiable seducer, has attracted the imagination of many writers in Spain and beyond; Zorrilla, whose romantic version of the play will be described, Molière, Byron, and Bernard Shaw. Tirso is represented by some thirty plays on biblical subjects, national and historical themes, and on fictional plots of amorous intrigue. Tirso was also a master of prose style. His best-known nondramatic work is *Los cigarrales de Toledo* (*The Orchards of Toledo*), whose plot supposes that a group of friends agree to spend one day together in the orchard of each in turn, and the owner of the *cigarral* will be obliged to entertain the group. It is, as the plan would lead one to suspect, a miscellany of materials, including poetry, tales, a *comedia*, and a short novel.

The last great dramatist of the Golden Age is Pedro Calderón de la Barca (1600–81). His enormous contribution to baroque drama in Spain crowns the efforts of this period with perfect and exemplary theatrical expression. The religious currents of the Golden Age are given theatrical form in the *autos sacramentales*, short allegorical representations in one act and one scene, usually based on the Eucharist or man's redemption. Calderón considerably expands the traditional form of the *auto*, both in length and in theme, to include material from biblical sources, ancient or contemporary history, mythology or legend, which might have a bearing on religious matters. *El gran teatro del mundo,* (*"The World's a Stage"*) for example, uses a metaphor which was common literary property of his time—used by Shakespeare as well—in which the world is seen as a stage and men are but actors for a brief time; in *Sueños hay que verdades son* (*The Truth of Dreams; Dreams of Truth*), Calderón dramatizes the story of Joseph in Egypt, interpreting the dream of Pharaoh; in *El Divino Orfeo* (*The Divine Orpheus*) and *El laberinto del mundo* (*The World Maze*) he turns to Greek mythology, using as themes the story of the pagan divinity Orpheus and the triumph of Theseus in Crete. Even in the *autos* furthest removed from the traditional sources of Christianity, Calderón introduces allegorical or metaphysical reflections which return the drama to the Christian context. It is in his longer *comedias*, however, that his poetic and dramatic genius reaches its perfection.

The *comedia* for which Calderón is best known is *La vida es sueño* (*Life Is a Dream*), which develops the deepest and most fecund metaphysical reflection of which Calderón is capable. When Prince Segismundo of Poland is born, his mother dies in childbirth, there are monstrous storms and prodigies of nature, and the royal astrologer, reading the infant's horoscope, informs King Basilio that, according to the stars, the child will grow up to be a tyrant and will place his foot on his own father's head. Basilio, horrified but unwilling to have the infant slaughtered, decrees that he shall be kept locked and chained in a remote tower, having no human contact but that of a servant and teacher, Clotaldo. Segismundo languishes in these conditions unaware of the outside world. The king decides to test the prediction. He orders that Segismundo be drugged, brought to the palace, and dressed according to his rank. When Segismundo awakens he is told that he is the royal prince. Angry at his long confinement and deprivation, he becomes despotic and vicious in every act, he hurls a courtier from a balcony and attempts to rape the beautiful Rosaura. Basilio orders that Segismundo be drugged again, returned to the tower, and told that all that has happened in the palace has been a dream. The old king names as his successor a noble of the court, but a popular uprising frees Segismundo and demands that he be put on the throne as rightful king. Battle is waged and Segismundo is victorious. As a result of his experience, Segismundo undergoes a profound change of character. Which is the dream, he asks himself—his life spent in chains like a wild beast, or the privileges of the royal crown? Or may they not both be dreams, and the reality something else entirely? The only epistemological and moral constant he can discover is one of moral rectitude, *obrar bien*, to do good whether waking or sleeping, since he cannot know which is the reality. When King Basilio is brought to him as a captive, the victorious Segismundo fulfills the prophecy by placing his foot on his father's bowed head, then tenderly lifts the old man to his feet, offers him the crown again, and displays every sign of humility and moral temperance.

The sources of the ideas to which Calderón gives dramatic life in *La vida es sueño* are many: the Buddha legend, one of the tales from *The Thousand and One Nights*, and perhaps the Oedipus cycle of Sophocles as well as certain ideas of Plato. What counts most in the work, in terms of philosophy, is the unequivocal affirmation of man's free will—"the stars may incline, but they do not compel"—to determine his own fate, good or bad, and hence his moral responsibility for his actions. It is also a striking dramatic statement of the ultimate question, What is reality? In terms of poetry *La vida es sueño* contains some of the best dramatic verse in the Spanish language. Segismundo's soliloquy early in the play occupies a unique place in Spanish literature, comparable to Hamlet's "To be, or not to be." Segismundo, in chains, laments that he, while superior in every way to the lower forms of life, lacks the one great good, freedom:

Nace el ave, y con las galas	A bird is born, and with the frills
Que le dan belleza suma	
Apenas es flor de pluma,	That give him matchless beauty
O ramillete con alas,	

*Cuando las etéreas alas
Corta con velocidad,
Negándose a la piedad
Del nido que deja en calma;
¿Y teniendo yo más alma,
Tengo menos libertad?*

Scarcely is he a flower of feathers
Or a bouquet with wings,
Before the ethereal wings
Quickly set him free,
Refusing for himself the peace
Of the nest he leaves behind;
And I, having the greater soul,
Must I have less liberty?

*Nace el bruto, y con la piel
Que dibujan manchas bellas,
Apenas signo es de estrellas
(Gracias al docto pincel),
Cuando atrevido y cruel,
La humana necesidad
La enseña a tener crueldad,
Monstruo de su laberinto:
¿Y yo, con mejor instinto
Tengo menos libertad?*

The beast is born, and with his hide
Adorned with lovely patterns
Like starry constellations
(Designed by the divine brush)
Then fearless and cruel,
The demands of nature
Teach him to be ferocious,
A monster in his lair:
And I, with higher instincts
Must I have less liberty?

Not all of Calderón's drama is theological or philosophical. Of great popularity were his plays of vengeance for affronts to family or marital honor, such as *El alcalde de Zalamea* (*The Mayor of Zalamea*) and *El médico de su honra* (*The Doctor of His Own Honor*), and a number of plays of romantic intrigue such as *La dama duende* (*The Phantom Lady*). It is impossible even to list the variety of Calderón's plays in a limited space; the author had, at his death, completed more than one hundred works in many theatrical genres.

Summary

The Golden Age of Spanish literature, a period extending roughly from the middle of the sixteenth century to the end of the seventeenth, is a time of enormous productivity in the novel, poetry, and theater. The pastoral novel and the novel of chivalry gradually pass from vogue and are replaced by the picaresque novel. This form introduces elements of realism, didacticism, and the depiction of life on the lower social strata. Spain's greatest novel, *Don Quijote de la Mancha,* is written in this period but cannot be said to belong to any of these genres, although it contains some elements of all three. Lyric and narrative poetry are cultivated by most of the major writers. The literary abuses of Gongorism and *conceptismo* run their courses of overelaborate intellectualism. Religious poetry is a vehicle for the expression of Spanish mysticism and comprises some of the finest lyric verse of the period. The theater experiences a growth and popularity comparable to or exceeding that of the Elizabethan theater in England. Both religious and secular drama are represented. Two dramatic forms dominate the Golden Age; the *auto,* a short religious representation usually based on biblical events or allegorical treatment of Christian doctrines, and the *comedia,* with many scenes and several acts. The *comedia* takes its themes from history, legend, folklore, and novelistic plots and may be tragic or comparatively light in treatment. A third form is the *entremés,* a short farce or burlesque with rustic or lower-class figures. The outstanding dramatists are Lope de Vega, Calderón de la Barca, and Tirso de Molina.

CHAPTER 5

THE AGE OF REASON

The influence of cultures, literatures, and languages foreign to Spain itself has been noted throughout Spanish history. One should be equally aware, however, of a basic and self-perpetuating substratum, a "something" Spanish to be influenced. When we examine the greatest works that Spain has produced—the *Poema de mío Cid,* the *Libro de buen amor,* the *Celestina, Lazarillo de Tormes, Don Quijote,* the theater of Lope and Calderón —we find works which certainly show an awareness of earlier or even non-Spanish models, but which are in a powerful sense unique, deriving their value from insights, language, character, and ideas recognizably Spanish. From time to time, owing perhaps to historical movements or to movements of the spirit, artistic manifestations so incontrovertibly Spanish as the *Libro de buen amor* or the etchings of Goya may appear. Spain's Golden Age represents an abundant flowering of this phenomenon. At other times, the typically Spanish product seems to be lost or waylaid by overwhelming foreign influences and may disappear in a welter of imitations of styles currently in European vogue. Such a period is the eighteenth century. The influence here is predominately French, and may in part—though not entirely—be explained by the presence of members of the house of Bourbon on the Spanish throne.

The eighteenth century, known as the Age of Reason, represents a playing-out of the creative impulse which, building on the expansive and imaginative spirit of the Renaissance, had produced with such astonishing literary fecundity in the sixteenth and seventeenth centuries works of unequaled value in theater, poetry, and the novel. We may, in a simple metaphor, look upon the fourteenth and fifteenth centuries as a period of discovery of new, vast, and fertile areas of imagination and artistic expression. The sixteenth and seventeenth centuries represent periods of exploration, consolidation, and brilliant development of the new realms. The eighteenth century is one of cataloguing, describing, and systematizing what had been done and found. The original creative drive degenerates into pedantry and didacticism, the original Humanist scholarship decays into editions, encyclopedias, and pettifogging details, and the original crisp and economical style which had been dominant from Juan Ruiz to Quevedo disintegrates into a prose which becomes overblown, verbose, and precious. While it is true that these tendencies were latent in seventeenth-century literature, and are even to be found in some of the best literature of the period, they are held in check by the more positive creative values. Yet one's outlook on the eighteenth century should not be completely negative, for it was also a period of consolidation in which the intellectual and rationalizing spirit of the Enlightenment seeks to bring system and order into the higher reaches of human experience, like a prim and determined housemaid tidying up after an irresponsible but admittedly inspired artist.

Particularly to be noted are the currents of "scientism" which French thought had developed, which sought to bring the same exactitude and logic into human affairs that had proved so fruitful in mathematics and the physical sciences. This is the case throughout Europe, where the *"philosophes,"* satirized in Voltaire's *Candide*, sought to resolve all of the problems besetting civilized man in programs to organize and advance human knowledge.

Early in the century the National Library was formed in Madrid (1712) and, with the co-operation of the state and private individuals, began to amass collections in many areas of learning, important among them being the acquisition of Oriental and Arabic materials. The growth of the National Library was aided by the granting of special privileges, such as priority purchaser in the public sale of books and libraries and the mandatory receipt at publication of a copy of every literary work printed in Spain. The great learned academies were formed shortly after. These were organized bodies of scholars whose function was not only to collaborate on major projects —such as dictionaries and encyclopedias—but, in a sense, to legislate taste as well. The *Academia Española* was founded in 1713 and given official recognition in 1714. The first fruit of the *Academia* was the *Diccionario de autoridades,* published in six volumes between 1726 and 1739. Such a dictionary is a vital step in the life of any unified culture, creating basic standards of literary usage. Following the *Diccionario* was the publication of the *Ortografía,* a manual of style, and the *Gramática.* The *Academia de la Historia* was founded in 1735 and was given official recognition in 1738. In addition to the *academias* which received official recognition, a number of private—and highly fashionable—groups formed for the purpose of historical and literary investigation and research. The centers of literary activity were Madrid, Seville, Barcelona, and Salamanca, and each had its *academia* or *tertulia* (literary group). Most influential, perhaps, was the *Academia del Buen Gusto* (*The Academy of Good Taste*) which served as a basic instrument for the establishment of the canons of neoclassical literature.

Of great importance to the literary atmosphere of the time was the proliferation of learned and literary periodicals. These journals contained reviews, literary and scientific articles, correspondence, and of course frequently became the arena for disagreements and polemics of all sorts. A comprehensive list of titles would be a long one; some published only a few issues, to be replaced by others with new titles. Some were so restricted in material or point of view as to have almost no public or general readership. A few of the more influential are: *Memorial literario y curioso de la Corte de Madrid,* which was published with occasional suspensions between 1784 and 1808; the *Diario curioso, erudito y comercial* (1755-58); *Diario de los literatos de España* (1737-42). The particular importance of these journals lies in the reinforcement such publications provided for the currents of erudition and criticism which are the hallmarks of the eighteenth century. The effect of propagating and communicating the work of individual savants was to encourage the whole direction of an age more given to commentary than creation, more productive of organized erudition than of original thought. Studies in bibliography and literary history also assume importance in this period.

The early part of the eighteenth century is largely a ramification of the trends which had dominated the latter part of the seventeenth century. The picaresque novel, diluted by *pícaras* and adventuresses, by the mixture of poetry, short stories, and short *entremeses* or theatrical pieces, and by the tendency to convert the genre into reminiscences or novels of manners, had lost its sharpness and bite. The inherent weakness of the picaresque novel is a tendency to become so episodic that it merely rambles, and this is the fate of several late survivals. The curious *Vida de don Diego de Torres Villaroel* is the semipicaresque autobiography of a brilliant and erratic adventurer who alternated a career as professor of mathematics at the University of Salamanca with the sale of very popular almanacs and horoscopes. He accurately predicted the death of Louis I of Spain in 1724 and thus established his fame as an astrologer. His autobiography details a number of scrapes and contentions with occasional periods of exile from Spain. It is, however, autobiography and so should not be classed as a novel.

There is some interest to be found in *Gil Blas de Santillana,* by the French Hispanist, translator, and adaptor Alain René Lesage (1668–1747). There has been discussion as to whether Lesage was indeed the author of the work or whether he merely adapted the novel from a now lost Spanish manuscript. *Gil Blas* is a mélange of stories, anecdotes, adventures, travels, and political history of the period 1588–1649, with no unity other than the rather vacuous personality of the hero. It is highly derivative of earlier picaresque novels, published memoirs, and historical accounts, and is probably a mere eclectic creation of the French writer. Whatever the truth may be, the novel does have charm, flashes of brilliance, and served to introduce the Spanish *pícaro* to the world beyond the Pyrenees. *Gil Blas* was retranslated into Spanish by José Francisco de Isla, "restored to his homeland and his native tongue by a Spaniard anxious to see that no one makes fun of his nation," as the full title reads. Father Isla (1703–81) is also the author of *La historia del famoso predicador fray Gerundio de Campazas* (*The History of the Famous Preacher Brother Gerund of Campazas*). This is intended as a satire on the overblown oratorical style current in the pulpit, and is, unfortunately, as overblown as the vogue it satirizes. It is primarily a didactic work, with discourses on logic, philosophy, poetry, history, music, medicine, theology, and mathematics. With the exception of some minor historical and pastoral works, the decline of earlier literary modes, this is all that the novel offers in the eighteenth century.

Poetry fares almost as badly. The pastoral vogue continued in verse, and most of the distinguished men of letters, under such pen names as Albino, Fileno, and Flumisbo Thermodonciaco, contributed to the perpetuation of the delicate fiction of bucolic love. The standards for this poetry were set early in the century by Ignacio Luzán (1702–54) in his *Poética, o reglas de la poesía en general y de sus principales especies* (*Poetics, or Rules for Poetry in General and of Its Principal Types*), published in 1737 and re-edited in 1780. Luzán, a member of the *Academia del Buen Gusto,* was educated in Italy and France, and his thought shows the influence which Muratori, Boileau, and Corneille exercised in European letters. The *Poética* has four sections, the first on the origin and essence of poetry, the second on the utility and enjoyment of poetry, the third considers dramatic poetry, and the fourth, epic poetry. There is little that is original in his literary theory. He defends the Aristotelian unities of time, place, and action in drama and propounds a didactic purpose for poetry in general: poetry should serve the end of moral instruction. Luzán's work would be of trivial importance were it not for the temper of the age, which accepted his precepts almost without reservation, making the *Poética* the catechism of good taste both for poetry being written and for the appreciation of the poetry of past periods. Such a critical apparatus tended to give sanction to the growing formalism and pedantry which afflicted all of Spanish literature of the period.

A revival of the two great "schools" of poetry of the sixteenth century, those of Seville and Salamanca, occurs in the latter part of the eighteenth century, but it is little more than a sad echo of the accomplishments of Herrera and Fray Luis de León. The revival in Salamanca was founded by Fray Diego González (1732–94), who devoted his life to the study of the works of Fray

Luis and to a revival of the spirit of lyric poetry which Fray Luis represented. A thoroughly humble man, González sought only to preserve and perpetuate a worthy literary tradition, but such was the vigor of his personality that he attracted a nucleus of some of the best poets of the period to Salamanca. One of the most arresting figures of the group was José Cadalso (1741–82), a pre-romantic who had traveled widely, distinguished himself as a soldier, knew several European languages, and who displayed a typically romantic personality rather out of place in so staid a century. Cadalso had a love affair with the actress María Ignacia Ibáñez in Madrid, for whom he wrote several poems. María died suddenly, and so grief-stricken was Cadalso that he refused to leave the church in which she was buried and had to be forcibly detained from disinterring her body. Cadalso achieved instant fame for a short satirical work in prose, *Los eruditos a la violeta* (*The Learned Men to the Violet*), in which he exposes the shortcomings of stuffy pedantry. More durable is his *Cartas marruecas* (*Moroccan Letters*), which appeared in the periodical *Correo de Madrid*. The author pretends to be a Moor traveling in Spain who makes a serious and well-intentioned appraisal of Spanish faults and virtues. *Noches lugubres*, published posthumously in the same journal, recounts in dramatic terms the attempt of the poet to disinter the body of his beloved. Cadalso came into contact with the school of Salamanca shortly after that episode, when he left Madrid to regain his emotional balance following the death of María.

One of the outstanding figures in the political life of the time was also a tangential member of the school, Don Gaspar Melchor de Jovellanos (1744–1811). Jovellanos' interests were encyclopedic in their scope, including agricultural reform, development of the mineral resources of northern Spain, the study of architecture, a proposal for the integration of the arts and sciences, various antiquarian and geographical studies, as well as two plays and a body of poetry. The plays, one of the genre known as lachrymose, the other, a historical drama, are strongly influenced by French neoclassical tragedy; ponderous and sentimental, they have little artistic value. His lyrical poetry is also weak and derivative. A series of satires and epistles, however, is of real worth. Jovellanos represents in its best light the values and accomplishments of an age which enshrined order, taste, and breadth of interests over dynamic creative ability. In an *Epistle to His Friends in Salamanca,* Jovellanos urged them to abandon the mannerisms of pastoral poetry and to seek a new and more direct mode of poetic expression. He was also active in the Sevillian school and was the author of a similar *Epistle to His Friends in Seville.*

A younger member of the school of Salamanca was the lyric poet Juan Meléndez Valdés (1754–1817), whose poetic gifts were among the most striking of the period. His work may be divided into two epochs. The first, following the tenets of the school, is strongly influenced by the major figures of the Renaissance, Garcilaso and Fray Luis. In this group are odes and eclogues, *romances* and *letrillas,* which revive and adapt both popular and learned forms of the sixteenth century to the modes of his time. A second period is marked by the presence of foreign influences—Locke, Leibnitz, Winckelmann, Montesquieu—and by the influence of Jovellanos. The deism of the eighteenth century is apparent in his ode, *El hombre imperfecto a su perfectísimo Autor* (*Imperfect Man to His Infinitely Perfect Author*):

> Señor, a cuyos día son los siglos
> instantes fugitivos; Ser eterno,
> torna a mí tu clemencia,
> pues huye, vana sombra, mi existencia.

> *Tú, que hinches con tu espíritu inefable*
> *el universo y más; Ser infinito,*
> *mírame en faz pacible,*
> *pues soy menos que un átomo invisible. . . .*

> Lord, to whose day the centuries
> are fleeting instants; eternal Being,
> turn thy clemency upon me,
> for my existence, vain shadow, is fleeing.
> Thou, who fills with thy ineffable spirit
> the Universe, and more; infinite Being,
> turn thy peaceful face upon me,
> for I am less than an invisible atom. . . .

We find in this poem a curious mixture of rationalist currents with mysticism; of the language of the deist, who sees God as an impersonal force, with the language of the ardent mystic for whom God is a personal, direct experience. Such anomaly is typical of the attempt to graft the new ideas of the Enlightenment onto the roots of the intense personalism which is central to Spanish literature.

The school of Seville offered less of real literary value. Its members sought inspiration in a revival of the poetry of Horace and Herrera, seeking thus to re-establish the glories of the seventeenth century, but to little purpose. As an example, we may mention Manuel María de Arjona, who translated two works of Horace and composed a number of pastoral and didactic poems, some occasionally anthologized.

In this century of criticism, didacticism, and interest in the ordering of knowledge, the most prepossessing figure is that of Fray Benito Jerónimo Feijóo y Montenegro (1676–1764), a Benedictine monk who was a professor of philosophy and later professor of theology at the University of Oviedo. His learning was truly encyclopedic and his interests varied widely. The major portion of his work is published in two large collections, *Teatro crítico universal* (the title is difficult to translate; *Universal*

Critical Exposition is an approximation), in eight volumes, and *Cartas eruditas y curiosas* (*Learned and Interesting Letters*), in five volumes. The *Cartas* is a supplement to the *Teatro* and contains a similarly wide variety of material. The whole is made up of essays and discourses on many subjects, scientific, humanistic, theological, and political. His interests may generally be grouped under three headings: (1) Scientific—with studies in astronomy, physics, mathematics, geography, and medicine; (2) Philosophical—with an examination of polemics and schools, a defense of skepticism, and a re-examination of Aristotelianism; (3) Literary—with important studies in philology and comparative linguistics, history, aesthetics, and education. Feijóo was especially vigorous in attacking superstition. He reflects the typical devotion to reason of the eighteenth century in his all-out attack against astrology, all forms of magic and divination, false miracles and prophecies, ghosts and other malefic spirits. He was open to the new currents and foreign influences of his time, but remained both a Catholic and a Spaniard, more willing to adapt new ideas to Spanish ways than to follow vogues for the sake of change. His long life was devoted almost entirely to study, and his voluminous writings, if at times repetitious and tedious, giving as much space to the trivial and obvious as to the important and original, represent the reflections of a mature and informed mind on most of the significant topics of his century.

The work of Feijóo was continued by his friend and disciple Fray Martín Sarmiento (1695–1771), also a Benedictine, who published a defense of the *Teatro crítico* against the many attacks which Feijóo's works elicited. He did important work in botany and other areas of natural history. His most important literary study is *Memorias para la historia de la poesía y poetas españoles* (*Notes on the History of Poetry and Spanish*

Poets), a work which shows very considerable insight into the history and aesthetics of early Spanish poetry. His critical apparatus is broader than that of Luzán and his judgments less dogmatic. His interest in the past is more antiquarian than literary and his work did not have the proclamatory character of Luzán's *Poetics*.

A minor genre which flourished in this period was the fable, largely inspired by La Fontaine. Tomás de Iriarte (1750–91) wrote a collection of seventy-six verse fables in various meters whose purpose was largely satirical. These are clever, acute, and charming pieces which make no claim to profundity. Typical is the fable of the Duck and the Snake. The Duck is preening and praising himself at the edge of a pool: "To what other animal has Heaven given such gifts? I belong to the water, to the land, and to the air. When I grow tired of walking, if I want to, I fly; if I want to, I swim." A clever serpent who was listening gave him a whistle and said, "Hey, pretty boy! There's no reason to be so proud of yourself. You can't cover ground like a deer, you can't fly like a falcon, you can't swim like a carp. So take this lesson to heart: the important and difficult thing is not to be a jack of all trades, but to do one thing really well." Frequently quoted as an example of his style is the quatrain:

Guarde para su regalo	Keep, as a special present,
esta sentencia un autor:	every writer this one verse:
si el sabio no aprueba,	if the wise man doesn't like
¡*malo!*	it, Bad!
si el necio aplaude, ¡peor!	if the fool applauds, still worse!

Iriarte antagonized a number of colleagues with his satires and wasted a good bit of time defending himself from attack. He was a writer of talent, intelligence, and humor. Two comedies of manners, *La señorita malcriada* (*The Ill-Bred Lady*) and *El señorito mimado*

(*The Pampered Darling*) are as good as any in the period.

A more traditional fabulist is Félix María de Samaniego (1745–1801). His *Fábulas morales* (*Moral Fables*) are mostly adaptations in verse of the fables familiar throughout Europe in the collections of Aesop and Phaedrus, some taken from La Fontaine and John Gay, while a few others are original. Samaniego wrote them at the request of his uncle for use in seminary instruction.

The theater, until the end of the century, suffered the same paralysis that had overtaken the novel and lyric poetry. It was suffocated rather than inspired by the influence of French neoclassical tragedy and was straitjacketed by the "rules" of the academies. The application of this academic thinking was so excessive and absurd that the production of *autos sacramentales*, the short religious and morality plays, was prohibited by royal decree. These plays, products of a venerable tradition and containing some of the finest dramatic poetry in the language, were offensive to the most vehement arbiters of taste for their mixture of the sacred and the profane, the anachronistic mixture of historical and biblical figures, the use of allegorical figures, and the difficulty of classifying the works in terms of genre.

One of the leaders in the movement was Nicolás Fernández de Moratín (1737–80) whose three historical tragedies *Lucrecia, Hormesinda,* and *Guzmán el Bueno* had no popular success, despite, or perhaps due to, the fact that they offer a classic example of the taste and discipline of the academies. Moratín was a much better poet than dramatist. His *Fiesta de toros en Madrid* (*The Bullfight in Madrid*) brings to life the exotic color and excitement of eleventh-century Madrid under the Moors. The hero of the narrative is El Cid, Rodrigo of Vivar, who enters Muslim-held Madrid to fight a bull in the *fiesta*, and makes a vow that he will not remove his helmet until he has taken the city from the Moors. According to one critic, the work is "perhaps the most perfect poem written in Spanish in the eighteenth century."

Toward the end of the century the mold began to crack sufficiently to allow some life back into the theater. Leandro Fernández de Moratín (1760–1828), the son of the poet and playwright Nicolás, did not entirely depart from the idea of order and a restrictive form for the drama—he accepted the classical unities and the need for moral purpose in the drama—but he allows fresh theatrical elements to find a place in his *comedias*. Moratín admired the French, Italian, and English tragedy and indeed wrote excellent translations of two comedies of Molière. He was the first to translate *Hamlet* into Spanish, but he did not feel bound to imitate foreign models in his own work. His best play, a work of stylistic perfection within its limits, is *El sí de las niñas* (*When a Girl Says "Yes"*). The plot is simple: the convent-educated young Paquita is promised by her parents to the rich and honorable but elderly Don Diego. Paquita is much in love with his nephew, Don Carlos. Deeply disturbed to find that Paquita is already promised in marriage, Don Carlos is prepared to go to any lengths against his unknown rival. When he learns that the rival is his own kindly and generous benefactor, his uncle, the case seems hopeless. Don Carlos and Paquita resign themselves to fate. Don Diego learns of the situation, however, and, deeply moved by their self-sacrifice, renounces his own claim and sponsors the marriage of the two. The value and originality of the work are not to be found in the rather saccharine plot of the play, but in the use of a contemporary theme, in the characterizations of the figures, and in Moratín's championship of young love against the rigorous demands of a social system which allowed little latitude for personal choice. In his more complex satirical play, *La comedia nueva*, Moratín strikes a telling satirical blow at the critical vogue for grandiose historical tragedy. His protagonist is a dramatist who is financially ruined when his play fails on opening night. He is then hired by a well-to-do sympathizer as an estate administrator because, although his play writing is bad, his penmanship is good.

Moratín is really more important for his influence on the succeeding generation of playwrights than for his own dramatic work. In cutting through the dead wood of the conventionalized theater of his time, writing his plays in fluent and believable contemporary dialogue, and taking his themes from the life around him, he prepares the way for writers who will enlarge upon these new techniques. If his plays occasionally fall into the artificiality of the sentimental comedy of manners, they nonetheless create a drama more closely related to the life and experience of their times than was the neoclassic tragedy. While the academies sought to establish neoclassic tragedy as the dominant theatrical form of the era, these plays proved generally unpopular and very different from the theatrical fare which the public wanted and would pay to see. The popular form was represented largely by the musical theater, the *zarzuela*, and the *sainete*. The *sainete* is a work in the light popular tradition of the earlier *pasos* and *entremeses;* they were generally regarded by the critics and writers of the eighteenth century as being beneath their notice. As a happy result, this popular form escaped the general petrification of the period and offers some delightful, if frequently inconsequential, moments of theater. The great master of the form was Ramón de la Cruz (1731–94), who had a rare genius for depicting the customs and types, particularly of the capital city of Madrid, from scrubwomen and chestnut vendors to the upper middle class. His scenes are taken from life, and often suffer the defects common to quick sketches. Yet the breath of life, the color, the movement, the crisp, piquant language of his works give the *sainetes* a vigor which the turgid neoclassical tragedy lacked. A prolific writer, Ramón de la Cruz presumably wrote more than four hundred *sainetes*, of which no complete collection has been made. The themes range from low comedy through the bittersweet irony of love lost to action which is close to tragedy.

Summary

The eighteenth century almost wholly petrified the enormous literary drive of the Spanish Golden Age into a lifeless and stuffy formalism. Originality, wit, and literary sparkle were largely stifled by adherence to literary "rules" derived from classic poetry and drama. The influence of French, Italian, and English writers was great and Spanish writers frequently limited themselves to translation and imitation. The false and dictatorial sophistication of neoclassic standards was implemented and imposed to a great extent by the foundation of academies of literature, language, and history, and by the growing domination of the literary scene by literary and critical journals, newspapers, magazines, and other periodicals. At the very end of the century there is a resurgence of vitality and originality in the theater. Replacing the dead hand of formalism and the domination of foreign models, the *sainetes* of Ramón de la Cruz, essentially vignettes of daily life, have considerable popular vogue. The *comedias* of Moratín restore contemporary idiom and themes to Spanish drama at the very end of the century.

CHAPTER 6

THE NINETEENTH CENTURY

Throughout Europe the first half of the nineteenth century is dominated by a new current of emotionalism and rebellion which has been given the name "romanticism." In a large sense this abundance of life, thought, ideals, and literature may be seen as a rebellion against the formalism of the preceding century, its reliance on reason —in philosophy and science—and its constant reference to the ideals and standards of ancient Greece and Rome. Romanticism sweeps away these restraints in search of a strong and unhampered immediacy of expression, in which the deepest feelings, the most urgent passions of the writer are communicated to the audience. A poem or a tragedy would have been judged in the eighteenth century primarily by reference to its form: is it a perfect ode in terms of rhyme and meter? Is the content meticulously adjusted to the verse form chosen? Does the play abide scrupulously by the classical unities? Do the ideas develop in a perfect harmony of logic? This intellectualism is overthrown by romanticism; the criteria of evaluation become emotional: Does the work evoke an overwhelming emotion of terror or of joy? Does it communicate the writer's deepest passions and desires? Thus the cleverness and sophistication of the well-balanced and reflective intellectual—the writer par excellence of the Age of Reason—give way to the wild and impassioned lyrics of the disordered, suffering, emotional genius.

Romanticism, as a literary movement, has its origins in England and Germany. It moves, both as a literary influence and as an interpretation of human experience, through France and Italy to Spain, losing something of its strength on the way. In Germany, romanticism is embodied in the works of Wagner, Beethoven, Goethe, Hegel; in England, by Sir Walter Scott, Wordsworth, Coleridge, Lord Byron, Keats, Shelley. Spain can boast of no such giants of romanticism, although these currents influence a number of writers of talent, particularly in poetry and the drama.

Literary movements are never so abrupt or obliging, however, as to adjust themselves neatly to calendars and to centuries. The tide of neoclassicism lingers in Spain for at least two decades of the nineteenth century while the currents of romanticism gather force. The works of Manuel José Quintana (1772–1857) represent the conservative literary strain. A disciple of Meléndez Valdés and Jovellanos, Quintana never fully accepted the excesses and the new literary freedom of romanticism. He was essentially a poet of restraint and discipline whose themes were largely patriotic and national, as in his celebrated ode *Al combate de Trafalgar* (*To the Battle of Trafalgar*). Quintana was also a literary critic and historian, journalist, and biographer. He wrote neoclassic tragedy in verse, but with little success (*El duque de Viseo* and *Pelayo*). The work of Quintana that has survived as a literary influence is his patriotic verse and various odes which celebrate political events. These poems certainly show an awareness of romanticism, a new life and lyricism, a depth of feeling and emotionalism which is a notable advance from the bucolic nostalgia of the school of Salamanca. In other ways, too, Quintana approximates the interests of the romantics. His ode *La fuente de la mora encantada* (*The Fountain of the Enchanted Mooress*) expresses the fascination which the exotic past held for the romantics and explores the rich colors, textures, and ornamentation of the Moorish world with all the sensuality of the romantic poet:

La media luna que ardía	The half moon that blazed
cual exhalación radiante	like a radiant sigh
entre las crespas madejas	among the curling locks
de sus cabellos suaves,	of her fine hair,
mostraba su antiguo origen	showed off her ancient origin,
y el africano carácter	and the African nature
de los que a España trajeron	of those who brought to Spain
el alcorán y el alfanje.	the Koran and the scimitar.
Mora bella en sus facciones,	Mooress lovely in her features,
mora bizarra en su traje,	Mooress exotic in her costume,
y de labor también mora	and also Moorish work
la rica alfombra en que yace,	the rich carpet on which she lies,
toda ella encanta y admira,	all of her enchants and delights,
toda suspende y atrae	all astonishes and attracts
embargando los sentidos	robbing the senses
y obligando a vasallaje.	and obliging one to vassalage.

The theater of Manuel Bretón de los Herreros (1796–1873) continues the line of development established by Moratín in his *comedias*. In *Marcela, o ¿cuál de los tres?* (*Marcela, or Which of the Three?*) a young widow is assiduously courted by three men, one a windbag, another a fop, the third a gloomy pessimist. Marcela turns them all down to live her own life. The play had considerable success and is still of some interest for its delineation of middle-class types in sharply drawn characterizations. *Muérete y verás* (*Die and See What Happens*) presents the case of Pablo, who goes off to the wars leaving his inconsolable fiancée behind. News comes of his death in battle and the fiancée promptly finds a new suitor and announces her coming marriage. Pablo, in fact merely wounded, returns to find his funeral *in absentia* underway and the wedding about to begin. He learns that while the fiancée had lost no time in grieving over him, her sister has secretly loved him all along and is suffering in silent grief. The "dead" Pablo makes his appearance, confronts the perfidious fiancée, proclaims the constancy of the sister, and marries her.

We find in these plays a sharpness of characterization and a breadth of social satire which is of some interest, but there is nothing conceptually new that is not to be found in Moratín. One of his plays, *Elena,* has some romantic aspects, but it does not give adequate expression to the new currents; it is, in fact, so bad a play as to be almost unreadable.

A minor literary form developed in the 1830's, serving as a bridge between the intellectualism of the neoclassic period and the freer forms of the romantic era. It also carried on the tradition of popular satire which had been a basic, or at least recurrent, element in Spanish literature since the late Middle Ages. This is the *costumbrismo* developed in essay form in the journals, gazettes, and newspapers which had become such an influential literary medium. Many of the major Spanish writers of the nineteenth century began their careers as *periodistas,* or literary journalists. Their *costumbrismo* took the form of sharp, witty, often acerbic depiction of the urban society of their times. They usually dealt, as in the *sainete,* with archetypes: the fop, the actor, the newly rich, the pretentious, etc. There is an intellectual, urbane, personal tone to these articles which reflects the neoclassic penchant for criticism and rationalism, and at the same time introduces a romantic element of the writer's direct and immediate relation to his material. Themes range from the mildly lampooning character sketch to quite overt criticism of the values and usages of the times, of the prevalent and ruling ideas and vogues. Some critics have seen in these pieces a foreshadowing of the attitudes of the Generation of 1898.

One of the earliest of these writers is Ramón de Mesonero y Romanos (1803–82). In his *Escenas matritenses* (*Scenes of Madrid*), he picks up and dissects the chit-chat and gossip of the cafés, at the same time bringing to the fore some of the most typical foibles of the bourgeoisie. His prose is a delightful example of a light, urbane, well-bred and well-read, cosmopolitan style. As an artist, Mesonero does not reach very high, but he attains effectively the results he seeks. He is amusing and entertaining, never viperish or waspish, and remains delightful to read as a writer who knows his times and both the amenities and follies they represent.

Mariano José de Larra (1809–37) uses the same literary vehicle, but the results are quite different. A suicide before the age of twenty-eight, Larra remains an enigmatic, embittered figure in a period which was generally expansive and optimistic, for all its political turmoil. Larra contracted an unhappy and unbearable marriage at the age of twenty and soon sought consolation from outside sources. With the brief triumph of liberalism and the return from exile of the Duke of Rivas, Larra was named deputy to the *Cortes* (Parliament) of Spain, a position he managed to hold for all of nine days. His failure in political life and a series of amorous crises seem to have exacerbated a growing pessimism and depression. Following a particularly tempestuous scene with his current mistress, he shot himself a month and a half before his twenty-eighth birthday.

Larra was the best-paid journalist in Spain of his day. Most of his articles appeared under his pen name, "Fígaro," in several of the more important Spanish journals. His early work displays the typical *costum-*

brismo of his period: a brilliant, urbane, charming style in which he dwells on the foibles and shibboleths of bourgeois Madrid, recording the figures and ideas, preoccupations and interests of his contemporaries. As his pessimism grows, the tone deepens and darkens. He pillories the intellectual backwardness of Spain, the hypocrisy, vulgarity, and vapidity of his contemporaries, the triviality and ostentation of the middle class, and the suffocating bureaucracy that sustains it. Soon Larra begins to look into himself and he finds a spiritual vacuum as horrendous as that which surrounds him externally. In *Día de difuntos de 1836* (*Day of the Dead of 1836*), the most bitter and revealing of the articles of "Fígaro," he has a vision of Madrid as a vast cemetery, wherein justice, honor, culture, truth, solvency, and national spirit have been laid to rest. At the end of the article, he is shocked to discover yet another tomb: his own heart, with the epitaph "Here lies Hope."

There is much here to remind us of Quevedo's *Sueños:* the biting, hopeless satire, the superb ability to reduce pomposity and sham by the most economic means, and the abrupt delineation of a vision which puts the whole of contemporary society into a new and grotesque—or macabre—context. Larra was probably the best prose stylist of his day. His work is always clear, concise, direct, and free of the penchant for puns and conceits which makes Quevedo so difficult to read. The romantics claimed him as their own, as much for his precocity, brilliance, and ill-starred life as for his defense of liberal causes and his insistence on the freedom of the artist to create as a law unto himself. The Generation of 1898 saw him as a precursor of their own interests in terms of his individualism and his preoccupation with the ills of Spain. From a present standpoint, he is to be seen as a superbly gifted writer, trained in the canons of neoclassic purity of form, but artistically open to the new currents of romanticism; a writer possessed of intelligence, knowledge, sensitivity, and a wide comprehension of his times. As a man, he was an embittered, unstable manic depressive. If Larra had survived his emotional crisis there is every likelihood that he would have been a major force in molding and creating the literature of the nineteenth century.

The first great figure of Spanish romanticism is Don Angel de Saavedra, Duke of Rivas (1791-1865). His earliest work is neoclassical in orientation, but while a political exile in Malta and England as a result of his liberalism at home, he came into contact with the works of Sir Walter Scott and Lord Byron. On his return to Spain he published his long narrative poem *El moro expósito* (*The Foundling Moor*). The poem is a retelling of the epic theme of the seven princes of Lara. Romantic aspects of the work are abundantly evident in the choice of a theme taken not from classical antiquity or mythology but from Moorish Spain, and in the elements of violence, mystery, terror, and exoticism which surround the plot. Other narrative poems of Rivas revive the national past with artistic success, particularly the series of *Romances históricas* (*Historical Romances*), published in 1841. These are based on various events and personages of the past and show Rivas' talents for sumptuous and animated description at their best. If historical accuracy is somewhat stretched, it is in the interest of poetic truth.

The production of *Don Alvaro, o la fuerza del sino* (*Don Alvaro, or the Power of Destiny*) in 1835 was the first great dramatic success for romanticism in Spain. Don Alvaro, a handsome *caballero* of mysterious origin, asks for the hand of the noble Doña Leonor. When he is refused by the girl's father, the Marqués of Calatrava, Don Alvaro attempts to elope with the girl, but he is discovered in the act of arranging the elopement. A quarrel ensues in which Don Alvaro accidentally kills the marqués, who dies cursing his disobedient daughter. Don Alvaro, believing Doña Leonor also dead, goes off to the wars in Italy, where he saves the life of her older brother. The two become close friends, neither knowing the identity of the other. When the truth is found out, the brother challenges Don Alvaro to a duel, and is killed by him. Don Alvaro, overcome with remorse, retires to a monastery to live a life of repentance. Doña Leonor, also remorseful for her relatively innocent part in the death of her father, has become a recluse on a nearby mountain. Neither knows of the presence of the other. Four years pass. The second son of the marqués has meanwhile dedicated himself to finding the murderer of his father and brother. In America, he learns of Don Alvaro's exotic past and traces him to the monastery. There he confronts the penitent with his past and challenges him to a duel. Don Alvaro refuses, not wishing more blood on his hands, but is finally goaded to accept. Leaving the precincts of the monastery, they fight in a violent storm, their blows punctuated by thunder and lightning. The brother is mortally wounded and Don Alvaro shouts for help for the stricken man. Doña Leonor appears on the scene. Her brother jumps to the conclusion that she has been all this while cohabiting with her father's murderer. With his last strength, he stabs his sister. Seeing the two dead, Don Alvaro leaps from a precipice to his death.

One sees in this play the most typical facets of romanticism: violence, guilt, horror, mystery, ill-starred love, adventure, and exoticism. The Duke of Rivas consciously violates the "unities" of neoclassic drama; his drama takes place over a long period of time, the action occurs in several different localities, and the complexity of the plot, with wild coincidences, revelations, and recognitions, violently distorts the neoclassic passion for neatness. Yet the play has important qualities lacking in the more orderly tragedy of the eighteenth century: a grandeur and a range of passions which provide a compelling movement to the drama, offering an operatic magnitude of theatricality. It is, in fact, the source of one of Giuseppe Verdi's finest works, *La forza del destino*.

Francisco Martínez de la Rosa (1787-1862) had much in common with Rivas. Also a liberal, his public career fluctuated between exile, prison, and the highest offices in the constitutional government. His early work, too, is neoclassical. His play *Moraima* depicts the civil wars of the Moors in the last days of their possession of Granada, and *Edipo*, one of the best tragedies of the nineteenth century, revives the legend of the Theban king. Martínez responds to the currents of romanticism with *La conjuración de Venecia* (*The Conspiracy of Venice*), produced with great success in 1834. It is essentially a historical drama with romantic overtones, not fully within the new currents. The action concerns a plot in Venice of 1310 to overthrow the tyranny of the Tribunal of Ten, presided over by Morosini. Morosini's niece and her secret husband, Rugiero, are implicated in the plot and when the rebellion fails Rugiero is sentenced to death. It is discovered that Rugiero is the son of Morosini, but even this cannot save him from the sentence of death for his part in the conspiracy. Rugiero dies and Laura goes mad. An earlier historical drama, *Aben Humeya*, originally written in French and later translated by the author, revives the Moorish theme of the last days of Granada and also contains some nascent feeling of romanticism in its violence, exoticism, and sentimentality.

Antonio García Gutiérrez (1813-84), soldier, journalist, public official, and dramatist, joined in the tide of romanticism with a number of dramas on historical themes, but is remembered primarily for *El trovador*, on which the libretto of Verdi's opera *Il Trovatore* is based.

His work is essentially shallow and excessively given to coincidence and the exaggeration of theatrical effects. It is romantic drama at its most flamboyant and is of little interest today except as a vehicle for Verdi's music. Another of his plays, *Simón Bocanegra*, was used by Verdi as the basis for one of his less successful works.

Juan Eugenio Hartzenbusch (1806–80), was the son of a German cabinetmaker and a Spanish mother. His work is varied and elegant, and he was both creative writer and scholar. His studies of the Spanish baroque theater contributed much to the revival of interest in Lope de Vega, Calderón, and Tirso de Molina. He wrote a collection of fables, a group of *costumbrista* articles, short stories, and poetry. As a dramatist, Hartzenbusch is best known for his version of *Los amantes de Teruel* (*The Lovers of Teruel*), a plot which had been used repeatedly before: Diego Marsilla and Isabel de Segura have been in love since earliest childhood. When Diego asks for the hand of Isabel, however, he finds that he is not the only suitor; the rich and noble Don Rodrigo de Azagra is also taken with the beauty of Isabel. Diego is refused by her family on the grounds that he is too poor to provide a proper match. He requests a period of time in which to make his fortune; the request is granted. Diego goes off to the wars and, in a series of travels and adventures, including his capture by Moorish pirates, manages to become rich. He returns to Teruel a few hours after the allotted period and finds that Isabel has just been married to Don Rodrigo. Diego dies of pure heartbreak and, taking his hand in hers, Isabel falls on his body and expires of the same malady.

José Zorrilla (1817–93) traveled widely and lived in France, Mexico, and Italy; his earlier travels were undertaken to avoid his wife's jealousy and domination. In Mexico he was named director of the national theater by the

Emperor Maximilian. Following Maximilian's death he returned to Spain and supported himself by giving readings of his poetry and eventually received official recognition and some support from the state. His lyric and narrative poetry and his *leyendas,* retelling traditional folk tales and legends, brought him early fame. The *leyendas* capture the flavor and simplicity of the Spanish past. Some are "miracles" of the sort that Berceo had used in his *mester de clerecía:* a young gallant gives his word of marriage to a girl before an image of Christ. After consummating the union, he absents himself for a time. On his return to Toledo he denies the promise of marriage and the girl takes her complaint to court, naming as her only witness the sacred image. The image is brought in to testify, signifying by the movement of a hand that the girl is telling the truth. In another *leyenda* Zorrilla uses a popular tradition of Madrid: Juan Ruiz and Pedro Medina are close friends who find themselves in love with the same girl. They cast lots to determine which shall have her, and Medina wins. On the wedding day, Medina is mysteriously stabbed and dies before he can name his assassin. Ruiz continues his attentions to the fiancée and finally wins her promise of marriage. He buys a fresh sheep's head for the wedding feast and is carrying it home under his cloak when the attention of the police is called to the fact that he is leaving a trail of blood behind as he goes along the street. They ask Ruiz to show them what he has under his cloak; when he opens it he finds that he is carrying the severed head of Medina, whom he had treacherously murdered on the other man's wedding day.

Zorrilla's lasting fame is founded on his version of the Don Juan theme in *Don Juan Tenorio.* The play follows the general outlines of the Tirso version with some additional touches and expansion. Zorrilla introduces Brígida, a new personification of the character of Celestina and Trotaconventos; he incorporates a popular tale of the rake who witnesses his own funeral in a macabre vision. Finally, the shade of his beloved Doña Inés appears to redeem the ne'er-do-well. At the end, a troop of skeletons, ghosts, and the statue of the Comendador gather around Don Juan to drag him down to hell. Inés appears, driving off the phantoms and informs Don Juan:

Yo mi alma he dado por ti,	I have given my soul for you
y Dios te otorga por mí	and God extends to you
tu dudosa salvación.	through me your doubtful salvation.
Misterio es que en comprensión	It is a mystery whose understanding
no cabe de criatura,	is not given to mortal man,
y sólo en vida más pura	and only in the purer life
los justos comprenderán	the saved will understand
que el amor salvó a don Juan	that love saved Don Juan
al pie de la sepultura. . . .	at the foot of the grave. . . .

Angels appear, the sweet odor of flowers fills the theater, the music changes from funeral dirges to "a sweet and distant music," and Don Juan makes his final speech of contrition:

¡Clemente Dios, gloria a ti!	God of forgiveness, glory to Thee!
Mañana a los sevillanos aterrará el creer que a manos de mis víctimas caí.	Tomorrow the Sevillians will be horrified to think that I fell into the hands of my enemies.
Mas es justo; quede aquí al universo notorio que pues me abre el purgatorio un punto de penitencia,	But that is just. Let it be proclaimed to the universe that purgatory was opened to me by a flicker of penitence;
es el Dios de la clemencia el Dios de Don Juan Tenorio.	the God of forgiveness is the God of Don Juan Tenorio.

Don Juan falls at the feet of Doña Inés and the two expire. From their mouths issue their souls, represented by two brilliant flames which lose themselves in space to the sound of heavenly music.

Many critics, and Zorrilla himself, have commented on the serious defects of the play. Zorrilla survived the first performance by almost fifty years and never ceased to condemn his own work as a toy of his youth and inferior to his best drama. The adverse criticism has centered on the loose structure of the play. It is constructed in two parts and seven acts, and there is a lapse of some five years between the opening and closing scenes. In spite of the criticism, the drama has had enormous popular success and is still annually produced in Spain on All Saints' Day. The aspect which best accounts for its great and continuing popularity is its inescapable Spanishness in terms of characterization, attitudes, dramatic movement, and the language in which it is set. If not a great work of art, Zorrilla's *Don Juan* is clearly a work of great popular appeal.

One of the most romantically appealing figures of the period, in terms of his short, adventurous, and ill-starred life, is José de Espronceda (1808–42). While still in his teens he was involved in the activities of a clandestine liberal society and was forced to flee to Lisbon as a political refugee. He had only five pesetas in his pocket when he arrived in the Portuguese capital. He paid three pesetas for a health certificate and then threw the remaining two in the river, "not wanting to arrive in such a splendid city with so little money." While in Lisbon he met and fell in love with Teresa Mancha, the daughter of an exiled Spanish brigadier. Her father sent Teresa to England and the young poet soon followed her there. Espronceda's liberal political convictions took him on to Holland and Paris, where he fought in the Revolution of 1830. When he returned he found that Teresa had been married off to a wealthy merchant, but, undaunted, he persuaded her to run off with him. Their life together was stormy, however, and Teresa finally abandoned the poet and their four-year-old daughter. He completely lost track of her until, sometime later and quite by chance, he saw her body laid out for her funeral in a house in Madrid. Espronceda died in Madrid of a throat infection at the age of thirty-four. His great talent was for description, but it sometimes becomes excessive in his verse, as in these lines from his poem *El verdugo* (*The Executioner*):

> *El tormento que quiebra los huesos*
> *y del reo el histérico ¡ay!*
> *y el crujir de los nervios rompidos*
> *bajo el golpe del hacha que cae,*
> *son mi placer.*

> The torture that cracks the bones
> and the hysterical scream of the convict
> and the crunching of broken nerves
> under the shock of the falling ax
> are my pleasure.

Espronceda's major work is a poem on a theme related to the Don Juan legend, *El estudiante de Salamanca* (*The Student of Salamanca*). In this poem, the arrogant and high-flying young aristocrat Don Félix de Montemar, after a series of heartless seductions, follows the veiled figure of a woman who beckons him down a dark and winding street. He is led to the scene of a funeral procession and perceives to his horror that the corpse is himself and the funeral he is attending is his own. This denouement had appeared in earlier works and probably goes back to medieval folklore, but the macabre events, the student's journey through the deserted streets of the shuttered medieval university town, the sense of urgency and impending doom, are all properly romantic. In his second important long poem, *El diablo mundo* (*The Devil World*), Espronceda takes his theme from Goethe's *Faust* and ambitiously attempts to symbolize the whole of human aspiration and disillusionment in the story of Adam, an old man supernaturally restored to youth to experience the heights and depths of human life. The poem is unfinished, owing to Espronceda's early death. It was, the poet himself realized, too grand a theme for his talents, but the work contains many passages of real literary value.

The second canto of *El diablo mundo* contains his famous *Canto a Teresa*, an elegy in which the poet expresses his love, his grief for the dead girl, his remorse for their unhappy past, and his awareness that life goes on in spite of personal tragedy.

> *¿Quién pensara jamás, Teresa mía,*
> *que fuera eterno manantial de llanto*
> *tanto inocente amor, tanta alegría,*
> *tantas delicias y delirio tanto?*
> *¿Quién pensara jamás llegase un día*
> *en que perdido el celestial encanto*
> *y caída la venda de los ojos*
> *cuanto diera placer causara enojos?*
>
> *Aún parece, Teresa, que te veo*
> *aérea cual dorada mariposa,*
> *ensueño delicioso del deseo,*
> *sobre tallo gentil temprana rosa,*
> *del amor venturoso devaneo,*
> *angélica, purísima y dichosa,*
> *y oigo tu voz dulcísima y respiro*
> *tu aliento perfumado en tu suspiro.* . . .
>
> *Gocemos, sí; la cristalina esfera*
> *gira bañada en luz: ¡bella es la vida!*
> *¿Quién a parar alcanza la carrera*
> *del mundo hermoso que al placer convida?*

*Brilla radiante el sol, la primavera
los campos pinta en la estación florida:
truéquese en risa mi dolor profundo . . .
Que haya un cadáver más, ¿qué importa al mundo?*

Who might ever have thought, my Teresa,
that it would be an eternal fountain of grief,
Such innocent love, such joy,
Such delights and so much delirium?
Who might ever have thought a day would come
in which the celestial enchantment gone,
and the blindfold fallen from our eyes,
what gave such pleasure would cause us pain?

Still it seems, Teresa, that I see you
light as a golden butterfly,
delicious dream of desire,
early rose on a slender stalk,
blessed delirium of love,
angelic, purest, and happy,
and I hear the sweetness of your voice, and I breathe
your breath's perfume in your sighs. . . .

Let us enjoy life, yes; the crystalline sphere
spins bathed in light: beautiful is life!
Who can call a halt to the whirl
of the beautiful world that calls us on to pleasure?
The sun shines radiantly, the spring
paints the fields in the flowery season:
Let my profound pain be changed to smiles . . .
That there is one more cadaver, what does it matter to
                                          the world?

    As the currents of romanticism paled somewhat toward the middle of the nineteenth century, a new generation of writers brought a spirit of controlled literary craftsmanship to Spanish letters—a "second romanticism" quite distinct from the revolutionary beginnings of the movement in choice of themes and in language. No longer obsessed by the churchyard and the midnight pealing of church bells, by veiled figures leading young libertines to their doom, or death and high drama on windswept mountain crags, these writers retained the sensitivity and directness of romanticism without its excesses. Chief among these is the poet Gustavo Adolfo Bécquer (1836–70), whose *Leyendas* (*Legends*) in prose, and *Rimas* (*Rhymes*), short verse compositions, reflect a spirit of tender melancholy and gentle despair, mixed with fantasy and an acute awareness of the more subtle aspects of nature, both human and external. The *Leyendas*, a group of tales with fantastic or supernatural overtones, are written with charm and clarity of language. The *Rimas* are dominated by a pervading sadness and subjectivity; and their themes are mostly built on the poet's awareness of the passage of time, of the nearness and solitude of death, and the bittersweet aspects of love. The spirit of his work is announced in the first of his *Rimas*:

Yo sé un himno gigante y extraño
que anuncia en la noche del alma una aurora,
y estas páginas son de ese himno
cadencias que el aire dilata en las sombras.

Yo quisiera escribirle, del hombre
domando el rebelde, mezquino idioma,
con palabras que fuesen a un tiempo
suspiros y risas, colores y notas.

Pero en vano es luchar; que no hay cifra
capaz de encerrarlo, y apenas ¡oh hermosa!
si, teniendo en mis manos las tuyas,
pudiera al oído cantártelo a solas.

I know a vast, strange hymn
Which announces a dawn to the night of the soul,
And these pages are cadences of that hymn
Which the air diffuses in the shadows.

> I would like to write it; of man
> Conquering his rebellious, grudging language
> With words which would be at one time
> Sighs and laughter, color and music.
>   But it is a hopeless struggle; there is no symbol
> Grand enough to hold it, and scarcely, O beautiful one,
> Holding your hands in mine,
> Could I sing it into your ear when we're alone.

Of somewhat more robust nature and a more vivacious attitude toward life was Ramón de Campoamor (1817–1901). The sharpness of his wit and his penchant for philosophy caused him to reject both the pomposity of the neoclassic writers and the tenebrous violence of the early romantics. In his *Poetics*, Campoamor gives a clear and forthright idea of his aesthetic principles. "Poetry," he says, "is the rhythmic representation of a concept or idea by means of imagery, expressed in a style of language which could not be more natural or more concise if it were to be said in prose." Thus Campoamor declares his poetic ideal to be that directness and economy of style which had traditionally marked the best and most typical moments of Spanish letters. All of his poems are short and intense, with subtle overtones of wry humor or sadness. Like Bécquer's lyrics, there is more of the formless melancholy of a rainy Sunday afternoon than the violent passions of Espronceda or the Duke of Rivas. His best work is found in two collections, the *Humoradas* and the *Doloras*. The term *doloras* is coined by Campoamor from the Spanish word *dolor*, pain or suffering, and is used by the poet to indicate the grief, wistfulness, and emotional pangs which most of the poems contain. Using emotional contrasts as a basic means of expression, and calling upon the dissimilarity of the subjective and external worlds as a means of highlighting the lesser struggles of the soul, he creates an incisive and insighted verse that never fails to move the reader. Campoamor lacks the lyricism of Bécquer and his poetry suffers, as some critics have felt, from triviality and a basic vulgarity.

A very considerable flowering of Spanish theater marks the latter part of the nineteenth century. Here too, there is an atmosphere of restraint and order which the early romantics lacked. The sense of form and literary control which the neoclassic theater had overvalued, loosened and made flexible by the "sociological" theater of Moratín and Ramón de la Cruz, broadened by the personalism of the romantics, produces in this period a theater which is at once vivacious and intense, concerned both with ideas and characterization, which mixes prose and verse without hesitation, depending less on coincidence and violence for its dramatic effects, and insisting on logic and verisimilitude in its plots. López de Ayala (1828–79), in *El tanto por ciento* (*Such and Such Per Cent*), builds a complicated and up-to-date drama around a love affair menaced by the sleazy dealings of an economic opportunist who has the confidence of both parties. Manuel Tamayo y Baus (1829–98) accomplished a major tour de force in *Un drama nuevo*, a play-within-a-play which has for its characters members of the theatrical company of William Shakespeare. The comic character Yorick begs to be given the part of the tragic hero in Shakespeare's new play, and the author agrees. The envious leading man, Walton, is thus forced to accept a lesser part, and takes his revenge by nurturing an incipient love affair between Yorick's wife and the young actor Edmund. This situation corresponds closely to the play that is being presented, and the last act sees the explosion of Yorick's jealousy on stage as he murders Edmund. Shakespeare informs the audience that what they have been applauding as drama is real-life tragedy, and urges them to pray alike for the murderer and the victim.

José Echegaray (1832–1916) represents the most complete fusion of romantic and realistic elements in the theater of this period. He was well-read in contemporary literature and in the great works of the Golden Age, successful in his professional life as a civil engineer and later as minister of the interior, and the first Spaniard to be awarded the Nobel prize for literature (1904). His long life was marked with success and prosperity. In spite of this, his drama centers on conflicts of conscience, suicides, duels, and adultery. Too often Echegaray's plays come very close to melodrama. He approaches the moral dilemmas of his theatrical characters as if they were engineering problems to be solved, and so lacks the psychological penetration into personality and character that is found in the dramas of López de Ayala and Tamayo. Despite these overtones of artificiality, his plays are impressively and intensely theatrical. Echegaray's best-known work is *El Gran Galeoto,* a thesis-drama; the point is to show that society, with its gossip and prying into private affairs, often provokes what it most condemns. The thesis is represented theatrically in a complex domestic situation: Don Julián, elderly husband of the lovely and virtuous Teodora, has befriended a penniless young writer, Ernesto, and has taken him into his house. Although the motives and morals of all three are above reproach, unfounded gossip, by suggesting that Ernesto is the lover of Teodora, soon renders the situation impossible. Ernesto agrees to fight a duel with the leader of the gossips to protect the good name of Teodora. Don Julián will not allow this, and insists that it is his duty to defend his wife's honor. In the ensuing fight he is fatally wounded. Circumstances lead the dying man to believe the gossip and he dies cursing his wife and Ernesto. The family of Don Julián throws Teodora out of the house in disgrace, but Ernesto comes to her defense, proclaiming that society, through false gossip and unfounded suspicion, has murdered an honorable man and slandered an innocent woman. Together they leave forever. *El Gran Galeoto*—the title refers to the episode of Francesca da Rimini in Dante's *Inferno* and is difficult to translate—is a belated product of romanticism fused with the tendencies toward social comment of the theater of Moratín.

Frequently described as the best historical drama of the nineteenth century is *El haz de leña* (*The Bundle of Kindling*) by Gaspar Núñez de Arce (1834-1903). The action is based on events of 1568, when Don Carlos, the lame and mentally afflicted son of Philip II, plotted to seize power by freeing the Lowlands from Spanish domination. Don Carlos was apprehended in an attempt to flee Spain and was placed under close surveillance. He died shortly after in circumstances that were regarded by most of Europe as decidedly suspicious. The religious struggles of the period become an important element in the play, in which Don Carlos is aided by Protestants seeking religious freedom, as well as political independence, for the Lowlands. The "bundle of kindling" refers to the pile of wood used to burn heretics at the stake. The play speaks out strongly for liberalism and freedom of conscience and certainly reflects the author's personal convictions regarding his own troubled times.

The novel did not flourish in the atmosphere of neoclassicism of the eighteenth century, nor was there any work of importance in this genre produced in the early pangs of romanticism. It is difficult to find good reasons why this should be so; perhaps the neoclassic writers felt that the novel violated the rules of unity and precision. Few novels were written in Spain in the time of Enlightenment, and those few were dull and characterless prolongations of the picaresque novel, biographies and autobiographies, and didactic and philosophic imitations of French models. The early period of romanticism is dominated by lyric poetry and theater; the first novels never develop beyond third-rate imitations of the English, German, and French romantics. Toward the middle of the century an effort is made to overcome this vitiating influence and a few readable historical novels appear. Probably the best of them is *El señor de Bembibre* of Enrique Gil y Carrasco (1815–46), which concerns the extinction of the order of Knights Templars in Spain. The action and figures are conventional in their sentimentalism and romantic excesses, and the plot bears a resemblance to Scott's *Bride of Lammermoor*. The descriptions of landscape are outstanding, however, and the beginnings of the regional novel can be clearly seen in this work. The novels of Francisco Navarro Villoslada (1818–95), *Doña Blanca de Navarra*, *Doña Urraca de Castilla*, and *Amaya, o los vascos en el siglo VIII* (*Amaya, or The Basques in the Eighth Century*) are also worth mentioning. Villoslada's creation of character, the authenticity of the reconstruction of historical events, and the sustained interest in the movement of significant moments of Spanish history combine to create works of some literary interest.

Toward the middle of the century a new type of novel made its appearance. Its setting was contemporary or near-contemporary, its themes were for the most part sociological, and its most distinguishing mark was the description of local countryside and of the way of life typical of isolated towns and villages. This is the regional novel of the *costumbristas,* writers who built their novels around the unique and picturesque qualities of various regions of Spain. The result of this *costumbrismo* was a happy one. Spain is enormously varied in dialects, folklore, dress, and way of life in general. This variety and color offered a very natural and rewarding field for the novelist, and these qualities had been emerging in the better historical novels.

The first writer of this "modern" novel is Cecilia Böhl

de Faber (1796–1877) daughter of a German Hispanist and a Spanish woman from Cádiz. Writing under the pen name of "Fernán Caballero," she gained renown for her regional novels of Andalusia, particularly *La gaviota* (*The Sea Gull*). The heroine, Marisalada, is called the sea gull for her unusual vocal ability to imitate the song of birds. A German surgeon who is passing through the village falls in love with her, marries her, and takes her to Seville. He educates her and opens her eyes to the bigger world, but Marisalada soon falls in love with a bullfighter and betrays her husband. She goes on to Madrid and becomes the toast of the capital as a singer. The bullfighter is fatally gored, the surgeon learns of her infidelity and departs for America, Marisalada loses her voice through an illness, and, totally disillusioned, marries the barber in her home village. The novel is marred by the heavy-handed moralizing of the author, who loses no opportunity to point out the innate corruption of mankind and the degrading effect of sophistication on rural simplicity. Despite this tendency, "Fernán Caballero" brings a vivid realism and descriptive ability to scenes which were immediate and pertinent to the Spanish life of her period, centering on a real and believable here-and-now.

A further step toward realism in the novel is taken by Juan Valera (1824–1905) in his immensely popular *Pepita Jiménez*. The story of blossoming love between the young widow Pepita and the seminary student Luis is complicated by the conflicts of love and the religious vocation, and various external handicaps to their felicity. Still, love conquers all eventually, with the sly help of several interested and well-disposed parties. Valera was a classicist and intellectual by nature, and these qualities sometimes override the mastery of form and amenity of style which constitute the major virtues of his novel.

Valera was, in a very broad sense of the term, a man of

letters. Widely read, widely traveled, and well educated, he served in the diplomatic corps in many capitals of Europe and America. The poetry, plays, and the novels which followed *Pepita Jiménez* were not particularly successful, but his historical and political writings were important. Valera was also one of the outstanding literary critics of the period: he was one of the founders of the *Revista de España,* where much of his work appeared. His studies of romanticism, the eighteenth century, Cervantes, the Russian novel, the literary trends of his own time, and of aesthetics in general were major contributions to the literary awareness of Spain in the nineteenth century.

The figure of Armando Palacio Valdés (1853–1938) follows logically after that of Valera in terms of the breadth of his literary interests. He first established himself as a critic, writing in the *Revista de España* and later publishing *Semblanzas literarias* (*Literary Sketches*) and *La literatura en 1881* in collaboration with the critic "Clarín." His abundant series of novels can be loosely divided into four "regional" categories: Asturian, with settings in the coastal villages of the northern coast (*Marta y María, El idilio de un enfermo*); urban, with settings in the more intense political and literary life of Madrid (*Riverita* and *Maximinia, El origen del pensamiento*); Valencian (*La alegría del capitán Ribot*); and the series for which the author is best known, with settings in Andalusia (*Los majos de Cádiz, Los cármenes de Granada*). To this last group belongs the novel on which Palacio's fame rests most securely, generally regarded as his best work, *La hermana San Sulpicio* (*Sister San Sulpicio*). A young poet-doctor from Galicia meets the novitiate Gloria Bermúdez (Sister San Sulpicio in her religious order), and falls in love with her. He soon learns that there is a month left before she takes final vows, and that she is considering abandoning the convent. He follows her to Seville, takes residence in a boardinghouse which is liberally populated with "types" of all sorts, and proceeds to court her as best he can. The major impediments to their romance are a domineering mother who insists that Gloria remain in the convent and take her vows, and a rival suitor who is more of a pest than a threat. Finally the doctor deposits Gloria in the house of a sympathetic friend, chases off the rival, and marries Gloria.

La hermana San Sulpicio is the regional novel at its best, with brilliant scenes of Andalusian life, the bullfight, flamenco dancing, drinking bouts in the taverns, and a broad portrayal of the character of southern Spain. The secondary characters are drawn sharply, clearly, and without exaggeration; the novel is infused with a realism and vivacity that have given it popularity far beyond the boundaries of Spain. Palacio Valdés is, after Cervantes, probably the most widely read and translated author Spain has produced.

Sensitive to the powerful currents of naturalism which pervaded French and Russian novels of the nineteenth century, the well-read and much-traveled Countess Emilia Pardo Bazán (1852–1921) sought to transplant new points of view to Spanish landscapes and adapt them to Spanish tastes. With the publication in 1883 of *La cuestión palpitante* (*The Throbbing Question*), a critical essay on the experimental novel of Zola and naturalism in general, a major polemic was initiated. Pardo Bazán accepts the function of the novel to explore in minute detail the effect which society produces on human character. She does not, however, accept the rigid determinism of Zola and French naturalism, which sees the individual as the helpless pawn of social forces; rather, she attempts to harmonize the doctrines of naturalism with those of Catholicism, affirming the free will of the individual to choose, within physical and social limitations, his own moral destiny. Pardo Bazán was a feminist and an intellectual. She defended the public rights of women with ardor and was counselor of public instruction and professor of Romance literature at the University of Madrid. Her works of literary criticism are abundant, sensitive, well written, and intelligently conceived. Most important are those books and articles which introduce contemporary French and Russian literature to Spain (*La revolución y la novela en Rusia*, 1887; *Lecciones de literatura; La literatura francesa moderna*, 1910–14). Her best novels are regional, describing life, customs, and landscapes of her native Galicia, that foggy and Celtic corner of northwestern Spain. Her most representative works are *Los pazos de Ulloa* (*The Mansions of Ulloa*) and its continuation, *La madre naturaleza* (*Mother Nature*). The techniques of naturalism, at least as Pardo Bazán conceived the movement, are evident in both. The works are a study of the physical and moral ruin of the minor Galician nobility. In their isolation and poverty they sink ever more into a quagmire of moral and social decay. Don Pedro Moscoso, Marqués of Ulloa, carries on a squalid affair with the servant Sabel, by whom he has a son, Perucho. His relations with the servant continue after his marriage to his cousin, the delicate and ethereal Nucha. Their marriage produces a daughter, Manuelita, and the mother dies shortly after.

In the second novel, Manuelita and Perucho are drawn together through their loneliness and sensitivity, unaware of their kinship. Unwittingly, they develop an incestuous relationship. When they learn the truth, Perucho goes off alone to seek his fortune and to forget the past, while Manuelita enters a convent. The force behind the two novels is the mental, physical, intellectual, and political corruption of rural Galicia and the inevitable effect of this environment on its inhabitants. There is particularly in *Los pazos de Ulloa*, deep psychological insight into major and minor characters. The marqués is a man of action to whom no action is possible in the moldering society of petty rivalries and politics; he is a warrior and a leader with no battles to fight and no one to lead. Decadence and degeneracy are the only certain outcome.

Leopoldo Alas (1852–1901) has an importance in the nineteenth century both as critic and novelist. Writing under the name "Clarín" ("Bugle"), he was the most feared, most respected, and most widely read critic in the Spanish-speaking world during the last two decades of the century. His criticism, if not always fair or kindly, was usually relevant, perceptive, and constructive when a given work contained material of value. Published in several volumes (*Solos de "Clarín," Mezclilla, Palique,* and other titles), his articles and reviews are still considered of major importance as literary criticism. When Clarín published his novel, *La regenta*, in 1884, he sought to fuse regionalism and naturalism with what both had lacked until then, a penetration into unique personalities that went beyond the nascent and implicit psychologism of earlier novels—as one critic has put it, Clarín conceives the novel as a study of souls. In *La regenta*, the title figure Ana Ozores is an unusually beautiful young lady married to the distinguished and elderly Don Víctor Quintanar. When her husband retires to the rainy, drab city of Vetusta (modeled on Oviedo, where the author lived most of his life) the childless Ana finds her life of complete emptiness and utter stasis unbearable. She becomes obsessed by the attractions and overtures of a local Don Juan, Don Alvaro Mesía. Her one outlet in a provincial city where card playing and gossip are the only social activities is the church. Her attempt to fulfill herself in an assumed piety and religious mysticism is, however, essentially hypocritical and reflects nothing real within her. The outcome is an adulterous relationship with the cynical Mesía, who later kills her husband in the latter's attempt to defend Ana's honor in a duel. The plot contains the perennial elements of a young beauty married to an elderly gentleman, the ennui and triviality of social life in a provincial capital, the narrowness and hypocrisy of provincial morality, and criticism of a local clergy which is ambitious, domineering, and more concerned with its image than with its spiritual function. The excellence of this long, complex, two-volume novel is found in the psychological accuracy with which the characters appear and move before us, not in terms of clinical dissection but rather as organic entities.

Clarín was also an outstanding writer of short stories which were published in several collections (*Pipá, El gallo de Sócrates, El sombrero del señor cura*).

Pedro de Alarcón (1833–91) is best known for his farcical novel of intrigue, *El sombrero de tres picos* (*The Three-Cornered Hat*). Widely read and translated, the novel has been made famous by the ballet of the Spanish composer Manuel de Falla. Alarcón takes his plot from a popular story of village life and gives it a touch of verve and dash which had not been seen in Spanish prose since the seventeenth century. The mill near Guadix is a popular rendezvous for the gentlemen of the town, who are attracted by the miller's lovely—and virtuous—wife. The Corregidor, a high city official, is an elderly libertine who plans an assault on that virtue. He contrives with the help of some unprincipled friends to keep the miller, Lucas, occupied while he slips into the mill late at night, to take whatever advantage of the situation he can. Unfortunately for his plans, he falls into a ditch and arrives at the mill soaking wet, with all thoughts of seduction driven from his mind. Lucas, suspicious of the Corregidor, returns to the mill and sees the aristocratic clothing hung by the chimney to dry. Deciding to give the Corregidor tit for tat, he dresses himself in the other's clothing and goes off to play the same trick on the wife of his rival. Alarcón gives a moral and acceptable ending to what was originally a bawdy country jest: Lucas has no more success with the wife of the Corregidor than the old libertine had with the virtuous Frasquita. The popularity of the work is based on the perfection of dialogue and the searchingly true-to-life representation of the characters. In its realism, it has been compared to the gayer paintings of Goya and to the *sainetes* of Ramón de la Cruz.

José María de Pereda (1833–1906) is distinguished for his regional novels of the mountains and fishing villages of northern Spain, in the area of Santander. *Sotileza*, a complex story of love and life among the fishermen of Santander, is outstanding for its re-creation of the scenery and customs of the remote area. *Peñas arriba* reflects to some extent the life of the author in the character of Marcelo, a young man living the good life in Madrid, who is taken, almost against his will, to live with his uncle in a mountain village near Santander. Marcelo at first finds the new life boring and depressing, but gradually as he sees more and comes to respond to the beauties of the land and the simplicity of his uncle's friends, he loses his desire to escape to the city. When his uncle dies, Marcelo decides to remain in the village and marry Lita, a village beauty. Pereda's novels have movement and an impressive awareness of the natural beauty of the area he loved. His literary style is clear and uncluttered, and one critic has remarked that Pereda is the greatest master of prose dialogue since Cervantes.

More familiar to the American reader are the novels of Vicente Blasco Ibáñez (1867–1928) through translations and movie versions of considerable popularity. *Blood and Sand* and *The Four Horsemen of the Apocalypse* are perhaps best known; unfortunately they represent the author's most sensational, not his best, work. Blasco

Ibáñez is strongest in writing of the countryside and peasantry of his native Valencia, as in *La barraca*, a powerful treatment of the work, customs, and life of the semitropical citrus orchards of the region, enlivened by animosities and self-destructive revenge which keeps the novel hovering somewhere between tragedy and melodrama. *Flor de mayo* brings a similar crude strength to the description of the life of a coastal fishing village which alternates its legitimate occupations with occasional smuggling expeditions. *Cañas y barro* is set in the rice paddies of the Albufera, a lake near Valencia, and here again the magnificent treatment of local color, both human and landscape, acquire a power and majesty which is reflected in the dynamic action of the novel.

Blasco Ibáñez has been called by some critics the "Spanish Zola" for the naturalistic bent of his novels. It is true, especially in his early regional novels, that we encounter the detailed description, the predominance of action over reflection, a rapid and occasionally careless style, characters brutalized by their environment, and a deep and unregenerate pessimism—that are typical elements of French naturalism. He was originally a newspaperman and he writes as one would who is concerned with action and the reporting of action. His protagonists are fighters, and whether they fight against their social, political, or natural environment, their lives are harsh, direct, and elemental.

In the latter part of the nineteenth century, Benito Pérez Galdós (1843–1920), both in terms of his massive literary production and the overwhelming power, variety, and general excellence of his work, towers over his contemporaries. His most ambitious project was the four series of *Episodios nacionales*, a monumental collection of novels which explore the turbulent history of Spain in the nineteenth century, "an epic in novel form." In forty volumes, they trace the history of Spain from the

Battle of Trafalgar in 1805 and the inroads of Napoleon on the peninsula, through the War of Independence and the period of political chaos of the Carlist struggles. A fifth series, of six volumes, brings the work up to the period of the first republic. These works are not "history" in a narrow sense; Galdós is concerned with the impact of events on the lives of people, not with the minute details of political and military events. Of the total collection, the first two series have been generally judged superior to the later novels.

Staggering as the sheer volume of the historical series may be, Galdós is perhaps better known for his "social" novels, in which he studies minutely the life and values of the middle and lower classes. In *Doña Perfecta* and *Gloria* we see the ruinous and tragic outcome of provincialism and religious bigotry. In *Misericordia*, Galdós investigates with shattering touches of realism a squalid world of physical and spiritual poverty in which ingratitude and brutal materialism are shown in bright relief against the charitable, forgiving, and saintly figure of the servant Benigna. In the four novels of the Torquemada series, Galdós analyzes the passion of avarice with a clinical scrupulousness of detail. Francisco Torquemada, the usurer-financier, is perhaps the most humanly understandable of all the misers of literature. A man capable of grasping only the most obvious and concrete values, Torquemada is at a loss to understand the more subtle torments that life inflicts upon him, such as the death of his gifted son, his own almost involuntary success in business, the affliction of a deformed, idiot son as the fruit of his second marriage, and the fulfillment of his social ambitions in later life.

In all of his novels, Galdós reveals a dramatic flair; in many we find an unusual mixture of realism and sentimentalism; *Marianela* and *Misericordia*, for example, unabashedly tug at the heartstrings with almost maudlin pathos while at the same time developing scenes of the most striking social realism with the acumen of a clinical observer. What stands out unmistakably in the work of Galdós is an enormous novelistic creativity which can transform the banal, the sordid, even the saccharine into the texture of human experience. It is indeed a mystery why Galdós remains almost unknown outside of Spain as a major literary genius, comparable in his creativity to any literary figure the Western world has produced. As one critic has said, "Had the fecund creator of that vast procession of *Episodios nacionales* and *Novelas contemporáneas* been a Frenchman or a German, his fame would have been universal; being a Spaniard, it is hardly more than Peninsular."

The novels of Galdós give an almost encyclopedic résumé of the sins and virtues of the complex social and political structure of Spain in the social turmoil of the last third of the nineteenth century. If he sees little hope for the triumph of order, virtue, and logic in human society, his vision is expressed in the choice of themes and characters, in actions and decisions, and not in explicit statement. The moral quality of human choice is shown in its outcome, in the result of action and inaction. Galdós is critical of the established Church, of provincialism, of hypocrisy, of superficiality in the whole realm of human affairs. He is fascinated by the weakness—psychological, moral, and political—which is the dominant note in the creation of his characters and ambience. His best novels are psychological studies of the effect which tradition and the social environment have upon individuals. This places Galdós, in terms of critical labels, somewhere between the traditional Spanish realism of the picaresque novel and Cervantes and the new currents of naturalism in the European novel.

The greatest European influence on Galdós, as he declares, is Charles Dickens. In descriptive technique and in the creation of sly, witty, urbane, ludicrous, or compulsive characters there is a clear similarity in the two writers. But Galdós is as Spanish as Dickens is English, and so however comparable isolated details may be, the total effect is as distinct as the societies and ethos the two writers portray. Galdós, like Dickens, stands as a towering figure who brings his epoch to a close in the final and comprehensive enunciation of the totality of his century. Galdós wrote for the theater as well, but with mediocre success. He adapted some of his novels to dramatic form, but, dramatic though his novels are, they became paler and more constrained in theatrical form. Best known of his plays is *El abuelo* (*The Grandfather*), which in some respects is reminiscent of Shakespeare's *King Lear*.

Literary criticism and philosophy, particularly Thomistic ethics, metaphysics, and philosophy of history, flowered in the late nineteenth century. The astonishing erudition of Marcelino Menéndez y Pelayo (1856–1912) dominates the scholarship of the last twenty years of the nineteenth century and the first decade of the twentieth. Professor of Spanish literature at the University of Madrid and later director of the National Library, Menéndez y Pelayo wrote on most aspects of Spanish literature and aesthetics from the time of Seneca to that of his own contemporaries. His works still form the solid base for studies of Spanish thought and creative writing in most periods and most genres. Of his many-volume studies the most significant are *Origins of the Novel, History of Aesthetic Ideas in Spain, History of Spanish Heterodoxists,* and *Spanish Science*. Menéndez y Pelayo displayed his brilliance at an early age, publishing a translation of the tragedies of Seneca before he was eighteen years old and completing his doctoral degree at nineteen with a brilliant thesis on the Latin novel. His studies extended to the whole of European literature, finding sources, influences, and backgrounds in large areas of poetry, drama, and prose. No contemporary scholar of arts and letters has matched the breadth and penetration of his learning or rivaled the extent of his published studies, which make up some seventy volumes in the official collection of his works.

Summary

Following the uninspired and largely imitative period of formalism which most of the eighteenth century represents in Spanish letters, the nineteenth century bursts forth from its doldrums in a spate of emotional excess with romantic drama and poetry. The initial impulse is checked and refined somewhat in the drama and poetry of the second half of the century, with a revival of interest in form and a moderation of the cheaply theatrical effects seen in many of the early romantic works. The theater tends toward a deeper analysis of character, psychological motivation, and the social milieu. The novel becomes the dominant literary form of the second half of the century. Three main genres of the novel emerge, not always clearly separated: the historical novel, the regional novel, and the social novel. Derived to a certain extent from the earlier romantic currents is an interest in individual experience, in the national past, and in the contemporary social structure of the society. The sterile criticism of the eighteenth century, with its emphasis on rules of art and an unnecessarily precious sophistication, is broadened and humanized to present, not so much programs and recipes for the creation of literary works, as insighted and productive analyses of the contemporary and earlier literary product.

CHAPTER 7

THE GENERATION OF 1898 AND "MODERNISMO"

The Generation of 1898

The objective criticism which Galdós had brought to a society which possessed neither social integration nor direction, a society which had failed to solve the moral and political crises which the nineteenth century had thrust upon it, pointed the direction for a total revaluation of the complex structure of Spanish life of the period. A parallel has often been drawn between the novelistic undertakings of Cervantes and Galdós in terms of their expression of the whole fabric of Spanish life in their times. To many, *Don Quijote* represents an artistic summation of the totality of Spanish thought, values, and social experience at the beginning of the seventeenth century. In much the same way, given the difference in their times and talents, Galdós presents the *Gestalt* of the last third of the nineteenth.

For the Spain of Cervantes' times the problems of transition and adaptation were solved mainly by temporizing and resisting Protestantism, industrialization, the aims and demands of the bourgeoisie, the nascent autocracy of the American colonies, the growing disenchantment with an absolutist monarchy, and the pressures of burgeoning nationalism in Europe. These pressures had become explosive during the nineteenth century and had manifested themselves in the great tides of political, economic, and philosophic movements which were apparent throughout Europe, and which are reflected in Galdós' novels. In concrete terms, the increasing gulf between the values and mores of Madrid and the provinces, reflected in *Doña Perfecta*, the cynical opportunism of the bureaucracy seen in *Miau*, the pretension and snobbery seen in *Misericordia*, the hypocrisy and perversion of religion as a real ethical force seen in *Gloria*, all point to a coming social crisis of major proportions, a mounting crisis which would not be solved by temporizing.

The crisis came, however, from without, not within. The growing separation between Spain and the American colonies had progressively weakened the empire of Charles V and Philip II, and the final blow was the Spanish-American War, which ended a century of Spanish territorial loss. The whole of the nineteenth century is for Spain a dismal spiral of dwindling empire, resources, and national prestige in America and in Europe. The ignominy of suffering defeat at the hands of the new American nation, little more than a century old, which forced the realization that Spain was no longer an empire and very far from being a world power, made inescapable a radical revaluation of all facets of the historical entity that was Spain.

It is difficult to assess the impact of the war of 1898 on the consciousness of Spain. Journalists, poets, statesmen, novelists, and historians had for some time been vaguely and uncomfortably aware of a national indigence of the spirit, of a lack of dynamism and verve in public and artistic life. Most of them had shrugged this off and addressed themselves to immediate problems or had consoled themselves with the contemplation of the past glories of Spain. Those few who spoke out sharply and realistically were generally looked upon as alarmists and demagogues. On Spain's side, the war was fought lethargically and without real national commitment. Spain's defeat and the loss of the Antilles and the Philippines, along with lesser territories, was the shock that made the body politic become immediately and ruefully aware of the irrevocable nature of the losses the country had suffered since the Golden Age of power and dominion, of the utter decadence into which the country had allowed itself to drift. The literary result of this awareness is expressed by the Generation of 1898.

The "Generation of 1898" is a phrase coined by José Martínez Ruiz, "Azorín," (1873–1967), a critic of great insight and sensitivity in his treatment both of the Spanish classics and of contemporary authors (*Al margen de los clásicos, Clásicos y modernos, Lecturas españolas*). Azorín wrote in many forms—almost-novels (such as *Antonio Azorín*, from which he took his pen name, and *La voluntad*) that are, as he says, like life, essentially plotless "happenings"; memoirs of his youth and his travels (*Confesiones de un pequeño filósofo, El paisaje de España visto por los españoles*) and a sort of vanguard surrealist theater. His style is richly ornamented; he employs a rather recherché vocabulary to express ideas which are complex and as often hinted at as stated. He has a subtlety of mind which can be absorbing, once the reader is attuned to his rather slow and detailed exposition. His literary work after World War I is of less interest and only fleetingly captures the insights and lyricism of his work at the beginning of the century. The pseudonym Azorín, meaning a goshawk or a kind of falcon, fits his literary personality well: the bird that soars high over the surface and swoops down to pick out minutiae; the tiny, barely visible detail is his prey. He is enormously concerned with the details of his past, of his personal and cultural experience. He is taken up, as a writer, with an almost neurotic compulsion to recapture and re-examine past time. People, places, events, physical surroundings of his own and the national past, hold an extreme fascination for him. In this compulsion he is an embodiment of his own creation, the Generation of '98.

This designation is used very loosely to group together a handful of writers of very diverse abilities and interests whose major point of contact is their reaction to the tragic awareness of Spain's loss of national prestige following the Spanish-American War. The term is little more than a handy misnomer. Critics have disagreed as to which writers should be included in the group, and the writers themselves had no feeling of a shared literary program or of confluent ideas. Some of those generally included in the group were novelists, some dramatists, some essayists and critics, some poets, with a considerable crossing of literary lines. What unites the group, as it is generally conceived, is a deep awareness of the bad times on which Spain had fallen since its Golden Age of the sixteenth and seventeenth centuries and their awareness of a need for renovation in the political and esthetic life of the country.

Most of these writers began their literary careers around the turn of the century. One of the most interesting figures of the period, sometimes included in the group and sometimes seen as its brilliant precursor, was Angel Ganivet (1865–98), who committed suicide in the year that became the identifying symbol of the group with which he shared so many insights. The work which most closely identifies him with the Generation of '98 is the *Idearium español*. Ganivet manifests most of the preoccupations which will become the central concern and uniting theme of the Generation of '98: an attempt to understand Spain as an historical entity; a search for *lo español*, the essential Spanishness of Spain; a re-examination of the national past—political, geographical, literary, and artistic; a comprehensive assessment of the national character; and a comparison of Spain with other European powers—all of this in an effort to understand the *abulia* or paralysis of will, which made Spain incapable of dynamic action. Ganivet's suicide cannot be directly related to Spain's losses in the war of 1898, but certainly his preoccupation with the decline of Spain in every important aspect of national and cultural life may have contributed to the depression which finally led him to take his life at the age of thirty-three.

The very great interest which has been displayed in the Generation of '98 both in Spain and abroad has led to endless critical attempts to classify the group either numerically or in terms of their literary, social, or philosophic identity. None of these has achieved wide acceptance because of the very diverse talents and interests involved. The handiest system is an acronym coined by the journalist Corpus Barga from the initials of the most widely recognized members: VABUMB. Like the sound of a bomb going off, this word symbolizes the explosive and disruptive tendencies in both art and politics of those writers most closely associated with the group. They are Valle-Inclán, Azorín, Baroja, Unamuno, Maeztu, and Benavente.

Ramón del Valle-Inclán (1866–1936), the first member of the VABUMB series, is among the least closely related to whatever identity can be found in the Generation of '98. This exotic figure, muffled in a cape, disguised by heavy glasses and a straggly beard, unwilling ever to tell a prosaic truth about himself when he could think of a more interesting lie, was perhaps the finest and most perplexing prose stylist of his period. He is considered by some critics a post-romantic, and his settings are often Gothic, heavy-colored and heavy-shadowed, given to overtones of violence and mystery, fantasy and folklore, realism and surrealism. Valle-Inclán was a *gallego* and shared the *gallego's* repugnance for the Castilian language and environment, although he wrote in the one and lived in the other. And like the typical *gallego*, he went to the New World, if not to seek his fortune, at least to look around. Absent for a period from the literary cafés in Madrid, he informed his friends on his return that he had been to Mexico, "the only country in the world that is spelled with an 'x.'" Had he gone instead to Luxembourg the literary result might have been quite different, for the colors, warmth, and tropical exoticism of Mexico play an important part in his work.

Valle-Inclán is known to American readers through translations of his four *Sonatas,* named for the four seasons. They concern the amorous and political escapades of Valle-Inclán's Don Juanesque hero, the Marqués de Bradomín. *Sonata de estío (Sonata of Summer)* takes the marqués to the lush tropics of Mexico and the equally lush passions of *la niña* Chole. *Sonata de otoño (Sonata of Autumn)* has strongly Gothic overtones in the love-death theme of the marqués' passion for both the moribund Concha and her cousin Isabel. Valle-Inclán's unique literary embodiment, his alter ego, the Marqués de Bradomín, is a hero of the Galician past, the late blooming of a feudal nobility long since fallen into decadence. These novels bring to mind and undoubtedly show an awareness of the Countess Pardo Bazán's re-creation of the moldering and spiritually deformed nobility of the same intransigent region in *Los pazos de Ulloa* and *La madre naturaleza.*

In his theater and in some works of prose, Valle-Inclán created a unique and personal art form which he called the *esperpento.* He likens these works to the effect which is produced when the world is seen distorted in a funhouse mirror with both ludicrous and terrifying effect. This is what he saw as the function of the creative writer: to magnify and distort, to tell truths through grotesque and horrendous exaggerations of truth, to compound a lie and a distortion until it comes nearer to the truth than any pedestrian account of the facts could. His concept of literature is essentially poetic, that deformation of reality which is the artist's own creative view of the facts of objective existence. Valle-Inclán excels particularly in descriptive language, in the creation of mood and scenery that is rich in colors and overtones, nuances and shades. His characters are violent, willful, dramatic, intense. His settings, whether the *pueblos* of Mexico or the *pazos* of Galicia, are dank and murky, given to the pathetic fallacy, yet enormously evocative. He is extraordinary at describing landscapes, sumptuous interiors, complex states of mind and soul, and rapid, frequently violent, action.

Valle-Inclán was very much the anarchic individualist. He did not consider himself a part of any literary group or movement. Yet there are strong links of interest, outlook, and personality which relate him to the Generation of '98. His preoccupation with language, his evocation of the past of Spain, his creation of anachronistic heroes and settings that conjure up the decadent feudalism of Galicia, the bravura of his treatment of scenes and characters, and above all, his commitment to examine Spanish life and character in however bizarre a setting and however regionalistic a context demand his inclusion in the group.

Azorín has been mentioned above as the critic who defined and gave a name to the Generation of '98, and as the formulator of the basic ideas which give a unity to such disparate figures. It is important to see Azorín as an integral member of the group, not only because he gave it its name, but because he contributed to the total view which the generation holds. Azorín—with his falcon's eye —sought to capture the Spanish reality by capturing his own past and by defining that which is Spanish in the literary product of his generation, a generation seeking its own meaning in a historical and national context.

Pío Baroja y Nessi (1872–1956) was an enormously prolific and inventive writer from the Basque country. Best known for his novels of action, of adventures, of heroes who reject with sincerity and a certain scorn the stable and viable aspects of workaday life, Baroja was not an intellectual but a novelist of realistic or naturalistic bent whose point of view seems generally anti-intellectual. On occasion, he theorizes about the novel's form and style—quoting from Protagoras, Seneca, Dickens, Tolstoy, and Verlaine—but he comes back always to the central fact of his own creative activity: observations of life. His plots are rambling, structureless, often illogical, an unconnected series of anecdotes and scenes. For Baroja, the novel, like life itself, is haphazard and generally unpredictable. He is by no means a stylist of language like Valle-Inclán or Azorín. His prose tends to be abrupt and direct; his sentences seldom run beyond a dozen words and his paragraphs rarely exceed a half-dozen sentences. He does not describe, he does not prepare his scenes, and yet he is able to capture atmospheres and backgrounds, times and places, quickly and with exactitude through the reactions of his characters. His characters come forth and speak, sharply, directly. They rarely oblige us with discourse; they act, however wisely or foolishly, from whatever motives or convictions they may have. Baroja was nonetheless a man of background, of culture, of ideas. He gives the reader a feeling that he is anti-everything; that life is generally a hoax, that there is nothing to look for, fight for, hope for, pray for, except life itself. He would be a pessimist if he were more involved, a nihilist if he were less so.

Like Galdós, Baroja was a voluminous writer. A novel typical of his style is *El árbol de la ciencia* (*The Tree of Knowledge*), a strongly autobiographical work which traces the career of Andrés Hurtado from the beginning of his medical studies through his disillusionment as a physician in a small, backward village, to his utter rejection of life and his death by suicide. In this novel, Baroja displays contrasting aspects of his personality, giving in the history of Andrés his own experience of the altruistic impulse, and the philosophic basis of his rejection of altruism in the person of uncle Iturrioz, who keeps to his penthouse apartment, waters his potted plants, and spouts his Nietzschean rejection of human nature. All of nature is struggle, dog-eat-dog, survival of the fittest. Human civilization is the slow and still imperfect process that removes man from the realm of animal struggle. Individual effort to help the masses is necessarily futile and unappreciated. The best answer is to retire to an English club, eat sterilized food, drink bottled water, breathe only filtered air. Andrés rejects this cynicism and dedicates himself to life: to healing, to helping, to marriage, and to fatherhood. He fails completely. His wife and child die, a mockery of his knowledge and medical skill. Andrés commits suicide at the stunning realization of the impotence of the intellect and of the total futility of his attempt to project himself into a human future. Iturrioz is left to pronounce a cynical epilogue, unhappily aware that he has been all too right in his rejection of sentiment and altruism.

In other novels, Baroja is generally less philosophical and analytical of his own gropings. *Zalacaín el aventurero* concerns a man who rarely thinks at all—life is action and its consequences. Success, survival, failure, death—what can it matter? It is all experience, and that is life. Baroja wrote regional novels: *Las inquietudes de Shanti Andía* (*The Restlessness of Shanti Andía*) and novels of the low life of Madrid (a series of three novels given the collective title *La lucha por la vida, The Fight for Life,* which some critics have called picaresque works). There is always present in his work the conflict between action and reflection, the dilemma of the idealist, the gulf between theory and practice, which makes both extremes ineffectual and meaningless. The best one can do, Baroja seems to say, is to abstain from commitments.

Life goes on, there is no help for it, but not much point to it, either.

Miguel de Unamuno (1864–1936) is undoubtedly the figure of the Generation of '98 best known outside of Spain. The relationship which many critics have found in the writings of Unamuno to the European currents of existentialism has caused his name to gain wide currency even while his writings were relatively unknown. At present a considerable body of his most important work has been translated into English, German, and French. Unamuno, a Basque from Bilbao, demonstrated an outstanding intellect in his early schooling and took his doctorate in classical philology at the age of twenty at the University of Madrid. For a period of time following this he devoted himself to reading and private study and around the turn of the century began to publish essays and articles in literary journals and periodicals. Once sure of his vocation, he competed for a post as professor of Greek and Latin at the University of Salamanca in the murderous system of "oppositions" by which Spanish university posts are awarded. Unamuno became professor of Greek, Latin, and Romance philology at the ancient university and was eventually made rector, a position comparable to dean of the faculty or chancellor, as American hierarchies go.

His career was generally uneventful. He fathered a fairly large family and dedicated himself to teaching and writing. He encountered political difficulties under the brutal and politically hopeless dictatorship of General Primo de Rivera and was relieved of his university post and exiled to the Canary Islands. After a short time he was able to leave the limbo of Fuerteventura and go to Paris. There he found an intellectually stimulating atmosphere, colleagues, and supporters, but his heart and soul were always with "my tragic Spain." Accordingly, he got as near to the Spanish border as he could, settling temporarily in the Basque town of Hendaya. When the dictatorship of Primo de Rivera fell in 1930, Unamuno returned to Spain. He resumed his administrative and teaching duties in Salamanca to the great joy of liberal students, scholars, and politicians. He continued his placid and scholarly life in Salamanca until called upon to represent the republic as a deputy in Madrid. There his typically paradoxical view of life forced him into the role of loyal opposition on almost every issue. Unamuno had all the questions and no answers, could voice all the objections to a given line of action, but could offer no solutions. This was unfortunately true for the majority of the ruling body and was to a large extent responsible for the governmental chaos of the early thirties, which formed a political vacuum into which Francisco Franco stepped with the aid of the uncommitted military and the positive support of the extreme right. For a short time Unamuno supported the Franco movement, but soon came to realize that a military dictatorship was very far from the solution that he sought for Spain's many problems. In a speech which he delivered as rector of the university on October 12, 1936—less than three months after the beginning of the war—he spoke out sharply and unmistakably against the repressive anti-intellectualism of the military clique. Unamuno was immediately relieved of his post as rector and subjected to a confinement that amounted to house arrest. He died during the night of New Year's Eve, 1936, at the age of seventy-two.

Unamuno was one of the most widely read Spaniards of his generation in European and American literature. He was among the first Spanish intellectuals to read Kierkegaard, and found in the nineteenth-century Danish theologian a striking affirmation of his own views on fundamental questions of life, death, and man's place in the universe. An example of this coincidental agreement is found in the prologue to one of Unamuno's most searching short novels, *San Manuel Bueno, mártir*. Some months after he had written the novel, he tells us, he was reading Kierkegaard's *Either/Or* and came across the following passage:

> It would be the greatest possible joke on the world if one who had expounded the most profound of truths were not a dreamer, but a doubter. And it is not unthinkable that no one should be able to expound ultimate truth so perfectly as a doubter . . . He would be expounding a doctrine which might resolve everything, in which mankind could have confidence; but that doctrine would not be capable of resolving anything at all for its own author.

This is precisely the theme of Unamuno's novel: the martyrdom of the priest who is unable to believe in God, the afterlife, and the immortality of the human soul. This is, indeed, the central theme of all of Unamuno's most serious work.

The full statement of his thought is found in the monumental philosophic work *The Tragic Sense of Life in Men and Nations*. The basic philosophic problem that man faces, and before which all other problems pale into trivialities, is that of survival after death. If there is no afterlife, then man exists in a moral vacuum in which there can be no value and no real purpose, in which there is no more meaning to his highest ideals and aspirations than there is in the busywork of the ant, mindlessly constructing anthills which may be obliterated by the unthinking or malicious blow of a boot heel. The man of flesh and bone, he says, cannot accept rationally or emotionally the icy chill of oblivion after death; he must live as if there were purpose and continuity in a never-ending projection of self through this life and beyond the grave.

> One *must* believe in the other life, in the eternal life beyond the grave, and in an individual and personal

life . . . One *must* believe in that other life to be able to live this one, to bear it and give it meaning and finality.

His concept of the "other life" is not, however, the traditional Christian platitude of endless peace and eternal bliss.

But the soul, my soul at least, longs for something else, not absorption, not quietude, not peace, not extinction, but rather eternal approaching without ever arriving, endless yearning, eternal hope which eternally renews itself without ever resolving itself completely. . . . Or, in summation, if nothing remains there of the intimate tragedy of the soul, what kind of life is that?

Unamuno always saw the human problem in terms of the Spanish problem; being human and being a Spaniard were so closely linked in his mind that the two went together, and the failure of Spain to respond dynamically and creatively to the shocking blow of defeat in the Spanish-American War troubled him deeply. In a series of essays written in the first decade of the century he seeks to examine the Spanish mind and reality—his personal quest for a definition of *lo español*—in terms of language, literature, history, and the present social reality. He finds in the duality of Cervantes' great creations, Don Quijote and Sancho Panza, the embodiment of the duality of the Spanish spirit. Pride and idealism, a "quixotic" persistence in ideals against impossible odds, goes hand in hand with an earthy and stubborn common sense. One of his most provocative essays, "*¡Muera Don Quijote!*" ("Death to Don Quijote!"), establishes the gentleman of La Mancha as the symbol of past Spanish empire and the spirit of the *conquistadores*, while Sancho is the embodiment of the rugged, simple, eternal sanity of the *pueblo*, the enduring substratum of Spain. Unamuno's ideas and convictions were established in these early essays: they did not change substantially in the course of his life. In his last writings he still displays his concern with what he called the real human problem, personal immortality; his faith in the "subconscious" of Spain, the *pueblo;* and his deep suspicion of -isms and movements which would turn the individual into a mere component of the mass.

> It is a horrible thing, this sort of moral suicide of individuals on the altar of collectivity. To sacrifice each and every Spaniard to Spain—is that not pure pagan idolatry? There is no idea, however great it may be, which is worth the internal peace of the village, the true peace, the fullness of the life of the people. The individual destiny of man, since it matters to each and every human being, is the most human thing that exists.

Unamuno's total literary production is sizable. It includes a number of essays, many of them originally published in newspapers, on a wide variety of literary, linguistic, and social topics. His major novels, all quite short, are: *Niebla* (*Mist*), a Pirandello-like work in which the main character emerges from the story to confront the author and protest the things he is being made to do; *Abel Sánchez,* a chilling study of the passion of envy, based on the biblical account of Cain and Abel and also on Byron's poem *Cain;* and *Amor y pedagogía* (*Love and Pedagogy*), a study of man's attempt to seize the future through his children, to find his immortality through his progeny. *Three Exemplary Novels* reflect the spirit of Cervantes, particularly in the title, which Unamuno takes from the *Novelas ejemplares. El espejo de la muerte* (*The Mirror of Death*) is a collection of short stories whose central theme is, again, man's relationship to the central fact of his existence, his own finitude. Two collections of travel impressions, *Andanzas y visiones españolas* and *Por tierras de Portugal y España,* present

Unamuno's unique subjective relationship to the two countries so central in all his thought.

It might be said of his work that Unamuno lacks the painter's eye. He is essentially unresponsive to shapes, forms, and colors, and his language becomes curiously flat and conventional when he attempts to describe the external qualities of a scene or object. When he describes a city or a landscape, we are given, not the visual or surface impression, but rather the effect which the experience has on the "intimate reality" of the author himself, the literary or historical associations which it holds for him. His concern is always for immediacy and penetration into the most intimate aspects of his characters and settings. He explains what is for him the creative process in the prologue to his *Three Exemplary Novels:*

> Reader, if you wish to create living figures through art, tragic agonists or comics or novelesque figures, don't accumulate details, don't set yourself to observing external aspects of those who share your life. Rather, converse with them, stimulate them if you can; above all, love them and wait until one day—perhaps never—when they expose the soul of their soul, the person they wish to be, in a cry, in an act, in a phrase. And then hold onto that moment, bury it within yourself, and allow it to grow and develop like a seed, into the true person, the person who is truly real.

Unamuno wrote for the theater without great artistic success, probably owing to the essentially introspective nature of his mind and personality. His talent is analytical: he tells us about the mind and soul of his characters, and shows us what is going on below the level of overt action. When it becomes a matter of showing us these people in movement, we see only the humdrum routine or pastimes that have no dramatic intensity to them: playing a game of chess in a café, taking a walk through the streets or in the woods, working at some normal occupation or profession. This is not the material of the theater, it does not project. As a result, his dramas tend to be stilted and pedestrian. Two works have been produced with some success, *El otro* (*The Other One*), a dramatic treatment of his novel *Abel Sánchez,* and *El hermano Juan,* a reworking of the Don Juan theme.

A large quantity of poetry of very uneven quality completes the literary production of Unamuno. The same shortcomings and virtues that are found in the whole of his work may be seen in his poetry: it is largely unmusical and universal, deriving its value from emotional and intellectual content. For Unamuno, poetry was enormously important. He felt that in poetry a writer had the greatest likelihood of attaining the immortality of fame, and it must be remembered that the search for immortality was always the motive force in his life and the continuing theme of his very diverse writings. His finest poetic achievement is *El Cristo de Velázquez,* a tribute to the painting of that title and a reflection on the meaning of the Christ figure in his own fervent but highly individualistic faith.

¿En qué piensas Tú, muerto, Cristo mío?
¿Por qué ese velo de cerrada noche
de tu abundosa cabellera negra
de nazareno cae sobre tu frente?
Miras dentro de Ti, donde está el reino
de Dios; dentro de Ti, donde alborea
el sol eterno de las almas vivas.
Blanco tu cuerpo está como el espejo
del padre de la luz, del sol vivífico;
blanco tu cuerpo al modo de la luna
que muerta ronda en torno de su madre
nuestra cansada vagabunda tierra;
blanco tu cuerpo está como la hostia
del cielo de la noche soberana,

de ese cielo tan negro como el velo
de tu abundosa cabellera negra
de nazareno.

Of what art thou thinking, thou, dead, my Christ?
Why does that veil of hushed night
of thy abundant black hair
of Nazarene fall over thy forehead?
Thou art looking within thyself, where is the kingdom
of God; within thyself, where dawns
the eternal sun of living souls.
White thy body is as the mirror
of the father of light, of the livening sun;
white thy body in the manner of the moon
which, dead, revolves about its mother
our tired, vagabond earth;
white thy body is as the Host
of the sky of the sovereign night,
of that sky as dark as the veil
of thy abundant black hair
of Nazarene.

These lines are typical of Unamuno's complex, often tortuous syntactical line, and of the intellectualism of his imagery. These qualities pervade his novels, plays, and essays as well. One of the major critical difficulties in dealing with any aspect of his work is the frequent mixing of genres. Unamuno had little patience with formal criteria; when critics objected to the lack of traditional form in his novels, he simply invented a new term, *nivola*, to describe his prose fiction, and continued to write as his creative sense led him. He had equally little patience with what to him were the trivialities of poetry—rhyme and meter. In this regard, we may say that as he lacks the painter's eye for visual metaphor he lacks the musician's ear for rhythms and verbal melody. In spite of these shortcomings his work is always suffused with his very personal and individual insights and preoccupations, with the beauty of a personality that could be gay, jocular, austere, and passionate at the same time.

Of minor literary importance in the Generation of '98 is Ramiro de Maeztu (1874–1936). He was not a man of creative literary talent, nor did he attempt the sort of creation that we find in Baroja or Valle-Inclán. He is rather a journalist whose interest was primarily political. His early career was largely polemic and iconoclastic in character. His newspaper articles attacked all things Spanish as being backward and hopelessly out of touch with European culture. He joined with Azorín and Baroja in an informal alliance of minds which came to be known as *"los tres"* (The Three). What they shared was a rebellious, liberal, "Europeanizing" point of view and a conviction that broad reforms in all areas of Spanish life were necessary. The influence of Nietzsche is apparent in the fundamentally pessimistic and nihilistic attitudes which underlie his writings at this time.

In 1905 Maeztu went to London as a news correspondent and resided there for a number of years, later traveling on the continent and finally returning to Spain. When World War I broke out he returned to England as a correspondent. His experience of England, France, and Italy during the war produced a radical change in his ideology. He became an ultraconservative, ultrareligious Rightist. He declared his support of the dictatorship of Primo de Rivera, broke off with his erstwhile liberal friends, attacked the ideas and writings of Unamuno, and declared his own earlier works fit only to be burned.

He organized a politically oriented group called *Acción española* (Spanish Action) and edited a periodical of the same name. Through this political activity he exercised an important influence on Spanish youth of his time. The most important work of his liberal period is *Hacia otra España* (*Toward a New Spain*) in which he compares his country unfavorably with England and Germany and argues for completely restructuring, industrializing and Europeanizing Spain. In his reactionary second period he reverses his stand completely. *La crisis de humanismo* (first published in English under the title *Authority, Liberty and Function*) holds that the humanistic ideal has failed in Western society and that man can find fulfillment and redemption only in traditional Catholicism, first recognizing his own radical corruption. He links the function of the state with the purpose of the Church: the sole aim of human life is Christian salvation, and the organization of the state must be conducive to this end.

His last important work is *Defensa de la Hispanidad* (*A Defense of the Hispanic World*). This book centers upon the historical civilizing and missionary role of Spain in the New World, and proclaims the need for the establishment of a second Spanish empire which would embody the ideals of the Spanish state of the Golden Age. The contemporary model for such a complex is clearly the relationship of Britain to the commonwealth. Despite his break with Azorín, Baroja, and other figures of the Generation of '98, Maeztu belongs in the same historical and literary setting. His conclusions and mode of action are not those shared by the rest, but his appeal to the national past for an understanding of current problems, his tendency to represent *lo español* through such key literary figures as Don Quijote and Don Juan Tenorio, and his firm conviction, in both periods, that Spain and Spaniards must act decisively in a period of national crisis, place him at least tangentially within the ranks of the group of '98.

The last of the group in the VABUMB sequence is Jacinto Benavente (1866–1954). Benavente was primarily a playwright, although his contribution to criticism and journalism was of some importance. The corpus of his dramatic production is very large; from 1894, the year in which his first important play was produced, to his death sixty years later, he wrote on the average of three or four plays a year. Much of this enormous production is trivial and repetitive. Not more than a dozen of his plays have real merit or originality, but those display grace, skill, urbanity, a superb command of language, and a fine sense of theater, opening the way to a new type of drama. Much as Moratín made new areas of experience and a new type of dramatic language available to the playwrights of the coming century at the close of the neoclassic period, Benavente gives life and fluidity, imagination and a new area of rhetorical possibility to a theater that had become lachrymose and stagy, plot-bound and sham in its language, its emotions, and its view of life. With Benavente, the theater becomes a subtle, artistic creation in which heroic movement, bohemian orations, deathbed declarations, contrived situations, and the cliché thesis so abundant in the nineteenth century are rejected for psychological penetration and a satire so subtle that it is at times completely lost in Benavente's tendency to preach and moralize. While the nineteenth century put too much action on the stage with too much of the broad gesture and dramatic revelation, Benavente's theater goes to the extreme of dramatizing too little. His plays have been called with reason drawing-room comedies. Hardly anything happens in the best or the worst of his theater. Snobs sit around and talk about each other, revealing the intrigues and foibles of others, and in the process they reveal their own souls.

But this is not all of Benavente. His theater is cast in a mold that could easily be trivial, but he does not always succumb to his own weakness. Three saving graces elevate his best moments to a very respectable place in European literature of the period: his command of language and the ingenuity with which he turns a phrase; his enormous sense of theater and what will play well before an audience; the multiple psychological dimensions which he is able to bring to his characters. Many of his plays are social drama of the sort that Echegaray had established as the dominant dramatic form in Spain in the previous generation, but they are free of the melodramatic duality which is always present in Echegaray. Benavente's people are usually—not always—civilized and sensitive, aware of the conflicts within themselves, and aware of the extent to which their passions conflict with the social norms. This conflict is generally kept inside, and therein lies the subtlety of the situations. An example of this is Benavente's first produced play, *El nido ajeno* (*The Other Bird's Nest*). The wealthy, adventurous, attractive Manuel returns after many years of absence to spend some time with his older brother José Luis and his sister-in-law María. Manuel and María are much attracted to each other in a perfectly Platonic way and spend considerable time together. The husband's suspicions are aroused less by the actual circumstances than by old rumors that Manuel is in fact a child of adultery— the adultery of their mother with a close friend of José Luis' father. This has long disturbed María's husband, and it now takes on immediacy with the return of Manuel and the obviously warm friendship which springs up between Manuel and María. José Luis faces up to the issue and asks his brother to leave. Manuel knows of the suspicions concerning his parentage, but has convincing evidence that they are no more than idle gossip. He realizes, nonetheless, the extent to which he is disturbing "the other bird's nest" and prepares to leave. On his farewell he gives María a brotherly kiss on the forehead and is overwhelmed with the realization that he is indeed in love with her.

There is a strong similarity in this play to *El gran Galeoto* and perhaps to *Un drama nuevo*. The basic difference between *El nido ajeno* and the post-romantic drama is the containment of action and restriction of dramatic gesture. In effect, nothing happens. Manuel, in a thunderstruck instant of insight realizes that love, virtue, and honor are not such simple issues as he had thought; he is more the son of the man who loved his mother Platonically than he is of his biological father. He learns that there can be an adultery of the spirit far more significant than adultery of the flesh. He leaves with this new knowledge and insight, not in defiance of the world and society by carrying off María, but with a heightened awareness of the complexities of the human spirit.

In the restraint, control, and subtlety of his drama, Benavente comes closer to European ideas of theater than any other Spaniard of his time. But not all of his theater is so urbane. In *La malquerida* Benavente explores themes which would not be out of place for Valle-Inclán or the Countess Pardo Bazán. Esteban marries Raimunda, a woman who has a grown daughter by an earlier marriage. Esteban falls hopelessly and brutally in love with the daughter Acacia and conspires to have her fiancé murdered. The ultimate moment of tragedy comes when Raimunda opposes herself physically to the consummation of this shared lust and is murdered by Esteban. She knows that her sacrifice will cast a pall of horror on the two which will make their liaison forever impossible; her dying words are "Blessed be my blood, that saves like the blood of our Lord!" *La malquerida* is one of the strongest works in contemporary Spanish theater, but it is not characteristic of Benavente's total production.

Best known of his plays is *Los intereses creados,* a tour de force which employs the Punchinello figures of the Italian commedia dell'arte. Leonardo, an impoverished gallant, finds himself in financial straits. The only solution is to marry well. His servant, Crispín, undertakes to bring this about by serving as intermediary for the hand of the lovely Silvia, daughter of the rich and foolish Polichinela. He slyly creates the image of a rich and high-born Leonardo and, by manipulating the forces of greed and vanity, soon has the whole town involved in a conspiracy to bring about the wedding. A bit of discreet blackmail brings the old pirate Polichinela around, and all is arranged in a triumph of young love, achieved through the creation of very materialistic and self-serving "interests."

Benavente was the son of a renowned pediatrician, and something of his father's concern for children manifested itself in his work. Two of his children's plays are performed frequently in Spain and have become uncontested favorites with Spanish theatergoers from three to twelve years of age: *La cenicienta* (*Cinderella*) and *El príncipe que todo lo aprendió en los libros* (*The Prince Who Learned Everything from Books*). These are charming, light, fanciful, eminently playable pieces which have delighted generations of children and have merited the serious consideration of some adult critics.

Jacinto Benavente won the Nobel prize in 1922, the second Spaniard to have done so. Criticism has been generally apologetic for his work, finding much of it trivial and repetitive. His later plays did not nearly approach the positive qualities of the period before 1920; this, too, makes it questionable to award for his late work the accolades due Benavente for his best theater.

Writers on the Generation of '98 have sought to include Benavente in the group and several have managed to find a niche for him there. It is difficult to see that he really belongs in the ideological or creative company of Azorín, Unamuno, Baroja, and the rest. One does not feel, on reading Benavente, the anxiety, unrest, pessimism, self-examination, quest for values, and search for *lo español* that are seen in the most typical works of the group. The total impression that one gets from Benavente is the encounter with something very polished, very European;

the dramatization of the facile and obvious. This feeling for life and art is very far from the palpitating center of the Generation of '98.

Brief mention should be made of a number of playwrights who were active around the turn of the century and whose work, while not of great literary importance, had considerable success. Carlos Arniches (1866–1943) wrote a number of sharp, bright *sainetes* which captured, with broad satirical flourishes, the life of Madrid. His longer comedies are revived from time to time and invariably prove popular. Serafín Alvarez Quintero (1871–1938) and Joaquín Alvarez Quintero (1873–1944) were two brothers who collaborated to produce an extensive collection of short plays on Andalusian themes. They established in theatrical literature the archetypical Sevillian; shrewd, boisterous, sharp-tongued, and excitable. Their work falls, as does that of Arniches, within the *costumbrista*, or regionalistic, literature that constitutes one of the trends of the period. Their plays have the warmth and color, vivacity and charm traditionally associated with Andalusia.

More serious in nature but certainly not more effective as theater is the historical drama of Eduardo Marquina (1879–1946). *Las hijas del Cid* (*The Daughters of the Cid*) and *En Flandes se ha puesto el sol* (*The Sun Has Set in Flanders*) re-create moments of Spanish history in a superficial and hackneyed fashion. Marquina also wrote musical comedy and other light works which had popular appeal but which added little to the stature of the theater of the period. Gregorio Martínez Sierra (1881–1947) achieved enormous success with *Canción de Cuna* (*Cradle Song*). This is the saccharine and melodramatic treatment of the life of a girl who is abandoned as a child at the door of a nunnery. She is brought up in the cloistered atmosphere under the care of the nuns, all of whom have hearts of purest gold. The feminine psychology is sufficiently true and varied to lead most critics to assume the collaboration of the author's wife in the work.

Quite the opposite is the case of Jacinto Grau (1877–1958), whose theater has very real merit but has never achieved popularity. Grau lived outside of Spain for most of his life, in Central Europe and South America. He was a writer of depth and skill, devoted to large, philosophical themes presented in a polished and rhetorical, eminently "untheatrical," manner. His literary production was small; other than an early novel and a collection of essays his work is all dramatic, made up of two plays on the Don Juan theme, one on the parable of the Prodigal Son, and five more on various themes. He wrote quite consciously for a minority and, unlike Lope de Vega, was not concerned with the applause of the "vulgar herd." He has never received it, although his plays had some small success before intellectually inclined audiences in France and Germany.

Modernism

Closely connected with the revolutionary and renovating qualities of the Generation of '98 as a movement is another literary manifestation—modernism. Some Spanish writers of the period, particularly Antonio Machado and Valle-Inclán, play a part in both. The two movements are in no way antithetical; both are in reaction against the ideas and aesthetics of the nineteenth century, and both represent the attempt to revaluate human experience in the light of events which had shattered and made untenable the frames of reference which prevailed into the 1880's and '90's. The major difference between the two lies in the purpose and orientation of each. The Generation of '98 is essentially social and philosophical in its interests, while modernism is primarily concerned with style and the aesthetics of expression. It is not surprising that the Generation of '98 should find its best expression in prose, particularly the essay and the novel, while modernism is primarily developed in poetry. Further, and very basic to an understanding of the two movements, the Generation of '98 is exclusively Spanish, while modernism is a multinational esthetic renovation.

The modernist movement parted completely from the chatty and prosaic verse of Campoamor and from the wild and sentimental excesses of romanticism. It sought a new subtlety and elaboration of poetic language and a widening of the possibilities of rhythm and meter which would bring a new musicality to Spanish verse. The sources or influences on modernism are many, but they may be reduced to three major categories: French Parnassianism and symbolism, particularly through the work of Leconte de Lisle, Verlaine, and Baudelaire; Spanish poets of the pre-Renaissance, Renaissance, and baroque periods (Berceo, Juan Ruiz, Santillana, Garcilaso, Góngora); and in the New World, themes of Spanish-American and precolonial tradition. The poetry is highly individual and subjective; it is experimental in the sense that these writers sought always for innovation in form and content. Modernism was never a "way to write poetry" but rather a constant search for new forms of beauty and expressiveness, for new tonalities of language, for new rhythmic effects, often for a vivid pictorial representation of visual effects.

Modernism originates not in Spain but in Latin America, where French movements in literature had penetrated more readily and more effectively. The renovation which modernism represents had been in the air for some time in Latin America. The premodernists Gutiérrez Nájera, José Martí, and José Asunción Silva, in their poetry, that are typical of the movement. The name that must be given as the founder of the movement, however, is that of Rubén Darío.

Rubén Darío (1867–1916) was born Félix Rubén García Sarmiento in Metapa, Nicaragua. A prodigy of poetry, he began to publish at the age of twelve. This precocity earned him the nickname "the boy poet." He came into contact with French poetry in the 1880's and was profoundly moved by the new accents he discovered in his French contemporaries. In 1888 his book *Azul* (*Blue*) was published, containing poetry and some vignettes in prose. The book reached Spain and was reviewed by the novelist-critic Juan Valera, who recognized the striking originality of the poetry and prose. The book was an immediate sensation: its innovations made it impossible for poets to continue writing as they had in the past. These new directions were even more clearly outlined in *Prosas profanas* of 1896. The book is, despite the name, a collection of poems. Again the response to the new accents, themes, and rhythms was immediate and intense throughout the Hispanic world. While some critics found the new poetry shallow and ornamental, too exquisite and elegant for real substance, all recognized an enormous literary talent in the Nicaraguan poet. Typical of these innovations is his *Sinfonía en gris mayor* (*Symphony in Gray Major*):

*El mar como un vasto cristal azogado
refleja la lámina de un cielo de cinc;
lejanas bandadas de pájaros manchan
el fondo bruñido de pálido gris.*

*El sol como un vidrio redondo y opaco
con paso de enfermo camina al cenit;
el viento marino descansa en la sombra
teniendo de almohada su negro clarín.*

    Las ondas que mueven su vientre de plomo
debajo del muelle parecen gemir.
Sentado en un cable, fumando su pipa,
está un marinero pensando en las playas
de un vago lejano brumoso país.

    Es viejo ese lobo. Tostaron su cara
los rayos de fuego del sol del Brasil;
los recios tifones del mar de la China
le han visto bebiendo su frasco de gin.

    La espuma impregnada de yodo y salitre
ha tiempo conoce su roja nariz,
sus crespos cabellos, sus biceps de atleta,
su gorra de lona, su blusa de dril.

    En medio del humo que forma el tabaco
ve el viejo el lejano brumoso país,
adonde una tarde caliente y dorada
tendidas las velas partió el bergantín . . .

    La siesta del trópico. El lobo se aduerme.
Ya todo lo envuelve la gama del gris.
Parece que un suave y enorme esfumino
del curvo horizonte borrara el confín.

    La siesta del trópico. La vieja cigarra
ensaya su ronca guitarra senil,
y el grillo preludia un solo monótono
en la única cuerda que está en su violín.

The sea like a vast silvered mirror
reflects the lamina of a sky of zinc;
far-off flocks of birds stain
the polished background of pale gray.

The sun like a round and opaque window
with a sick man's pace climbs to the zenith;
the sea wind rests in the shade
having its black trumpet for a pillow.

The waves that move their leaden bellies
under the dock seem to groan.
Seated on a cable, smoking his pipe,
is a sailor thinking of the beaches
of a vague, far-off, misty land.

He is an old man, that sea wolf. His face has been burned
by the fiery rays of the Brazilian sun;
the violent typhoons of the China sea
have seen him drinking his bottle of gin.

The foam that carries iodine and saltpeter
has long known his red nose,
his curly hair, his athlete's biceps
his canvas cap, his drill blouse.

In the middle of the smoke his tobacco makes
the old man sees the far-off, misty land,
for which one hot and golden afternoon
his brigantine sailed with all sails set . . .

The siesta of the tropics. The sea wolf sleeps.
Now the gray scale covers everything.
It seems as if a soft and enormous shading pencil
might have rubbed out the line of the curved horizon.

The siesta of the tropics. The old cicada
tries out his ancient hoarse guitar,
and the cricket begins a monotonous solo
on the single string that he has to his violin.

We see in this poem the powerful and evocative visual imagery, the metaphors of color, texture, sounds, smells, and light, and the appeal to the exotic, the far-off golden lands, which are typical of much of Darío's verse. The musicality of lines and the flow of his verse are evident also, but he does not depend on rhyme or monotonously set rhythms to achieve it. The only unifying principals in this poem are assonance in *i* in the second and fourth lines of each stanza and a verse line made up not of measured syllables but of four metric beats. In some of his poetry Darío comes very close to free verse, and in other examples uses with great artistry the fixed and invariable forms of the thirteenth century, as well as those of later periods. He brings together every device that poetry had traditionally used in a synthesis that is original and commanding. We find not only the pictorial representation of the here-and-now, but also the nymphs and satyrs, lakes and swans, dashing princes and melancholy princesses of earlier poetry. Darío draws upon the exoticism of South and Central America as well as the *fin de siècle* salons of France, on the mythology and traditions of pre-Columbian civilizations as well as the Greek and Latin sources of Western inspiration. His well-known poem *To Roosevelt* adds another voice to the growing criticism of American influence in the Latin lands at the turn of the century. In his *Cantos de vida y esperanza* (*Songs of Life and Hope*) published in 1905, Darío's tone has deepened and clarified itself. He has come to a new awareness of his powers and purpose as a poet, and he is able to criticize clearly his earlier poetry:

> *Yo soy aquel que ayer no más decía*
> *el verso azul y la canción profana,*
> *en cuya noche un ruiseñor había*
> *que era alondra de luz por la mañana.*
>
> *El dueño fuí de mi jardín de sueño,*
> *lleno de rosas y de cisnes vagos;*
> *el dueño de las tórtolas, el dueño*
> *de góndolas y liras en los lagos;*
>
> *y muy siglo diez y ocho, y muy antiguo,*
> *y muy moderno; audaz, cosmopolita,*
> *con Hugo fuerte y con Verlaine ambiguo,*
> *y una sed de ilusiones infinita.*
>
> *Yo supe de dolor desde mi infancia;*
> *mi juventud . . . , ¿fué juventud la mía?*
> *Sus rosas aun me dejan su fragancia,*
> *una fragancia de melancolía . . .*

> I am he who only yesterday recited
> the blue verse and the profane song,
> in whose night a nightingale there was
> which was a lark of light in the morning.
>
> I was the master of my garden of dreams,
> full of roses and of gliding swans;
> the master of turtledoves, the master
> of gondolas and lyres on the lakes;
>
> and very eighteenth century, and very ancient,
> and very modern; daring, cosmopolitan
> strong as Hugo and ambiguous as Verlaine
> and an infinite thirst for illusions.
>
> I knew pain from infancy;
> my youth . . . , was it really youth?
> Its roses still have left me their fragrance,
> a fragrance of melancholy . . .

Darío continued to write poetry until his early death, but nothing new or unique emerged in his work after the publication of *El canto errante* (*Errant Song*), in 1907. His total work constitutes a major synthesis and revaluation of Spanish poetry; a veritable *ars poetica* in which all the major strophic and verse forms are represented in a way which gives them a new life, freedom, and flexibility. As Garcilaso had brought Italian forms to Spanish poetry, making possible the participation of Spanish poetry in the Renaissance, Rubén Darío brought the French Parnassian and symbolist forms to Spanish poetry and made possible the opening of Spanish verse to an entirely new realm of lyrical expression.

Darío visited Spain on several occasions and came into contact with the leading poets and literary men of the time. He was feted and lionized and indulged rather beyond his own capacities to resist. The bohemian excesses which his popularity permitted him had their effect on his health and on his work; there is a temptation to make a comparison with the career of Dylan Thomas, although the poets lived in dissimilar societies half a century apart.

All of subsequent Spanish poetry was affected by the impact of Darío's verse, but the movement itself was comparatively short-lived. The best poets of the period were profoundly influenced for a time, but before the first decade of the twentieth century had run its course, they had begun to move on to other techniques and to new syntheses.

The poet Antonio Machado (1875–1939) belongs to both the Generation of '98 and to the stylistic currents of modernism. His themes are closely related to the search for *lo español* in the landscape of Spain, in the diversity of its cultures, and in the visual, emotional, and historical impact of the land and its people. His poetic style is strongly influenced by Rubén Darío and the modernist feeling for language and imagery, but modernism was too much concerned with verbal adornment, with the exotic and sensual, to become a stylistic commitment for Machado. In his poem *Retrato* (*Self-Portrait*) he refuses to classify himself in terms of literary schools and movements.

RETRATO

¿Soy clásico o romántico? No sé. Dejar quisiera
mi verso, como deja el capitán su espada:
famosa por la mano viril que la blandiera,
no por el docto oficio del forjador preciada.

SELF-PORTRAIT

Am I a classicist or a romantic? I don't know.
                          I would like to leave
my verse as the warrior lays down his sword:
famous for the virile hand that brandished it
not prized alone for the skill of the smith who forged it.

His spirit was somber and austere, inclined toward simplicity and depth rather than surface brilliance. His life was divided between Andalusia and Castile, and his poetry has the spiritual qualities associated with both: color, lyricism, and excitement; austerity, mysticism, and introspection. This duality is clear in his *Canciones de tierras altas* (*Songs of High Lands*):

Soria de montes azules	Soria of the blue mountains
y de yermos de violeta,	and of violet wastelands,
¡cuántas veces te he soñado	how many times I have
en esta florida vega	dreamed of you
por donde se va,	on this flowery plain
entre naranjos de oro,	through which flows,
Guadalquivir a la mar!	among golden orange trees,
	Guadalquivir to the sea!

A series of dedicatory poems which Machado wrote for some of his contemporaries, imitating or parodying their style, themes, and the general tone of their poetry, are interesting as literary curiosities. One of these, which he dedicated to Unamuno on the publication of *The Life of Don Quijote and Sancho* captures particularly well the character of the *"fuerte vasco":*

Este donquijotesco
don Miguel de Unamuno, fuerte vasco,
lleva el arnés grotesco
y el irrisorio casco
del buen manchego. Don Miguel camina,
jinete de quimérica montura,
metiendo espuela de oro a su locura,
sin miedo de la lengua que malsina.

A un pueblo de arrieros,
lechuzos y tahures y logreros
dicta lecciones de caballería.
Y el alma desalmada de su raza,
que bajo el golpe de su férrea maza
aún duerme, puede que despierte un día . . .

> This Don Quijotesque
> Don Miguel de Unamuno, hardy Basque,
> wears the grotesque armor
> and ridiculous helmet
> of the good Manchegan. Don Miguel takes to the road,
> rider on a chimerical mount,
> giving the golden spur to his madness
> without fear of the slandering tongue.
>
> To a nation of mule drivers,
> bill collectors and gamblers and profiteers
> he gives lessons on chivalry.
> And the desouled soul of his nation,
> which under the blow of his iron mace
> still sleeps, may perhaps awake one day . . .

Antonio Machado also wrote in prose and, in collaboration with his brother Manuel, for the theater. His prose works offer a valuable insight into the poet's aesthetic ideology and literary values. *Juan de Mairena* is fictional biography, a patchwork of aphorisms, anecdotes, and literary and philosophical reflections. His theater, a half-dozen verse dramas, had some popular success but is not of great literary importance.

Juan Ramón Jiménez (1881-1958), Spain's third Nobel prize winner, in 1956, also came strongly under the influence of Darío and modernism. He was active in the literary circles of Madrid in spite of chronic poor health and occasional confinement in sanatoriums in France and Spain. As a poet and critic, he followed in his work the direction of constant reduction and purification. His initial interest in modernism led to the production of embellished and sensual work, employing long lines of verse, images of brilliant sound and color, and a vocabulary chosen for its refinement and elevated poetic diction. A typical—and beautiful—example:

> *Un pájaro, en la lírica calma del mediodía,*
> *canta bajo los mármoles del palacio sonoro;*
> *sueña el sol vivos fuegos en la cristalería,*
> *en la fuente abre el agua su cantinela de oro.*
> *Es una fiesta clara con eco cristalino:*
> *en el mármol, el pájaro; las rosas, en la fuente;*
> *¡garganta fresca y dura; azul, dulce, arjentino*
> *temblar, sobre la flor satinada y reciente!*
> *En un ensueño real, voy, colmado de gracia,*
> *soñando, sonriendo, por las radiantes losas,*
> *henchida el alma de la pura aristocracia*
> *de la fuente, del pájaro, de la luz, de las rosas . . .*

> A bird, in the lyrical calm of noonday,
> sings under the marbles of the sounding palace;
> the sun dreams living fires in the crystal,
> in the fountain the water opens its golden ballad.
> It is a bright festival with crystalline echo:
> on the marble, the bird; the roses, in the fountain;
> fresh, strong throat! Blue, sweet, silvery
> trembling, over the silken and recent flower!
> In a fantasy of truth I go, brimming with grace,
> dreaming, smiling, on the radiant tiles,
> my soul swollen with the pure aristocracy
> of the fountain, the bird, the light, the roses . . .

This early fascination with the more obvious possibilities of complex diction and metaphor wore off, and Juan Ramón came to devote himself ever more to the quest of *poesía desnuda,* a poetic art which would be a pure thing in itself, owing nothing to mannerisms, schools, literary manifestoes, vogues, or formulas. A frequently anthologized poem proclaims this quest:

> *Vino, primero, pura,*
> *vestida de inocencia;*
> *y la amé como un niño.*
> *Luego se fué vistiendo*
> *de no sé qué ropajes;*
> *y la fuí odiando, sin saberlo.*

> *Llegó a ser una reina,*
> *fastuosa de tesoros . . .*
> *¡Qué iracundia de yel y sin sentido!*
> *. . . Mas se fué desnudando.*
> *Y yo le sonreía.*
> *Se quedó con la túnica*
> *de su inocencia antigua.*
> *Creí de nuevo en ella.*
> *Y se quitó la túnica,*
> *y apareció desnuda toda.*
> *¡Oh pasión de mi vida, poesía*
> *desnuda, mía para siempre!*

She came, first, pure,
dressed in innocence;
and I loved her as a child would.
Then she began to adorn herself
in all sorts of costumes;
and I began to hate her, without knowing it.
She became a queen
showing off her treasures . . .
What meaningless, bilious wrath!
. . . But she began to undress.
And I smiled on her.
She kept for herself the tunic
of her ancient innocence.
I believed in her again.
And she removed her tunic
and appeared completely nude.
Oh passion of my life, Poetry
nude, mine forever!

Even more than Machado, Jiménez sought the most reduced, austere possible line of verse and the simplest conceivable expression of beauty. He brings this simplicity to his prose as well. His best-known work is *Platero y yo* (*Platero and I*), a narrative of the shared life of the poet and his donkey in his native town of Moguer, in Andalusia. In a series of short vignettes, some only a couple of paragraphs in length, the poet captures brilliantly the colors and figures of the Andalusian village and countryside. This book has been widely translated and has achieved almost universal fame.

Jiménez traveled widely in Europe and America. Following the outbreak of the civil war, Juan Ramón sought refuge in the United States, more for peace of mind and spirit than for political reasons. He lived, wrote, and lectured in the United States and Latin America for the remaining years of his life. He died in Puerto Rico in 1958. He was received always as a poet and intellectual who knew both his literary craft and the full world of Hispanic letters. The surface simplicity of his verse, especially in his later work, is the result of a lifetime of constant and conscious reduction of metaphor and language. Few poets of the Western world have so effectively controlled the poetic impulse to grandeur of phrase as he, yet there is not a line of his verse that might be called commonplace or pedestrian. Criticism is confounded by the poetry of Machado and Jiménez; each says so much in such highly personal and original ways that comment becomes superfluous and résumé almost impossible. These poets continue to be anthologized, translated, and quoted, and they will have a lasting influence on writers of Spanish verse. In transcending modernism they created styles so intimate that they cannot be formed into schools, and no label has been devised that can incorporate their intense individualism into literary movements.

Summary

In the latter part of the nineteenth century, a new literary and social awareness manifested itself in Spain, owing largely to the penetration of ideas and attitudes from Europe and America. This awareness was expressed in the literature of the time by the flowering of creative journalism and criticism, the essay, the naturalistic trends in the novel, and the social realism of Galdós. These developments set the atmosphere in which the Generation of '98 grew to maturity. The Spanish-American War brought inescapable and dramatic awareness to Spanish intellectuals of the plight of Spain—destitute of morale and leadership, suffering from *abulia,* or paralysis of the will, impoverished in spirit as well as in its national economy. The response of the leading writers of the period is diverse and contradictory, but has certain constant elements as its basis. These are a search for *lo español,* the essence or "Spanishness" of Spain; a deep concern for the *pueblo,* the village, and the peasant, which represent to most of these writers the heart and soul of Spain; and an almost compulsive re-examination of Spain's past and its traditions. The outstanding writers of the period were identified as the Generation of '98 by the critic and essayist Azorín, and may be symbolized by the made-up word VABUMB, formed by the initials of Valle-Inclán, Azorín, Baroja, Unamuno, Maeztu, and Benavente. Most wrote in several forms but excelled in only one or two. Valle-Inclán is known primarily for his novels and plays; Azorín for his critical essays; Baroja for his novels; Unamuno for novels, essays in many fields, and poetry. Maeztu, who did not really fulfill his literary potential, wrote political and sociological essays in two periods of his thought, the first profoundly liberal and the second strongly conservative. Benavente, the last of those generally considered as belonging to the group, was primarily a playwright.

A new current in poetry and the use of language makes itself felt in Latin America in the last decade of the nineteenth century. It is essentially the adaptation of French innovations to the Castilian language, but brings with it also a renovation and rebirth of traditional Spanish verse forms from the late Middle Ages, the Renaissance, and the baroque period. The major figure who introduces these new possibilities to Spanish poetry is the Nicaraguan Rubén Darío. He was enthusiastically followed by many gifted writers in Spain but the most outstanding poets, Antonio Machado and Juan Ramón Jiménez, soon sought their own paths of aesthetic fulfillment. The major period of modernism as an effective movement is short-lived, encompassing the period from roughly 1890 to 1910.

CHAPTER 8

SPAIN IN THE TWENTIETH CENTURY

The first decades of the present century represent a severe crisis in the national life of Spain in all dimensions. The country had long since ceased to figure in European politics as a major power, and the collapse of what remained of the overseas empire in 1898 reduced the nation once again to its peninsular state. The disorganized and impoverished situation was further complicated by internal dissension, class struggle, and regional separatist movements. As a result, it was practically impossible, as well as politically inadvisable, for Spain to participate in Europe's first world war. The country remained in a state of paralyzed neutrality, factionalized by the ideals of nationalism and civil order which the teutonic nations represented and the liberalism and social justice proclaimed by England and France. This left Spain in an anomalous state, allied neither to the victors nor the vanquished; once more, it could be said, Europe stopped at the Pyrenees.

This relative containment had, nonetheless, certain literary advantages. European literary influences in this period penetrated in a rather delayed and diffuse manner, and Spanish writers continued to mine their own historical and social experience for themes and creative attitudes. The Generation of 1898 remained active as a productive force well into the thirties, and the influence of Modernism in opening new esthetic and linguistic horizons gave enormous impetus to innovations in poetry. Building upon this adventurous spirit, Juan Ramón Jiménez had divined a new quest for the poet: the search for pure poetry—"*poesía desnuda*." Such a label, however, is essentially intuitive, and can cover a wide variety of content. Purification generally means elimination. What shall be eliminated from poetry to make it "pure" without destroying its essence as poetry? Shall it be pure sensation or emotion, purged of social message or intellectual content? Shall it be pure intellection, reducing the subjective, human element to the vanishing point, as mathematics and symbolic logic might seek to do? Or is it some more metaphysical purity that the poet must seek? The major poets who accept this quest as a valid and compelling pursuit make their hypotheses on the nature of "pure" poetry in the course of their work.

A rallying point for this new poetic sensibility, which rejected so much of the immediate past, presented itself in a historical framework. The year 1927 represented the tercentary of the death of the baroque poet Luis de Góngora. Góngora's commitment to linguistic renovation and to an elitist esthetic appealed irresistibly to an unusually talented generation of university-trained poets. The influence of the Generation of '98, with its emphasis on *lo español* and Spanish cultural history, *Modernismo* with its interest in language, rhythms, and metaphors, and the new search for poetic purity, all conjoined in a most unusual moment. Góngora, so long neglected in poetic syntheses, represented precisely the point of new orientation from which a generation of superbly gifted poets might direct its quest. But literary movements are never entirely homogenous. Starting from a given point —in this case, the esthetic of Góngora—the itineraries of the individual poets were very different. Like the Generation of '98, the Generation of 1927 falls apart as a movement when we begin to look in close detail at individual work and concepts. New influences, such as surrealism and Marxism, which were only minimally present in the previous generation, now assume important roles. We can best understand the innovations and directions of Spanish literature in the twentieth century if we proceed by examining the major genres and their transformations: poetry, theater, the essay, and the novel.

Poetry

Pedro Salinas (1891–1951) shared with his friend Juan Ramón Jiménez the desire to reduce the elements of form and rhetoric in poetry, and his early work displays this tendency clearly. Salinas goes farther than Jiménez, however, and reduces the thematic content as well. His mature poetry revolves around one primary theme—love. This is not the anguished, passionate declamation of the romantic, nor is it the erotic itinerary of a Don Juan. It is a sophisticated and refined awareness of the beloved, an elevated responsiveness to the person and to the objects which represent her, in a pantheistic conviction that the nature of all reality is love. This fragment from Salinas' *Razón de amor* provides a typical example of his verse:

> *Pensar en ti esta noche*
> *no era pensarte con mi pensamiento,*
> *y solo, desde mí. Te iba pensando*
> *conmigo extensamente, el ancho mundo.*
> *El gran sueño del campo, las estrellas,*
> *callado el mar, las hierbas invisibles,*
> *sólo presentes en perfumes secos,*
> *todo,*
> *de Aldebarán al grillo, te pensaba.*
> *¡Qué sosegadamente*
> *se hacía la concordia*
> *entre las piedras, los luceros,*

> *el agua muda, la arboleda trémula,*
> *todo lo inanimado,*
> *y el alma mía*
> *dedicándolo a ti!*

> To think of you tonight
> was not to think of you with my thoughts,
> I alone, from myself. Thinking of you
> along with me went the whole extensive world.
> The great sleep of the fields, the stars,
> in silence the sea, the invisible plants,
> only felt in dry perfumes,
> everything,
> from Aldebaran to the cricket, thought of you.
> How restfully
> the harmony developed
> among the stones, the stars,
> the mute water, the trembling tree groves,
> every inanimate thing,
> and my soul
> dedicating it to you!

The theme of love takes on many ramifications in Salinas' later work. His focus is not so limited that it excludes landscape, work and relaxation, even social commentary. His poetry is intimate, personal, fervent. It is a "poetry of the second person," usually addressed to the beloved, but occasionally it takes on a more ample tone. There is always a supreme sensitivity to language and the sound of his lines, with their flexible and subtle rhythms.

Salinas was known primarily as a poet, but his work in other genres was extensive. He took his doctorate in literature at the University of Madrid and later taught and lectured at Cambridge, Wellesley, and Johns Hopkins. His critical work is significant; *Reality and the Poet in Spanish Poetry* is well known to the English-speaking world, and his studies of the poetry of Jorge Manrique and Rubén Darío are important contributions. His version of the *Poema de mio Cid* in modern Spanish verse is widely read and used in the study of the great medieval epic.

Jorge Guillén (1893–) is still active as a poet and lecturer. His verse, too, seeks purity, and some critics have seen him as overly intellectual, overly abstract, "dehumanized." Yet there is in his poetry a great joy of living, a remarkable openness to human experience, an awareness of beauty expressed with a magnificent control of language and metaphor. As Salinas' poetry centers itself in the theme of love, Guillén's orientation is to *things*, to the world of objects and events. Guillén's poetry is highly polished and most carefully elaborated. The major part of his work is contained in the *Cántico*, which he has continually revised and enlarged over the years in its various editions since 1928. In its latest form it contains over three hundred poems of varying lengths. *El huerto de Melibea* (*The Orchard of Melibea*), published separately, is a lyrical ballad which recreates the tragedy of Calisto and Melibea, originally given form by Fernando de Rojas. Guillén was influenced, as were all the poets of his generation, by French poetry, particularly Valéry and Claudel, whose works he translated. He also participated in the Góngora revival, and the tone of the baroque master is occasionally identifiable in Guillén's poetic lexicon and syntax.

Dámaso Alonso (1898–) is the poet-scholar-teacher who most effectively contributed to the revival of interest in Góngora in the late twenties and early thirties. His study, *La lengua poética de Góngora*, won the National Prize for Literature and his prose version of the *Soledades* has contributed effectively to the understanding of that very complex poet's imagery. As a teacher, Dámaso Alonso has inspired generations of students of Spanish literature in the major academic centers of Europe and

America. Critical and annotated editions of important Spanish texts, collections of literary essays, pioneer work in stylistic analysis, carefully prepared anthologies, all have added to his stature as a universally respected scholar. Dámaso Alonso is an equally impressive figure as a poet. Five major collections of verse, dating from 1921 to 1955, trace the development of power and control which gives astonishing expression to a growing conceptual depth and complexity. His thematic preoccupation is similar to that of Unamuno: man's place in the universe, human destiny, and the relation of God to the world of man's anguish and aspiration. His most significant collections, *Hijos de la ira* (*Children of Wrath*) and *Hombre y Dios* (*Man and God*), contain poems of bitter depth and frustration in which mystic and existential elements assume a personalism, a confessional tone which goes to the innermost reality of the man himself.

Vicente Aleixandre (1898–) is one of the few major poets of his generation who both survived the war and remained in Spain during that difficult period of privation and intellectual repression which the post-Civil War period represented. Aleixandre offers no constant point of view in his poetry. He participated marginally in the Góngora revival and surrealist elements appear, especially in his early work, such as *Pasión de la tierra* (*Earth Passion*). His verse is most often given in free form. It is essentially erotic poetry and it speaks a very personal message. Night, the senses, physical being, involvement in love and the physical caress, are important elements of his work. The poetic line may be brief or complex and the rhythms agitated or serene. We find in his verse a shout or an observation, a description or a startling declamation. His poetry has been described as "anarchic" in the sense that no central theme is found, as is the case with Salinas or Guillén, and no constants appear which might be called the "rules of the game" for Aleixandre's poetry. The most recent evaluations of his poetry have tended to see in Aleixandre a romantic who, attracted by the lexical freedom and liberty of metaphor of the surrealist movement, let himself go in the direction of looseness of style and linguistic association. Beyond this, however, is his feeling that from within himself he can mine the universally and eternally valid human qualities which all poetry seeks: another hypothesis on the nature of "pure" poetry. As Spain's most recent Nobel laureate (1977) many critical works, anthologies, and editions are being prepared and dedicated to the work of a poet who might otherwise have remained a secondary voice in his generation. Much more notice had been accorded to others of the group of 1927, perhaps owing to their broader involvement in lecturing, teaching, and publishing literary criticism; perhaps owing to the retiring nature of Aleixandre himself. Neither an academic nor a critic, Aleixandre's unperturbed way of life kept him apart from the involvement in international literary circles which others of his generation sought and enjoyed. A typical, brief example of his poetry:

MATERIA

Cadencia y ritmo
y augur
de cosas que tu aventas
con tus dedos abiertos,
hacia mis ojos, recargados
de tu sospecha.
  Comezón dolorosa
de tu ausencia,
y lento repasar entre las cosas
nuevas
y entre las viejas.
  Y cegadora nota última
—confirmación de la sospecha

que gravitaba en mis ojos—
cuando sucede la experiencia.
He buceado en la noche,
hundido mis brazos
—materia de la noche—,
y te he tropezado entre mis
      dedos,
concreta.

MATTER

Cadence and rhythm,
and diviner
of things you push away
with your fingers spread,
toward my eyes, overloaded
   with your jealousy.
 Painful gnawing
of your absence,
and slow return among things
that are new
and among the old.
 And sight-depriving final
      note
—confirmation of the suspi-
      cion
that settled down in my
      eyes—
when the fact becomes real.
I have bottomed like a diver
   into the night,
sunk deep my arms
—substance of night—,
and I have encountered you
   between my fingers,
concrete.

The period after World War I saw the upsurge in Spain, as elsewhere in Europe, of many sporadic new movements in poetry. Called the "epoch of the -isms" by some critics, young poets sought new directions, new commitments, and issued new manifestoes. Such movements as futurism, vanguardism, creationism, ultraism, surrealism, and expressionism made their appearance in the innumerable, usually short-lived little magazines of the period. These movements and esthetics attracted their devotees who had their say and then succumbed to other vogues. Most of the poets of importance in the period had brief flirtations with one or more of "-isms." Surrealism, of course, exercised a decisive and lasting influence, and both creationism and ultraism gained the allegiance for awhile of several major figures. Creationism sought to "make a poem like Nature makes a tree"; the Chilean poet Vicente Huidobro defined the quest in his *ars poetica*:

> *¿Por qué cantáis la rosa, ¡oh! poetas?*
> *¡Hacedla florecer en el poema!*
> *El poeta es un pequeño dios.*

> Why do you sing about the rose, O poets?
> Make it flower in your poem!
> The poet is a small god.

Ultraism was a Spanish synthesis of several foreign movements which had held their sway over lyric poetry. In the words of the poet-critic who is said to have coined this ultimate -ism, Guillermo de Torre, it "has tended as a preliminary toward the genuine rehabilitation of the poem. That is, toward the capture of its purest and most imperishable elements—imagery, metaphor—and toward the suppression of parasitic qualities which do not really belong to it: the anecdote, the narrative theme, erotic effusion."

Active in several of these movements was the very eclectic Gerardo Diego (1896–   ). Diego has experimented with traditional forms as well as the most far-out aspects of neo-Gongorism and innovations of the post–World War I period. His work includes religious poetry, evocation of monuments and countryside, verbal playthings, deeply moving sonnets, poetry based on his extensive travels. This enormous variety of style, theme, and attitude makes it possible to find reflected in his poetry almost every movement of significance in twentieth-century Spanish poetry. It would be impossible to choose a typical example of Gerardo Diego's work; one would have to cite a dozen of his most diverse poems. Nor can we speak of linear evolution in his styles; in the same collection, product of the same year, may be found quite opposed and distinct approaches. Gerardo is a skilled musician and an *aficionado* of the bullfight. These intrests are reflected in his poetry in a variety of ways. A series of dedicatory poems to Beethoven, Debussy, Schubert, and other composers expresses his deep response to their music. Beyond this, the rhythmic subtlety and the awareness of sound in his poetry lend tonal qualities which are clear evidence of his musical sensibilities. The publication in 1956 of *Egloga de Antonio Bienvenida* brings together some of his verse which uses the bullfight as its theme. His sense of the color, tradition, order, and ceremony of the taurine art gives a sensation of the event which is unsurpassed in poetic form.

The poetry of Salinas, Alonso, Guillén, and Diego has as a common denominator its intellectualism, introspection, and a generally cerebral quality. University-trained scholars, lecturers, teachers, it is hardly surprising that they should see their own poetry to some extent in the light of their critical methodology, thus allowing them to create on the dual planes of poet and critic.

The reserve and introspection which may be felt in the poetry of this group runs counter to another tendency which is never completely absent in Spanish poetry:

the popular voice which seeks its themes not in the inner world of analysis and self-probing, but rather in the color, fire, and passion of life observed. Two poets who represent this tradition of popular themes and folklore elements are Rafael Alberti and Federico García Lorca.

Rafael Alberti (1902–   ) received scant formal education. He left school when he was fifteen years old. His first interest was painting and he had some early success as a minor cubist. He turned to literature during an illness which forced physical inactivity upon him for a while. Despite his lack of academic preparation, Alberti is a man of wide literary and intellectual formation. He participated in several of the postwar literary movements and indeed some of his poetry suffers from over-erudition. Along with his participation in various movements and vogues—neo-Gongorism, surrealism, *ultraísmo*—Alberti cultivated a simple, singing line in some of his poetry which relates directly to the life of the Andalusian *pueblo*. A significant part of his poetry and poetic drama contains overtly polemic political themes. A collection of his most evocative verse, *Sobre los ángeles* (*Concerning Angels*) was published in 1928, and still stands as a major work of his generation. An example:

EL ANGEL DE ARENA
Seriamente, en tus ojos era la mar dos niños que me espiaban,
temerosos de lazos y palabras duras.
Dos niños de la noche, terribles, expulsados del cielo,
cuya infancia era un robo de barcos y un crimen de soles
                                             y de lunas.
Duérmete. Ciérralos.
Vi que el mar verdadero era un muchacho que saltaba
                                             desnudo,
invitándome a un plato de estrellas y a un reposo de algas.
¡Sí, sí! Ya mi vida iba a ser, ya lo era, litoral desprendido.
Pero tu, despertando, me hundiste en tus ojos.

THE SAND ANGEL

Seriously, in your eyes the sea was two children who peered at me,
fearful of ties and harsh words.
Two children of the night, terrible, expelled from heaven,
whose childhood was a theft of boats and a crime of suns and moons.
Sleep. Close them.
I saw that the real sea was a boy who hopped naked,
offering me a plate of stars and a siesta of algae.
Yes, yes! Now my life was going to be, it already was, a free coast.
But you, awakening, drowned me in your eyes.

Federico García Lorca (1898–1936) is without doubt the most widely known Spanish poet and playwright of the twentieth century. Through translations into all of the major European languages and frequent productions of his dramatic works abroad, the subtle, intense, smoldering quality of his imagination is familiar to a very large reading public. Lorca's poetry is so intensely personal that it cannot really be related to movements or schools, although a surrealist note is almost constant, and the influence of the modernists and the major French poets is certainly there. His themes are death, blood, sex, violence, and often the world of the child. Lorca was a native of Granada and all of the most picturesque elements of the life of Andalusia enter into his poetry; colors, fragrances, the traditional violence, abandon, and independence of the Gypsy, the sensuality of the Moorish temperament, and the rhythms of flamenco music. His major collections of poetry on these themes are the *Canciones* (*Songs*), the *Poema del cante jondo* (*Poem of the Deep Song*), and the *Romancero gitano* (*Gypsy romance*). Here, in some of the most striking metaphorical language to be found in contemporary Spanish poetry, in rhythms as compelling as those of the flamenco guitar, and in colors as dark and menacing as those of the late paintings of Goya, is described a world of earth and blood, violence and death, religiosity and uncontrolled passion.

SORPRESA

*Muerto se quedó en la calle
con un puñal en el pecho.
No lo conocía nadie.
¡Como temblaba el farol!
Madre.
¡Como temblaba el farolito
de la calle!
Era madrugada. Nadie
pudo asomarse a sus ojos
abiertos al duro aire.
Que muerto se quedó en la calle,
que con un puñal en el pecho
y que no lo conocía nadie.*

SURPRISE

There he was dead in the street
with a dagger in his breast.
No one knew him.
How the street lamp flickered!
Mother.
How the little street lamp flickered!
It was very early morning. No one
could look into his eyes
open to the hard air.
And there he was dead in the street,
and with a dagger in his breast
and no one knew him.

Lorca's poetry employs a relatively large and constant set of symbols: the moon, horses, bulls, knives, water, the Sierra Morena, a mountain range of Granada; the colors silver, green, crimson; flowers, the wind, night, and dawn —almost always in some relation to the theme of violent death. The masculine world is conceived in terms of sweat, horses, knives, and labor in the fields. It is a world of incomprehensible violence, vengeance, struggle, and death, from which the poet withdraws in awe and horror. Lorca visited New York and neighboring areas in 1929 and the result of his experience was the long poem *Poeta en Nueva York* (*The Poet in New York*). He was particularly attracted to the life of Harlem, finding similarities there to the gypsy world of the Sacromonte in Granada.

The influence of Lorca has been great in modern Spanish poetry. The lyrical quality of his verse, the terse intensity of his imagery, the shock of his metaphor, and the electrifying dramatic force of his poetic statement set him apart from other poets of his generation. These qualities are strongly present in his major theater, comprising the plays *Bodas de sangre* (*Blood Wedding*), *Yerma*, and *La casa de Bernarda Alba* (*The House of Bernarda Alba*). Here songs, metaphor, verse, and prose dialogue are used with sureness and economy to produce true tragedy; the same stark, direct qualities that are to be found in Sophocles. These three plays are often referred to as a trilogy by critical writers, as they have similar themes, similar treatment, and all represent tragic aspects of rural life and morality.

In *Bodas de sangre*, erotic passion conflicts with family honor as the bride runs off with her married lover on her wedding day. She and the lover fully realize that they will be relentlessly hunted to death by the new husband and the girl's family, that the whole fabric of Spanish social organization will demand a blood revenge. They are utterly helpless victims of their passion, however, and have no more power to resist than did Phaedra and Hippolytus in Euripides' tragedy. The inevitable outcome is given magnificent theatrical realization through the use of folk poetry, choruses, personification of Death as a beggarwoman; the appearance of the moon as a character, and the death of the male figures at knifepoint. The women are left alone, childless, seeking to understand a life that so utterly destroys human values.

In *La casa de Bernarda Alba* we see an exclusively feminine household of five ugly virgins ruled with relentless rigidity by the widowed mother, Bernarda. The one male figure, fiancé of the eldest girl, functions as a catalyst to produce explosive tensions in the household when he begins an affair with the youngest sister, Adela. The tragic resolution is prefigured when a village girl is discovered to have murdered her illegitimate child. Bernarda joins the vengeful and self-righteous villagers, shouting from her doorway:

BERNARDA: Let them all come with clubs of olive wood and hoe-handles, let them all come to kill her.
ADELA: No, no. Not to kill her.
BERNARDA: And let her pay, who trod upon decency. (*Outside is heard a woman's scream and the noise of a crowd.*)
ADELA: Let her get away! Don't you go out there!
BERNARDA: Finish her off before the *guardia civil* comes! Flaming coals in the place where she sinned!
ADELA: (*clutching her belly*) No! No!
BERNARDA: Kill her! Kill her!

Finally Adela defies them all and prepares to run away with Pepe. When Pepe appears, Bernarda fires at him with a shotgun, and although she misses him, Adela is led to believe that he is dead. She runs into her room, hysterical, and hangs herself, thinking that all escape is now impossible. Even with this, Bernarda can think of only one thing: the respectability of her household. The play closes on a note of indomitable hypocrisy:

BERNARDA: Cut her down! My daughter died a virgin! Carry her to her room and dress her as a virgin. No one must say a word! She died a virgin. Tell them to ring the church bells twice at daybreak. And I want no cries of grief. Death must be looked upon face to face. Silence! (*To one of her daughters.*) I have said to be quiet! (*To another daughter.*) Tears when you are alone! We will drown ourselves in a sea of mourning. She, the youngest daughter of Bernarda Alba, died a virgin. Do you hear me? Silence, I say silence! Silence!

(*Curtain*)

In both plays, human needs and passions come into conflict with the totally inflexible social order of small-town Andalusia, where appearance and good name are the only ultimate and acknowledged values; a conflict that can only be resolved in blood. In both, the male figure is an enigma of passion and violence; a lion, a bull, a stallion. Lorca understood far better the closed-in, protected world of women. His psychological penetration of the male is slight. One might as well try to psychoanalyze a cyclone as to penetrate beyond the crude surface power of his men. He has, on the other hand, a deep, lyrical, intuitive understanding of women. Bernarda, Adela, and the other girls emerge with strengths and frailties, with depths and colors of considerable complexity.

In *Yerma* the theme is quite different. Yerma—the name means "barren"—is married but childless. Her hopes of pregnancy diminish month by month and she is in complete despair on learning that her husband not only cannot give her children, but does not want them. She goes for help to an old woman who is reputedly wise in these matters. The hag leeringly suggests that there is one sovereign remedy for the situation, and that her son would be quite willing to oblige for the occasion. Yerma rejects adultery as a solution. Her sense of honor and her concept of herself do not allow so crass a way out of her predicament. When her husband seeks to console her, telling her that they are happy, they have land and money, they need nothing more, that, in fact, children would destroy the happiness they have, her world crumbles completely. As he embraces her, she strangles him, crying, "I have killed my son!" Knowing that she is morally incapable of having children by a man other than her husband, by his death she is sealed off forever from motherhood.

The three plays are unmistakably linked in theme. Passion against accepted morality—whether it be the personal integrity of Yerma or the fanatical hypocrisy of Bernarda Alba or the doomed eroticism of *Bodas de sangre*—provides the sulphurous amalgam that must as surely end in blood as the *hubris* of Greek drama. They are equally linked in terms of dramatic technique. Three tightly drawn acts establish the situation, intensify the conflict, and resolve the action in necessary and inevitable tragedy. In this external sense Lorca follows the rules of Spanish classical drama, particularly the theater of Lope de Vega. His use of folklore themes is another point of contact with drama of the Golden Age. The songs of reapers in the field, the lullabies of lonely women, the chants of washerwomen by the river, all serve to root his drama in the soil and sociology of the Spanish *pueblo*.

Lorca also wrote comedy and other light theatrical pieces. *Así que pasen cinco años* (*Let Five Years Pass*) is a surrealistic play which at times verges on the unintelligible. *La zapatera prodigiosa* (*The Shoemaker's Prodigious Wife*) is pure light farce. Lorca displayed a theatrical talent certainly equal to his magnificent gifts as a poet. In all, he was one of the truly creative figures of his century. His death at the age of thirty-eight, under circumstances which are even now not clear, stilled the most promising talent of his generation in Spain.

A generation of gifted poets began to publish work of very considerable merit in the brief period of the Spanish Republic, 1931–1936. As the previous generation had found inspiration and a point of departure in the poetry of Góngora, this group looked to the esthetic of Garcilaso de la Vega, seeking a simpler line and a more direct imagery. Called by some critics the "Generation of 1936," as their manifestoes coincided with the four-hundredth anniversary of Garcilaso's death, they represent a return to the discipline of form and metrics and the use of more direct, less metaphoric language than was typical of the Góngora revival. It is not an esthetically aggressive generation, although it rejects the quest for "pure" poetry and any hard-lining adherence to the "-isms" of the twenties. The religious, surrealist, and existentialist tones are still evident, although considerably toned down in comparison to their expression in the poetry of the Generation of 1927. All are, again, university-trained intellectuals; major figures of the group are Germán Bleiberg (1915–), Leopoldo Panero (1909–1962), Luis Rosales (1910–) and Luis Felipe Vivanco (1907–).

The most exceptional talent of this generation—and it must be borne in mind that the concept of "generation" is a very blunt critical instrument—is that of Miguel Hernández (1910–1942), an almost entirely self-taught farm laborer and sheep herder from the province of Murcia, in southeast Spain. Influenced by his reading of Góngora, Garcilaso, and other Golden Age poets, he began to publish his earliest poetry in a local newspaper. In 1934 he went to Madrid, where his literary gifts were encouraged by Aleixandre and the Chilean poet Pablo Neruda, among others. His most important collection of poetry, *El rayo que no cesa* (*The Unceasing Thunderbolt*) was published in 1936 and established Hernández as a uniquely promising figure in a brilliant group. An example from that collection:

> *Por una senda van los hortelanos,*
> *que es la sagrada hora del regreso,*
> *con la sangre injuriada por el peso*
> *de inviernos, primaveras y veranos.*
>
> *Vienen de los esfuerzos sobrehumanos*
> *y van a la canción, y van al beso,*
> *y van dejando por el aire impreso*
> *un olor de herramientas y de manos.*
>
> *Por otra senda yo, por otra senda*
> *que no conduce al beso, aunque es la hora,*
> *sino que merodea sin destino.*
>
> *Bajo su frente trágica y tremenda,*
> *un toro sólo en la ribera llora*
> *olvidando que es toro y masculino.*

By one path the orchard-hands go
—it's the sacred hour of return—
with their blood bruised by the weight
of winters, springs, and summers.

They come from their superhuman labor
and go to the song, and go to the kiss,
and go leaving impressed on the air
a smell of iron tools and of hands.

By a different path I, by a different path
which doesn't bring me to the kiss, although it is time,
but wanders pillaging without a destiny.

> Under his tragic and menacing brow
> a lone bull cries on the riverbank,
> forgetting that he is a bull and male.

The perfect and classic form of the sonnet, wedded as it is to the world of the farm laborer and the poet's own dual sensibility, gives an idea of the range and originality of Hernández's genius. We might expect at most an imitation and rehashing of Golden Age themes and language from such an untutored, undirected literary formation, but the poet's intuition and grasp of what poetry is all about was so sure and immediate that his verse vibrates with personal vision and originality. Another tragedy of politics and the Civil War, Hernández died in prison at a time when he was beginning to achieve the full maturity of his astonishing talent.

Following the victory of the Nationalist forces in the spring of 1939, lyric poetry was probably the genre least affected by political pressures and the censor. Those writers most punitively affected by the Franco regime, with exile, imprisonment or death—and the list is a long one—suffered not so much from the verse they had published as from public stances they had taken in the chaotic politics of the thirties. The poetry written in Spain by the post-war generation generally continues the lines projected by the generation of the thirties in its devotion to form and refined clarity of expression seen in the Garcilaso revival. There is an ineffectual resurgence of the "-isms"; now, *postismo* and *introvertismo,* the latter a variation on surrealism. But the program, if it may be called that, of most of the post-war generation, is a reduction of poetic line and vocabulary with a premium on communication and social content. Poetry should have meaning for the moment we are living and, while in no sense advocating a specific type of social order or political regime, should address itself to the human condition, the *angustia vital* in which man lives out his days. The poets who subscribe to a sort of "poetic telegraphy," with verse seen as message and communication, are Victoriano Crémer (1908–), Gabriel Celaya (pseudonym of Rafael Mugica, 1911–), and Eugenio de Nora (1923–). Poetry should not be an end in itself, art for art's sake, but rather a "high calling to change the world." Blas de Otero (1916–), one of the most accomplished and committed poets of this period, calls for poetry to go public; to address itself to the "immense majority," not to confine itself to the esthetic minority for which Juan Ramón Jiménez and the Generation of 1927 first wrote.

There is considerable continuity in the development of Spanish poetry from the initiation of the Garcilaso ethetic to the present time, marked by devotion to perfection of form and clarity of expression. Significant figures of the present moment are Carlos Bousoño (1923–), Vincent Gaos (1919–), José Hierro (1922–), and Claudio Rodríguez (1934–).

With the passing of the Franco regime following the *caudillo*'s death, the stern, though often capricious, rule of censorship has practically ceased to exist. Almost anything which might be found in the bookstores of New York, London, or Paris can be published and circulated in Spain at present. There has been an enormous spurt of publication of material which, up to 1975, was rigorously forbidden. Translations of everything from Brecht to Mao, and editions of proscribed Spanish writers, have mushroomed and literally overflow the bookstores to stands set up in parks and boulevards. A great deal of poetry is being written and few students of literature neglect to publish a slim volume or two at their own expense, or at least contribute an occasional sonnet to the numerous little magazines that seem to appear and vanish overnight. What has not been heard since the Civil War is the great voice, what Gerardo Diego calls *tenores del cielo,* announcing a grand theme which might call for a lifetime of elaboration. The recent return to Spain of two Grand Old Men of the Generation of 1927, Rafael Alberti and Jorge Guillén, was widely celebrated in literary and political circles. The way is open, for the time being at least, for a revival or a totally new vision in Spanish poetry.

Theater

Spanish theater began to take some surprising turns in the early decades of the twentieth century. As seen in the previous chapter, the theater of Benavente showed signs of a return to sources and a rejuvenation from the heavy-handed social moralizing of the 19th century. The theater of García Lorca had major impact in Spain, Latin America, and, in translation, throughout the world. But as we re-see and re-read Lorca's theater, the situations stale and petrify; the plays become, in fact, a kind of situation tragedy, however enlightened by their poetic and theatrical qualities. The most original playwright of the early part of the century, especially in his theater written in the twenties, was Ramón del Valle-Inclán, referred to earlier as a member of the Generation of 1898. Valle-Inclán was publicly much better known for his novels and for the personal myth he created and maintained as a bohemian artist. His theatrical work, which makes up a sizable part of his total literary production, was largely neglected until very recently; roughly the last three decades. There were few productions, few editions, and little criticism of his work. This is not really surprising. His theater is complex, difficult to produce, and located at the polar extreme of the light entertainment or self-conscious melodrama which had generally been the dominant fare in Spanish theater. Violence, irony, shock, and a powerful attack on social hypocrisy in all the forms he could identify, presented in distorted imagery and in obscure, colloquial language, all combined to render the revolutionary esthetic of his *esperpentos* and his *comedias bárbaras* practically unintelligible to a naive public and a commercially oriented theater.

The *comedias bárbaras* form a trilogy set in the feudal backwaters of Galicia, in which the sons of a once-wealthy landowner connive to rob and finally kill the old man. Elements of folklore and witchcraft, pride and depravation, brutality, and magnanimity combine to produce intense drama. *Divinas palabras* (*Divine Words*) concerns the rivalry of two peasant women for the possession of a deformed and imbecilic child, who is a lucrative source of income in their begging at local fairs and religious celebrations. Adultery and again witchcraft enter into the the plot. The "divine words" of the title are those of Christ, judging the woman taken in adultery: "Let him who is without sin cast the first stone." Here, the context is utterly hypocritical. The wife of the village sacristan is caught *in flagrante* by the whole village, amusing herself with her semi-tramp lover. The sacristan lacks the courage to avenge himself as a Calderonian hero would, and finds his escape in the false piety of forgiveness. The play is so mordant, the human values so perverted, that it goes beyond satire to an almost demonic level.

His best known theatrical work is *Luces de Bohemia* (*Lights of Bohemia*), in which the author defines his unique esthetic invention, the *esperpento,* as the sort of image of reality and traditional values we might get from a series of fun-house mirrors. He uses popular street language, slang and dialectical terms, but not to create an effect of realism. His intention is wholly esthetic:

to create with these exaggerated themes and language, with a cast of characters composed of beggars, prostitutes, drunks, and pimps a sort of esthetic transmutation that will be truer to life than the superficialities of life itself. *Luces de Bohemia,* published in 1920, describes the last night of a blind poet, Máximo Estrella in "an absurd, brilliant, and starving Madrid." There is no traditional plot involved—the play is a "journey to the end of the night" as the penniless, blind poet goes from tavern to tavern, pawns his cloak to buy a round of drinks, lands in jail as a suspected anarchist, is bailed out by an old classmate, the Prime Minister of the current government, and finally collapses, dying, on his own doorstep as dawn breaks. There are no acts; the play is divided into fifteen scenes in which a quite large cast participates. The poet Rubén Darío appears briefly, as does the fictional hero of Valle-Inclán's *Sonatas,* the Marqués of Bradomín. True to his definition, the basis of the work is undeniably realistic, and some characters of Madrid's bohemian literary life are recognizable. But all is distorted, exaggerated, phantasmagorical, as in a fun-house mirror. The play is at least a decade ahead of the most advanced esthetic that post-war European theater produced.

There was little influence derived from the theater of Valle-Inclán between the twenties and the sixties. Those of his plays that saw production were usually short lived on the boards, or produced for very restricted audiences. However, for an in-group, the liberalization of theatrical concepts and the possibility of alternate esthetics led to further experimentation. There was a partial revival of some of Valle-Inclán's theater during the period of the Spanish Republic, but his name as a playwright was virtually forgotten in the theater of the Franco regime.

A totally different concept of life and its dramatic

representation is seen in the theater of Alejandro Casona (1903–1965). His major theme is the human tendency to escape from reality into fantasy, or the essentially hopeless attempt to force reality to conform to our desires. His characters typically seek fulfillment and salvation from their shortcomings in bizarre imaginings which are doomed to exposure and defeat. In one of his most popular plays, *La sirena varada* (*The Stranded Mermaid*), which won the important Lope de Vega prize, a young idealist sets up a home for the disillusioned in a haunted house by the sea. There he collects a band of interesting failures. Typical among them is a painter who is in fact blind, but who conceals his lack more from himself than from others by wearing a blindfold and declaring that he wishes to shut out the dreary colors of the real world to live among the vivd tones which only his imagination can supply. The "mermaid" is a girl who has been forced by circumstances into prostitution, and who has escaped from that life into the fantasy that she is an unworldly creature of the sea. The resolution of the play announces Casona's continuing thesis, that we must face up to life in whatever harsh reality it may present itself in order to make a livable adjustment. In learning that there is no escape into delusion or fantasy, we also learn that the truth is bearable, and we find the fortitude to come to grips with it. A similar situation is the motive force of *Prohibido suicidarse en primavera* (*Suicide Is Prohibited in the Spring*). Here the setting is a refuge for would-be suicides, who are led to work through their fantasies and despair to find a viable reality for themselves.

La dama del alba (*The Lady of the Dawn*) develops the theme of Death taking a holiday in the atmosphere of a rural village. Death here is a kindly figure who brings relief from suffering and tribulations while bearing her own ghastly burden: that everything she touches must wither and die. When her local mission is finally accomplished and understood, it is seen that all has worked to the best possible solution, and that Death in fact collaborates with life.

There is always a happy ending in Casona's plays, always an opening of new hope and new possibilities in the last act. His heroes and heroines find the means to face life with courage and optimism when they are forced to emerge from their cocoons of fantasy or bitterness; even Death comes as a happy ending. Such gentle sentiments can hardly produce high tragedy or gripping drama, but Casona can be delightful when taken on his own terms. One of his last works was a version of the *Celestina* of Rojas. It is clear that Casona's talent for dramatizing whimsical and charming eccentricities is not capable of giving theatrical presence to such superb tragedy as the *Celestina* represents.

The theater of Antonio Buero Vallejo (1916–) is the most innovating and varied dramatic product of the 1950s and 60s. In terms of theme, scenic effect, and originality of presentation, Buero stands out among his contemporaries as a writer of subtle and imaginative sensibility. His earliest vocation was to painting, and he began studies in Madrid's Academy of Fine Arts. His training was interrupted by the outbreak of the Civil War; he served on the Republican side in the medical corps. At the end of the war, Buero was imprisoned and condemned to death by military decree. This sentence was fortunately not carried out immediately; it was commuted some months later and gradually reduced, with the result that he was given conditional freedom in 1946. Buero did not return to painting, but rather began to write for the theater. His first work, *Historia de una escalera (History of a Staircase),* was produced in Madrid in 1949 with enormous success. Here, the lives of lower-middle class families are interwoven, with their frustrations, rivalries, and very limited hopes of bettering their economic conditions. Buero says nothing directly about the war or politics, but the implications of social injustice which reduce a generation to poverty and very limited personal horizons are clear. Two major plays deal with the blind: *En la ardiente oscuridad (In the Burning Darkness)* and *El concierto de San Ovidio (The Concert of Saint Ovid)*. In the first, the dramatic tension is generated from within the group of sightless inmates of an asylum for the blind; in the second, a small band of blind musicians is victimized by an unscrupulous promoter who exhibits them as a curiosity, as if they were trained seals. The metaphor of sightlessness is clear and perhaps oversimple. A group of people handicapped by lack of vision and the inability to organize their own lives are in one way or another victimized and frustrated by their limitations; an obvious and ironic parallel to the situation of a majority of the population of post-Civil War Spain.

Buero develops another system of metaphor in a series of biographical historical plays. In *Las Meninas*—the title is that of a major work of the painter Diego Velázquez—he dramatizes a critical episode in the life of the great baroque artist. Velázquez has painted a nude Venus, against the prohibitions of the Inquisition, and also, according to envious courtiers, portrayed members of the royal family as simple human beings rather than as glorified and majestic figures. Finally, after striking blows for human and artistic freedom and dignity, the play ends with the exoneration of the artist and his restoration to the king's favor. *El sueño de la razon* deals with the later years of the painter Francisco Goya, and takes its title from one of the master's etchings. The action takes place in the most degraded period in the reign of Fernando VII, a period of terror, torture, dynastic absolutism and foreign support of a tyrant. Goya, aged, deaf, and fatally ill, becomes a target for the vindictiveness of a reign which, having no popular support, vents its rage on all non-conformists: painters and writers and liberal politicians alike. Buero calls upon his extraordinary gifts as a scenarist to give great visual presence, with lights, projections of the most horrific paintings of Goya's "black period," and rapid shifts between the royal palace and the painter's studio in the outskirts of Madrid, to the rapid and violent movement of the action. Goya's deafness is an integral part of the play. When the elderly painter is on stage, the other actors speak in growls, squawks, and the cackling of hens; a totally incomprehensible cacophony, as the deaf Goya might have heard their speech. When the painter is absent, the actors speak clearly and in normal tones. Buero's political metaphor goes farther here, to tell us that a period of desperate tyranny and senseless, terrified repression can only result in injustice, pointless social paralysis, and total incommunication with the most civilizing and creative forces of the epoch. Buero's critics point out that, in these historical plays, he often exaggerates events, distorts history, and makes up characters and situations which have no historical foundation. The author repiles with a shrug; he is writing plays, not textbooks, and is more concerned with generalities of human experience than with historical detail.

El tragaluz departs from historical biography to present a confusing futuristic survey of contemporary problems. Two "beings" from the twenty-second century appear on stage and announce that the audience will see a recreation of a problem from the twentieth century. The problem is one of contemporary middle-class melodrama. An unscrupulous parvenu is making a great deal of money in questionable and chancy business transactions, and having an affair with his secretary. His younger brother has an idealistic repulsion for the shadier aspects of his brother's wheeling and dealing, and supports himself minimally through some translation and proofreading for his brother's publishing house. The key character—and he is a marvelous realization—is the senile, half-insane father of the two men. The old man spends his days cutting out figures from magazines and postcards, wondering who these strange people are, convinced that he has seen or known them somewhere, sometime. The play comes to a thundering conclusion when the father stabs the entrepreneur son with his ever-ready scissors, aware at last that the son has caused the death of a younger sister during the war years. The inevitable melodramatic touch is added when the idealistic proof-reader son decides to marry the pregnant mistress of his adventurous brother to save her from the street.

In all of Buero's work there is an irreducible element of soap-opera, of melodrama and the gimmick. *El tragaluz*—the title refers to the street-level windows which illuminate one of the interior sets—infuriates the sophisticated spectator because its flaws could be so easily remedied with a bit more taste and maturity of concept. Yet his dialogue is excellent, if a bit slow moving, his creation of dramatic character is very solid, and his sense of what will play scenically is outstanding. His painter's vision never fails him in the use of space and light, but his timing is poor. Speeches are often too long and carry too much message, too little feeling. Usually the message is obvious from the outset: he is talking about repression and social injustice, and the conditions of post-war Spain make it necessary for him to speak his piece from a temporal distance and in a historical or masked context. Buero's choice of heroes, the blind, the deaf, and in *La doble historia del Dr. Valmy,* the sexually impotent, make it clear that he sees around him a deformed and incapacitated society, capable now and then of joy, but ordained to battle against crushing social pressures.

An acrid polemic broke out between Buero, who, gaining the acceptance of Madrid's theatrical public and the censors, became to an extent an establishment figure, and Alfonso Sastre (1926–   ), who had constant difficulty with censorship and consequently little access to commercial production. Sastre opposed to Buero's easily accepted work—although Buero too had occasional difficulties—a "theater of the impossible" which would rebel against the strictures of government control in artistic concerns. Buero felt that a creative artist could work within repressive parameters and say what he wanted to say in metaphorical or allegorical terms, discreetly and indirectly, putting esthetic considerations above and beyond political caprices. Sastre would have none of this. He rebelled against a "theater of accommodation" and, like some of the poets of the period, called for a less esthetic, more committed theater centered on social problems and their effect on the human condition. Sastre, widely read in Marxist and existential theory, is not content with a theater of plots, happy or tragic endings, or a poetic vision of life. His theater is "experimental" and somewhat reminiscent of American theater of the Depression in the thirties. It is often given in a space without time, using minimal plot lines, animated by situational encounters and mordant, at times philosophic, dialogue.

Escuadra hacia la muerte (*Death Squadron*) is set in the Third World War. A group of military criminals has been placed in an advance position from which it is clear they will not emerge. They are idle, awaiting a killing charge of the enemy. A sadistic non-com, a professional soldier and death-worshipper, keeps the men in hair-trigger discipline and readiness. Each of the soldiers plays out and confesses the crime or weakness which has brought him to this death squadron. Finally, having broken into the rations of alcohol, all drunk, they kill the brutal corporal who represents by now the only order left in their lives. Some feel guilt, some feel freedom, some feel an existential loss. All know that their act will be discovered, that they can not go back, and that the enemy before them will wipe them out if they attempt to go forward. All, by their own acts or inaction, have placed themselves in the ultimate existentialist predicament, from which there is no escape and to which there is no solution. *Ana Kleiber* is a rather confusing and mysterious play involving re-encounter and murder, which brings up again the question of ultimate guilt in human relations. *La mordaza (The Gag)* deals with a family ruled by an iron-fisted, autocratic father who imposes, but does not adhere to, severe and inflexible moral standards. The theme in this work is hypocrisy and what Jean-Paul Sartre calls "bad faith with life."

Tierra roja (Red Earth) has a clear message and simple structure. It is a tense drama of a miners' strike in southwest Spain. Pedro, an old miner, is about to be ousted from his work and his house. Pablo, an idealistic young man new to the mines, resents this injustice and rouses his companions to a strike. The old man has been through all of this in his own youth; it is a replay of his own early attempts to humanize working conditions in minimally productive mines by revolutionary means. He can not dissuade Pablo from provoking an uprising which is of course promptly crushed, after bloodshed, by military force. The play ends with the old man shouting "We shall not move out tomorrow," moved to sacrifice himself and his family in the same hopeless cause for which others have shed their blood. In *Tierro roja*, Sastre places the theme of Lope de Vega's *Fuente Ovejuna* in the contemporary setting of a bloody miner's strike in what he rather sarcastically calls "the humble homage of a present-day Spanish playwright to the genius of Lope de Vega."

Sastre's art has suffered considerably from the entirely circumstantial fact that he has rarely seen his plays produced. Spanish censorship identified him early as an unruly voice in a politically sensitive medium. As a result, Sastre could not learn from his mistakes in theatrical presentation, could not hear the voice of the public and experiment with theatrical possibilities to the extent that more docile Spanish playwrights were able to do. Sastre's work has appeared in many editions and translations, but production of his plays has been largely limited, in Spain at least, to university and other nonprofessional groups. Sastre has written much theatrical criticism, essays, and articles about the theater which have been published widely in France, Germany, Latin America, and indeed in Spain. But his true calling, in spite of more than a dozen plays written and published, has been frustrated.

Buero Vallejo and Alfonso Sastre are the only Spanish playwrights who merit serious consideration, from a general, overall point of view, in the decades following the Civil War. Spanish theater during the Franco regime was generally reduced to light comedy, musical reviews, revivals of the Golden Age classics, and translations of American and European plays. Many skilled and competent playwrights—among them Joaquín Calvo Sotelo, Víctor Ruiz Iriarte, Alfonso Paso—have had numerous and successful productions, but their work has not merited attention on an international level. As one critic has said, "The Spanish Civil War opened an obligatory parenthesis in the theater." The parenthesis has not yet been closed by the appearance of truly overwhelming talent nor by a social atmosphere conducive to renovation in drama. It has been a theater of complacency and diversion, without resonance, originality, or commitment.

In the late sixties and early seventies, censorship was considerably relaxed in all literary genres. With the "miracle" of Spanish tourism, the country began to receive literally millions of foreign visitors per year, and foreign capital began to take an interest in the rehabilitation and economic development—many Spaniards would call it commercial exploitation—of the country. This massive contact led inevitably to a sophistication and opening of the censorial mentality, and works which would have been unthinkable a decade before began to appear as a matter of course. A variety of "underground" theater began to develop; this adjective has been over-employed to characterize a sort of anti-theater, or theater of the absurd, developed along the lines of American off-off Broadway productions. The influences are various and conglomerate. Valle-Inclán is being read and some of his shorter *esperpentos* produced; the avantgarde movement of *postismo*, mentioned in the section on poetry, begins to have theatrical expression; the influence of pop art and happenings comes to in-group popularity; foreign reviews and journals are being read; Spaniards are traveling abroad in far greater numbers than in the forties and fifties.

One of the first manifestations of this new consciousness is the emergence of café-theater: presentation of short original pieces in the intimate atmosphere of chic bars and cafés. This sort of ambience does not promise much for serious theater, but it gave an opportunity to some young writers with progressive ideas to try their skills before an audience. The themes were more frequently sexual than political, but in fact the censorship had been as ferocious against the one as against the other during the forties and fifties. In terms of major essays at full-length drama, there has been more attempt than success. Two directions are clear: serious social drama and absurd social drama. The first follows lines developed by Buero Vallejo and the main current of theater in Europe and America—a theater of plots and action, developed in the everyday logic of human situations—complete with message and denouement. Fantasy and poetry have their place in these works, as they attempt to avoid bourgeois melodrama. Carlos Muñiz, Lauro Olmo, and José Martín Recuerda, the latter to the greatest extent, represent a continuing line in the theatrical tradition of Valle-Inclán and García Lorca.

The second follows lines influenced by Lorca's surrealist farces, Hollywood's silent comedies, the more grotesque elements of the *esperpentos,* and embodies some of the more absurd and occasionally outrageous elements of the popular cartoon or comic book. In this group the more successful have been José Ruibal, Martínez Ballesteros and Fernando Arrabal. Many more names could be listed; the theater has always been an enormously attractive art form to Spanish writers, and there is a clamor at present to fill the forty-year gap between the innovative thirties and the present. Spanish television and cinema have developed to a level where many young dramatic writers can find commitment and satisfaction more easily than in the arduous and delayed, often problematical, undertaking of writing for the stage.

Essay

In the field of the critical essay, including philosophical, literary, and historical studies, the twentieth century in Spain has been extraordinarily fecund. Figures of international importance have built upon the tradition of literary investigation which culminated in the monumental bibliographical erudition of Marcelino Menéndez y Pelayo. The outstanding figure in a vigorous revitalization of medieval studies is Ramón Menéndez Pidal (1889–1968). His meticulous reconstruction of the one extant manuscript of the *Poema de mio Cid* introduced a new and rewarding perspective to the study of European epic poetry. His minute study of customs, language, geography, warfare, genealogy, dress, and jurisprudence of eleventh-century Spain in *La España de mio Cid* (*The Spain of the Cid*) achieves a level of scholarship which literary historians of other societies and other eras have sought to approach. His studies of historical grammar—of the linguistic development of Spanish from classical and vulgar Latin to modern Castilian speech—is a model for the formal study of any language in the Romance complex. His collection and study of the *romances*, anonymous short poems which are probably reworkings of earlier epic poetry, makes available a large body of popular verse of the fifteenth and sixteenth centuries, a blending of the narrative and lyrical traditions. It was Menéndez Pidal's unique preparation as a scholar which brought to Spain's historical past a lively and ebullient imagination, grounded upon the most impeccable scholarly techniques and breadth of historical investigation.

Schooled in totally different disciplines and the product of a younger generation was José Ortega y Gasset (1883–1955). Following his early studies in a Jesuit school in Málaga and his training at the University of Madrid, Ortega spent his most formative years in the German universities of Leipzig, Berlin, and Marburg. A curious mixture of Spanish humanism and German intellectual discipline resulted. Ortega's philosophical and critical work obtains an objectivity and universality which no other Spaniard of recent times has achieved. Several of his works are well known in English translation: *The Revolt of the Masses, Invertebrate Spain,* and *The Modern Theme*. Whether he is writing in the field of sociology, metaphysics, art, or literary criticism, it is always the subjective human reality which he considers. The central fact from which all philosophy begins, and to which it must always return, is individual experience. "I am myself and my surroundings," he says, with "surroundings" taken in its broadest sense of total awareness. A key phrase in his thought is the term *razón vital,* which, he explains, is one and the same thing as living, and living is "to have no recourse but to reason in the face of inexorable circumstances." Thus there are both pragmatic and existentialist sides to his thought.

Certainly Ortega is eclectic, and much of his originality is to be found in the themes he addresses and the language in which his ideas are expressed. He is a renovator of Spanish style, rather than an innovator. He gives to words, expressions, and metaphors the full meaty significance latent within them, but not normally brought forth in so forceful a manner. For this reason Ortega, in his preoccupation with language, may be seen as extending logically the interests of the Generation of '98 and the modernists. The theory of "generations" which Ortega helped to elaborate has proved useful as an effective tool in understanding historical and literary movements. A "generation" in his terms is a period of approximately fifteen years in which beliefs, points of view, and basic positions in art or in any aspect of history are generated and elaborated upon. There follows a similar period in which these new frameworks are put into effect, and in which they dominate the general scene. By the end of this period, new opinions, beliefs, and points of view will have been put forth by a new "generation." These will be established and elaborated and will enter the second phase of general acceptance. The concept of generations is one which goes far back into the history of Western thought, was revived and applied to social and cultural change by Comte, Dilthey, Ranke,

Mannheim, and many others, but reached perhaps its fullest critical elaboration with Ortega's thought.

Ortega's work is voluminous and many-faceted. He gave new form and significance to the essay, and much of his work appeared in journals and periodicals, especially in the important *Revista de Occidente*, which he founded in 1923 and supervised until 1936. Ortega was an inspiring teacher who held the chair in metaphysics at the University of Madrid. He left Spain at the outbreak of the Civil War, traveling and lecturing extensively abroad, and returning occasionally to Spain. He died in Madrid in 1955. Ortega was not strikingly original in his thought; he does not develop an original system of philosophy. Rather, he gives the Spanish language a philosophic vocabulary capable of expressing contemporary metaphysical, artistic, and sociological ideas. His training in Germany provided him with a vision of the world of human experience which he was able to express in terms understandable to the Latin ear, and with conceptual innovations which he was able to communicate to a Mediterranean public. Thus his work has an objectivity and a bloom of universality to it, while retaining a specifically Spanish sensibility.

Ortega is usually mentioned in connection with Unamuno; these two are seen by many as Spain's major philosophers of the twentieth century. They are alike in that they wrote voluminously on a variety of subjects, and in both, the basis of their thought is the human reality—the "man of flesh and bone" for Unamuno, the *razón vital* for Ortega—but the similarity ends there. Unamuno, widely read though he was in European and American literature, and universal as his themes may be, remained always immutably peninsular, rooted in the *pueblo* and the Spanish reality. Ortega seeks to Europeanize Spanish thought, to open doors to European insights, and to provide both the Spanish language and the peninsular mentality with the tools by which these insights may be grasped and expanded. Of the two, it is Unamuno who has left the greater legacy in terms of literary creation and the expression of basic human problems in dramatic, poetic and novelistic form, but Ortega who has had the greater influence in shaping contemporary Spanish thought and supplying the voice of his own "generation."

Of the same generation, and sharing the tendency to look toward Europe for intellectual fulfillment and the solution to many of Spain's problems is Salvador de Madariaga (1896–   ), professor of Spanish literature at Oxford. Madariaga, who writes equally well in English, Spanish, and French, is well known for his studies on Shelley and Calderón, for his biographies of Cortés, Columbus, and Bolívar, and for his perceptive analysis of recent social and historical phenomena in *Spain: A Modern History*.

A third figure in this generation was the physician Gregorio Marañón (1887–1960), an internationally known endocrinologist. Marañón gained literary renown equal to his scientific prestige in a series of biographical studies, including the seventeenth-century political eminence Gaspar de Guzmán, Conde-Duque de Olivares, the power behind the throne of Philip IV; the baroque artist El Greco; the humanist philosopher Luis Vives; and the mythical literary personality of Don Juan Tenorio. Marañón's approach to these subjects is a novel combination of solid historical, literary, and artistic research and well-based medical knowledge. Each study is an exhaustive case history given in depth, adding physiological and psychosomatic analysis on a highly sophisticated level to give plausible, multidimensional value to his subjects. He is the first, for example, to postulate and analyze the latent homosexuality of the Don Juan figure.

Ramón Gómez de la Serna (1888–1963) was a thoroughly versatile literary figure who wrote novels, studies of art, plays, biography, essays, and collections of his own unique invention, *greguerías*. The *greguerías* are an ingenious twisting of reality by means of language and metaphor to display something new, some unexpected facet of the world around us. "A rainbow is the ribbon that Nature puts on after she washes her hair." "The snail is constantly ascending his own staircase." "May not the secret of high tide be that somewhere, at a certain time, God goes into the sea for a swim?" It is for these aphorisms that Gómez de la Serna is most popularly known, for their arresting, mercurial quality and pithy brevity. His more serious work—although the tone of the *greguería* often creeps into other forms as well—includes important studies of El Greco and Velázquez, Lope de Vega, Oscar Wilde, and Valle-Inclán. The anecdotal quality and the lack of sustained movement in his novels and his theater make it difficult to attach real importance to either, according to present critical standards.

A number of distinguished scholars have done important work in Hispanic studies over the past three or four decades—linguistic, historical, literary, sociopolitical—and as more Europeans and Americans come to know Spain and its literary traditions, an ever greater interest is being manifested in the multiple facets of an intriguing and inexhaustible millennial culture. British and American Hispanism has been especially fruitful and prolific, and French, German, and Italian scholarship has contributed much of merit and interest. Many gifted and well-trained Spaniards have devoted their abilities to the understanding, revaluation, and dissemination of their culture. Several have been mentioned in other contexts; the names of Américo Castro, Joaquín Casalduero, Valbuena Prat, Guillermo Díaz Plaja, and Julián Marías must be added to the most minimal list of major scholars and critics who are well known in international terms.

Novel

The literary form in which Spain has been most original and prolific is without doubt the novel. From the earliest attempts in a modern European language to forge anecdotes, folklore, and apothegms into an organic whole—Don Juan Manuel's *Conde Lucanor*—to the first of the picaresque novels, *Lazarillo de Tormes*, to what has often been called the first modern novel, *Don Quijote de la Mancha*, to Galdós' magnificent re-creation and synthesis of a century of his nation's history and social experience in the *Episodios nacionales*, the novel has been the form in which Spanish literature has achieved perhaps its greatest distinction. The Generation of '98 made important contributions to, and equally important modifications in, the contemporary novel. Two of the most original writers of the group went so far as to dissociate their work entirely from the traditional label of the genre: Unamuno called his works of prose fiction *nivolas* and Valle-Inclán wrote *sonatas*. This was not mere idiosyncrasy or testiness on their part. Writers of the twentieth century were becoming aware that new directions were opening in the exploration of human experience and that a new relationship was developing both between the writer and his public and between the writer and his work. The new dimensions of poetry, represented primarily in modernism, surrealism, and all the other "-isms" brought forth in the period, were certain to have an effect in all areas of creative writing. The dominant tones of realism in Pardo Bazán and Galdós had faded rather considerably in the writers of '98, and those who followed would look for still other orientations.

Of the novelists immediately following the Generation of '98, Ramón Pérez de Ayala (1881–1962) is generally seen as the outstanding figure. As with most writers of his day, Ayala began his literary activities by publishing essays and criticism in newspapers and periodicals. His background included extensive training in both law and humanities. He was a classicist and intellectual through and through, and it is these qualities which are most striking in his novels. His work in several genres is extensive. Three volumes of poetry contain polished, semi-modernist pieces in which the influence of Rubén Darío and Machado may be clearly seen, along with those reflections of Berceo and Juan Ruiz which are typical of the movement. It is an intellectual poetry, completely in line with the aesthetic of the time and offering little of originality. An important study of the theater, *Las máscaras,* includes classical, foreign, and contemporary Spanish dramatic works seen from a standpoint which is almost invariably biased and partisan, exaggerated in one direction or another, but well written and generally interesting. It is with the novel that Ayala acquired his most enthusiastic public. These are usually divided into two groups according to length: a series of short novels of greatly varied content, and his full-length novels, which are to a certain extent autobiographical.

The short novels display a wide range of themes. One of the more typical is *Prometeo* (*Prometheus*), a thesis novel similar in theme to Unamuno's *Amor y pedagogía* but structured rather affectedly on the *Odyssey*. The protagonist, a professor of classics, comes to the conclusion that a perfect human being would be a man of both thought and action. He realizes that he lacks the capacity for action, and so sets about to seek out the perfect mate so that they may produce ideal offspring. The result is a ludicrous, ironic, even tragic, failure: a child who is subhuman in all important respects, whose short life ends in suicide. The use of mythological themes and parallels is frequent in Ayala and an anticlerical tone is usually present.

The longer novels are better known and more abundantly display Ayala's learning, prejudices, and essential inadequacy in novelistic structure. *A.M.D.G.* (*Ad majorem dei gloriam;* "To the greater glory of God," the motto of the Jesuits) is a prolonged diatribe against Church-run boarding schools, and presumably draws heavily on the author's experience, as he received a major part of his early education in a Jesuit school. Nothing of the obvious is lacking in Ayala's portrayal of a bleak and traumatizing atmosphere: fanaticism, sadism, perversion, and bumbling inadequacy of instruction. *Tinieblas en las cumbres* (*Darkness on the Peaks*) and *La pata de la raposa* (*The Fox's Paw*) revive the venerable theme of the rake/adventurer in his relations with various classes of ladies-of-the-world. These novels are almost plotless and depend heavily upon the author's style and ability to create moments of interest and literary value.

The most popular of Ayala's longer novels are *Tigre Juan* (*Tiger John*) and its sequel, *El curandero de su honra*. The latter title is a literary pun based on Calderón's *El médico de su honra*. The basic idea is that a man who has lost his husbandly honor is ill and can be cured only through a bloodletting of revenge. A *curandero,* however, is a village quack without degrees or medical qualifications. The novels thus reduce the conflict upon which Calderón built so much of his theater to the level of the village, of simple people, and occasionally to almost burlesque treatment.

In summing up Pérez de Ayala's contribution to the literature of his time, we are faced with a dilemma. His best work was produced in the decade from 1916 to 1926, a period particularly devoid of schools, trends, or ideologies in the Spanish novel. It was in 1924 that Ortega announced the death of the novel as a contemporary literary form. Certainly Ayala does little to revivify the corpse; certainly his works, either long or short, fail to measure up to the monumental production of Galdós or to the insights of Baroja. Yet his novels have style, and if they lack plot, they have movement and character. They more frequently offer carping criticism than point of view; they abandon realism of speech for an artificial perfection of style; the characters declaim rather than talk, and too frequently become caricatures. But the characters are interesting, particularly in the later novels; they have ideas and theses and even obsessions, which they can express and discuss with considerable charm, however unrealistic the dialogue may be.

As ideas dominate the novels of Pérez de Ayala, it is essentially description which intrigues and attracts the interest of another outstanding novelist who follows the Generation of '98, Gabriel Miró (1879–1930). A stylist above and beyond everything else, Miró has composed some of the finest paragraphs and pages of any prose writer of the century. Glowing, luminous, sensuous, his prose is flexible, colorful within the subtlety of its tones, but rarely affected or excessive in its own framework. Ortega, speaking of Miró's style, says, "I have read a few lines, perhaps a page, and have always been surprised at how well done it is. Nevertheless, I did not go on reading. What sort of perfection is this, that pleases but does not enthrall, which impresses but does not enchant?" One might say that Miró's prose is comparable to a painting in which every figure and every detail is perfect but which does not lead the eye from one segment to another, and from which one does not receive a total impression.

Miró's most important works have a religious orientation. *Nuestro padre San Daniel* (*Our Father St. Daniel*) and its sequel, *El obispo leproso* (*The Leprous Bishop*) are two of his major novels. His reputation rests, however, on a two-part work which is not properly a novel at all, though it is certainly novelesque: *Las figuras de la pasión del Señor* (*Figures from the Passion of the Lord*). As the title indicates, this is a series of portraits and studies, scenes and vignettes, associated with the Crucifixion. Miró brought all the skill he possessed to his depiction of the familiar figures of the Apostles and others associated with the New Testament drama, and to description of landscape, drawing on the features of his native Alicante, at the other end of the Mediterranean from the Holy Land and yet so similar in topography and color. Miró wrote with fervor, skill, and restraint, and yet he had a tendency to dialectical and archaic language, popular slang and technical terms, and items of vocabulary so rare and exotic that even the most literate Spaniard feels the need of a good dictionary from time to time in reading him. Inevitably this has made of Miró a writer for the minority. His literary qualities are generally recognized, but his work is rarely read in his own country and even more rarely translated abroad.

Among the many writers who fled Spain at one point or another during the civil war, two novelists received outstanding recognition. Ramón Sender (1901–) had acquired a solid reputation in Spain as a journalist and novelist before the outbreak of the war; he had won the National Literature Prize in 1935 with his novel *Mr. Witt en el cantón*. He fought on the Republican side during the war and was sent by that government to the U.S., where he gave a series of lectures in support of the Republican cause. Shortly after, he was sent to France as director of a pro-Republican gazette, *La voz de Madrid*. Sender, while strongly antifascist, had quarreled politically with both the anarchists and the communists, who represented the strongest "parties" on the anti-Franco side of the conflict. His personal dilemma was not unlike that of George Orwell. With the fall of Barcelona and the clear defeat of any variety of liberalism in Spain, Sender emigrated to Mexico and then to the U.S. He continues to write in exile: novels, articles, theater, and poetry, and he has taught and lectured in several American universities. His themes are generally autobiographical and social.

His longest work, *La crónica del alba* (*Chronicle of the Dawn*), consists of nine short novels written over a period of twenty-five years; they are a fictionalized treatment of his youth and adolescence. *Los cinco libros de Ariadna* (*The Five Books of Ariadna*) deals with the early years of the war and, in fictionalized form, the death of Sender's wife. *Siete domingos rojos* (*Seven Red Sundays*) concerns the attempt by a small group of activists to organize a general strike. The leaders lack the most rudimentary sense of order or of planning. They are impelled by a vague sense of revolutionary justice, but soon show themselves to be as rigid and repressive as the forces they are fighting. They are slaughtered by the police in a fairly routine action and even their funeral is a scene of disorder and factionalism. What lifts the novel above the level of mere reporting or political commentary is Sender's analysis of the psychology and impulses which lead small groups to seek political solutions in disordered violence, without thinking through the consequences of their acts, and without giving importance to the fact that they themselves will probably be the first victims of their political aggression. *Seven Red Sundays* has had considerable success in the U.S. since it was reissued in English in 1968. A similar theme lies at the center of *Requiem por un campesino español* (*Requiem for a Spanish Farm-Laborer*). Questions of personal guilt, the pragmatics of social idealism, and the meaning of humanity in such inhumane undertakings as revolution and war form a major part of Sender's preoccupations, and the autobiographic basis of most of his work is clear. His style is direct and quick, and although he was a friend of Valle-Inclán and in intellectual contact with the Generation of 1927, their esthetic and stylistic preoccupations are not to be found in Sender's work.

The expatriate who received widest international renown as a novelist of the Spanish civil war was Arturo Barea (1886–1957). *La forja de un rebelde* (*The Forging of a Rebel*) achieved best-seller status in half a dozen languages. It is autobiographical, beginning with the author's early youth in Madrid, recounting his experience during the Moroccan wars, the Civil War, and his exile. While the success of the book was extraordinary, undoubtedly owing to its timeliness and to the strong sympathies for the Spanish Republic felt abroad, it does not have the literary qualities found in Sender's work. It appeared at the most propitious moment for its theme and so was given a reception not really warranted by its artistic merits. A second novel, *La raíz rota* (*The Broken Root*) is the dispirited account of a Spaniard trying to return to his homeland and resume his old life there after a considerable period of exile. He discovers, of course, that "you can't go back" and is forced to accept the disillusionment of change. *La raíz rota* was less successful in every way than his earlier work and shows Barea to have been essentially a chronicler of events rather than a major novelist. Barea also wrote literary criticism and published a short book on Unamuno.

Another best seller on the theme of the Spanish Civil War was José María Gironella's (1917–   ) *Los cipreses creen en Dios* (*The Cypresses Believe in God*), written from a quite different point of view. Girondella had established himself as a novelist by winning the Nadal Prize for *Un hombre* (*A Man*) in 1946. *Los cipreses* is limited to events from 1931 to the outbreak of the Civil War in July of 1936 as they affect life in the provincial Catalan capital of Gerona. As ideologies become clear, as lines are drawn over which fratricidal battles will be fought, Gironella is able to give an objective yet moving and meaningful representation of the effect of political strife on lives yet remote from the center of conflict. The book was as popular in Spain as it was in translation abroad. *Los cipreses* was conceived as the first novel of a trilogy. The second part, *Un millón de muertos* (*One Million Dead*), covers the period of the war. It is certainly less successful as a novel, possibly because the events, the essentials of the experience, do not permit the necessary distance to acquire creative perspective. The third novel of the trilogy, *Ha estallado la paz* (*Peace Has Broken Out*) follows the principal characters of the first two novels in the aftermath of the war, as they regroup and try to adjust to the poverty and stagnation, disorder and reprisals in a situation where the line between victory and defeat is not always clear cut.

Camilo José Cela (1916–) made his reputation on his first novel, *La familia de Pascual Duarte* (*The Family of Pascual Duarte*), published in 1942, and has continued, in a varied and productive literary career, to occupy a major and aggressive position in Spanish letters for more than thirty-five years. *Pascual Duarte* caused a literary sensation with its focus on rural violence and brutality, its almost morbid concentration on the degrading and repulsive aspects of a life devoted to an almost mindless revolt against normal human relationships. The tone of the work was promptly given status as a trend by some critics and was baptized with the name *tremendismo*, signifying a style of realism which dwells on the gruesome detail, which magnifies the monstrous and inhuman aspects of experience.

The novel is presented as the fragmentary personal

account of a man sentenced to death for murder. He describes in scenes of great intensity the "family" which makes up the title of the novel: his bullying and drunken father, his nagging and unpleasant mother, his prostitute sister, a cretinous younger brother whose cries go unheeded as his ears and nose are nibbled off by a passing hog. A climax is reached as Pascual murders his mother, strangling her in her bed in a ferocious struggle. There is no reason or motive for the act; as in Poe's *The Tell-Tale Heart*, which the episode resembles, Pascual simply decides that the time has come to kill her, and so he goes about the task almost without emotion. It is this lack of emotion, this deadness of the spirit, that most defines Cela's *tremendismo*. It differs from the "disengaged" paralysis of feeling which we see in *L'Etranger* of Camus in that it selects the trivial gruesome detail to present a totally brutalized "reality" to the reader. The critics who saw this as an identifiable new direction were somewhat mystified by Cela's next novel.

Pabellón de reposo (*Rest Ward*) bears a superficial resemblance to Mann's *The Magic Mountain* and Maugham's *Sanatorium* in that it concerns the restricted life of victims of tuberculosis in a rest home. The tone here is very calm; nothing of *tremendismo*, of violence and brutality, of the world seen as a place of meaningless and inexplicable ferocity. Rather, under the exterior tranquillity of a way of life that is of necessity without event, we see the internal anguish and suffering of those afflicted with lingering and debilitating illness. It is a world in which hopes and anxieties must necessarily take the place of action. The author writes from experience and the insight gained is reflected in his penetration of the patients' private worlds.

In *Nuevas andanzas y desventuras de Lazarillo de Tormes* (*New Wanderings and Misfortunes of Lazarillo de Tormes*), Cela takes yet another direction. Reviving the long Spanish tradition of the picaresque ambience, he structures a novel which, while modeled on a venerable pattern, is more than an attempt to imitate the genre. In first-person narration, the new Lazarillo tells of his travels and adventures and describes the people he encounters in his life of wandering and beggary. Much of the interest of the book, as is the case with its sixteenth-century prototype, is found in the description of these marginal figures, which Cela creates with impressive artistry. Finally, Lazarillo sums up the lesson of his experience: "I was now a man, and fear, hunger, and calamity had been my only school." He reflects on "those happy mortals who are born, live, and die without having moved three leagues from the boundaries of their *pueblo*, and I thought, God knows with what anguish, what happiness it would be for me to stop and live out my days in the first houses I ran across. Why Providence would not permit it is something I do not understand; perhaps my flesh was marked with a sign which would not permit it to stop going and going, without sense or reason, from one place to another." Lazarillo then uses the metaphor of the rolling stone, which must look with nostalgia and envy on the moss-covered rocks that retain the pasture land.

Cela's first extended and really ambitious novel was *La colmena* (*The Hive*), published in 1951. Its setting is post-Civil War Madrid in its poverty and isolation. Cela does not revive the inhuman note of his earlier *tremendismo*, but nonetheless concentrates on a series of lives which are bleak or sordid or pointless, according to their circumstances. The title is perfectly indicative of the character of the work: the author takes the top off the human beehive of Madrid and shows us the swarming mass, involved in day to day activities. He uses a large number of characters—someone has counted 160— to show us the "mass man" of Ortega in action. The novel has no central theme, no plot, no direction, and no heroes. Yet there is movement, the feel of a city, excitement, and a range of emotion as broad as the number of "protagonists," a cross section of the lower middle class in postwar Madrid. Cela has a sharp ear for language and a penetrating eye for detail. The shortcoming of the novel is common to most works of this sub-genre: it tends to disintegrate and to become a series of short stories and vignettes more or less interwoven by chance, proximity, and superficialities. But Cela has given us a true picture—certainly the details are artistically true—of the life of the city at that time, and the lack of structure, the swarming, buzzing confusion, are a necessary part of the presentation of Cela's particular vision.

San Camilo, 1936, published in 1970, returns almost obsessively to the outbreak of the Civil War. The point of view is again panoramic; while *La colmena* has its center of action in a popular café, *San Camilo, 1936* sees events of the earlier period almost exclusively from Madrid's houses of prostitution. The intentional crudity of language and characterization is what one might expect of the chosen environment. This novel, like *La colmena*, is a pastiche of characters and intertwined situations, using clippings from newspapers and the texts of radio broadcasts to give momentum and a sense of immediacy to the narrative.

Cela is among the most prolific and original of contemporary Spanish writers. His work includes two volumes of poetry, the excellent *Viaje a la Alcarria*, among other descriptions of his travels in Spain, four collections of short stories and novelettes, a novel based on his travel to Venezuela, and collected essays and literary criticism. He is the editor of an important literary review, *Papeles de Son Armadans*. He is a gifted and impressive speaker who has lectured in many parts of the United States and Latin America. Cela has been accused of being his own best literary creation and, whether calculated or not, he is an effective self-propagandist. Of the novelists to emerge in the period since the Civil War, he is among the most read, the most discussed, and the most controversial. He is also among the most skilled, varied, and creative of his contemporaries.

The immediate and clamorous success of Carmen Laforet's first novel, *Nada* (*Nothing*), resembles in more than a superficial way the effect which *Pascual Duarte* achieved. A new direction in the Spanish novel was being announced by an unknown young author of clear and obvious talent. *Nada* is a novel of spiritual desolation with touches of a *tremendismo* that is more subtle and more sensitive than Cela's rather bludgeoning early style. Laforet (1921–   ) centers the novel on the experiences of a sensitive and lonely girl attending the University of Barcelona while living in a repulsive and neurotic environment, the ugly and forlorn apartment of distant relatives. None of the family is quite sane. They live in a masochistic symbiosis wherein their main purpose is to goad and torture each other. Andrea seeks refuge in the company of other students, but finds no substance and no solace there. The "nothing" of the title is the "being and nothingness" of Sartre, the vision of the abyss of Unamuno, the feeling of being flung into a a totally meaningless and alien world without values or constants. The existentialist qualities of "nausea" and "sickness unto death" are apparent in both Cela and Laforet, but in the latter there is greater personal awareness of the surrounding vacuum; in the former, perhaps a more inarticulate but vital communication to the reader. However great the temptation to compare *Nada* with Cela's *Pascual Duarte,* there are important differences: the style of narration, the urban against rural setting, the activism of Pascual, who initiates violence and provokes discord, against the passive sensitivity of Andrea and the more subtle, feminine insight into character and circumstance.

A period of some seven years went by before Carmen Laforet published another important work, and some critics could not resist the jibe, "*Después de* Nada, *nada* (After *Nothing*, nothing)." Even this cynicism, however, points up the importance of the work and the promise it showed. Her next novel, *La isla y los demonios* (*The Island and the Devils*) appeared in 1952 and had a rather mixed reception. While structurally and formally more impressive than *Nada*, it lacks the sharpness, the sense of encounter, of the previous novel. There is a misty, poetical, vague quality present throughout the work in scenes, characters, and descriptions which, in combination, make it a work of soft focus and minor tone.

These two novels have more than an obvious correlation to her own life. Born in Barcelona, she grew up in the Canary Islands. She returned to Barcelona at the age of eighteen, where she attended university classes. Before writing *La isla*, she visited the Canaries again, the setting of the novel, to refresh her impressions. *La mujer nueva* (*The New Woman*), her third novel, concerns the religious conversion of an adulterous wife, symbolically named Paulina. The novel penetrates deeply into the psychology of faith, with excellent delineations of character. Her technical skill grows visibly in each successive work, but it is only in *Nada* that Laforet has done something truly arresting and original. She has also published a number of interesting and sensitive short stories and vignettes.

The tone of emptiness and disillusion that permeates *Nada* is also found in the novels of Miguel Delibes (1920–   ), who won the Nadal prize for 1947 with *La sombre del ciprés es alargada* (*The Cypress's Shadow Is Long*). The setting of the novel is Avila, a provincial city walled in physically by the feudal bulwarks which are its most distinctive feature, and walled in psychologically by its poverty and isolation. The cypress casts its long shadow in the cemetery, and this becomes the dominant theme of the work. It is a pessimistic and chilling novel, finely written, with a love for detail and description. *El camino* (*The Road*) is set in the mountainous region of the north of Spain. An adolescent boy reaches the age to leave his home and his village to go off to school. The novel concerns his tension at leaving the beloved but rather boring scenes of his childhood to go off into a larger world that is both threatening and promising. Delibes' most powerful novel, and really a tour de force, is *Cinco horas con Mario* (*Five Hours with Mario*). In interior monologue, or stream of consciousness, a widow sits beside the body of her husband in a funeral parlor and reflects on their life together—the bitter, the tedious, the joyous. In terms of European fiction of the past two or three decades, Delibes offers nothing really unusual in technique or literary innovation. He writes well and sensitively, but leaves us with a feeling that not much has taken place in his novels.

As if announcing the emergence of a new literary force and perspective in the Spanish novel, a number of young female writers began to publish novels of significance within a few years after the appearance of *Nada*. Two of the most productive and skilled are Ana María Matute and Elena Quiroga.

Ana María Matute (1926–) brings a deep sensitivity and a sort of gentle nostalgia to scenes of childhood and rural life. Among her major novels are several which have won important Spanish literary prizes: *Fiesta al Noroeste* (*Fiesta in the Northwest*), *Pequeño teatro* (*Little Theater*). *Los hijos muertos* (*The Dead Children*) won the National Prize for Literature, and *Primera memoria* (*Earliest Memories*) was awarded the Nadal prize in 1960. This novel formed the first part of a trilogy, followed by *Los soldados lloran de noche* (*Soldiers Cry by Night*), 1964, and *La trampa* (*The Trap*), 1969. The trilogy, under the title *Los mercaderes* (*The Dealers*), deals with the impact of the Civil War on children who are far from the actual conflict, living in the Balearic Islands. Despite the safety and remoteness of the location, the corruption and factionalism of the war spreads its contagion, and the children, only indirectly aware of the roots and issues, are compromised, victims of lies and propaganda, and victimizers of each other. With the trilogy, Matute fulfills her early promise as a major novelist and brings yet another human dimension to the literature of this rending and deforming social calamity.

Elena Quiroga (1921–) represents rather contrasting currents in her novels. Her earlier work, including the Nadal prize novel *Viento del norte* (*North Wind*), is an updated and personal version of the naturalism developed by Pardo Bazán. *La sangre* (*Blood*) is a tour de force in which the narrator is a venerable chestnut tree, omniscient witness to scenes and events which have taken place in its presence. A second phase displays more sophisticated and modern novelistic techniques; it includes the work which is probably her best novel, *Algo pasa en la calle* (*Something Is Happening in the Street*). This work reminds us somewhat of early Joyce; brought together by the death of a professor, figures from his past life converge and interact to reconstruct his personality and to reveal their own. Quiroga is an experimental novelist, sensitive, imaginative, who seeks constantly to find new tools of expression. The risk she runs, and does not consistently escape, is that of falling into the use of gimmicks and the traps her own inventiveness create.

There is an extensive body of critical literature in Spanish devoted to the novel of the war years and the social consequences of the civil conflict. It is not a wild exaggeration to say that the Civil War gives a special cast to all serious literature written in Spain since 1940. The social upheaval caused enormous literary trauma which still has not subsided, possibly because the regime which followed the war made no attempt to conciliate the factions, but actively exacerbated the rancor and maladjustment of a severely shocked and crippled nation. Postwar conditions of unemployment and depression, isolation during the reconstruction and boom of post-World War II European economies, massive emigration for political or economic reasons, censorship of foreign news and all public forms of expression, created an atmosphere in which low-key novels of day-to-day existence were the most prevalent fare.

El Jarama—the name of a river which flows past Madrid—is an unusual and very successful experiment by Rafael Sánchez Ferlosio (1927–). It is basically a phonographic novel, almost all aimless conversation among a group of young working-class adults who come on bicycles from Madrid for a Sunday picnic on the river bank. The interchanges are completely banal and natural; the talk of sensible but unremarkable twenty-year-olds who make their living by long hours of work in garages and restaurants. There is horseplay, joking, sulking, and one of the boys gets a bit high on wine. A central event takes place: one of the picnickers is drowned. But this accident is not really plot—there is no plot. While the group is deeply affected, nothing is changed in the total situation. The novel simply captures and sustains the drabness of the moment in the lives of a generation which has grown up in urban poverty and is content with very small joys in a life of monotonous daily breadwinning.

Juan Goytisolo (1931–) is one of the major voices in Spanish literature at the present time. His earliest novels dealt with the same sort of material that we find in Matute's *Primero memoria*. *Juegos de manos* (translated as *The Young Assassins*) and *Duelo en el paraíso* (translated as *Children of Chaos*) explore the brutalizing effect of the war on children. The latter novel, which bears a resemblance to Golding's *Lord of the Flies*, is set in a school for refugee children in a small Catalan village. The children are accustomed to the sight of strafed or executed soldiers and civilians along the roads, and they despoil the corpses as a matter of course. Their play begins to imitate the adult world of summary wartime justice in tones which become ever more realistic. The school is finally converted by the children into "a true reign of terror, with its chiefs, lieutenants, spies, and informers. At night the dormitory becomes a den of serpents and leopards, a regular torture cell."

He creates an adult world of similar nihilism in novels which follow, *Fiestas* and *La isla* (*The Island*). He sees Spain as a nation of tense surface order and inner decay, isolated and bereft of spirit and morale. His people are perverts, idlers, dreamers, brutes, and sadists; all are victims and losers in a sick society. The disheartening contrasts between the gaudy wealth of the upper classes and the tourists who come to Spain because it is "cheap," and the grinding, hopeless poverty of the underdogs are brought forth in *tremendista* detail. Criticism of the regime is clearly implied in his depiction of a society that lives in its own filth, broken in spirit and incapable of protest except in isolated acts of pointless and perverse violence. In this period, Goytisolo is a sort of "angry young man" of the Spanish novel, writing in the tradition of Baroja, from bases in Paris and North Africa, and publishing his work outside Spain.

The novel of plot and social commentary, anecdote, and almost documentary treatment of lives and psyches bruised, maimed, and deformed by the consequences of the war gives way to a novel of more sophisticated literary style in the middle and late sixties. Juan Goytisolo is among the first to break with the simplistic realism and *tremendista* currents which dominated the Spanish narrative in the forties and fifties. He becomes interested in avant-guard linguistic and structural theory, and this interest is put to work in a collection of critical essays in *Furgón de cola* (*Wagon Train*). In his recent novels *Señas de identidad* (*Marks of Identity*) and *La reivindicación del conde don Julián* (*Count Julian*) the narrative content is greatly reduced in favor of a density of style and a depth of analysis of character and situation. *Señas de identidad* is the search for personal identity of a Spanish exile among the objects of his life, a search for objective proof that he has lived. *Count Julian* is another search-for-self, set in North Africa. It reaffirms the Moorish presence as a social, historical, and vital influence in the culture of Spain and the life of the present-day Spaniard. The title refers to the medieval tradition that Count Julian avenged the rape of his daughter by allowing the Moors to conquer the Visigothic kingdom in 711 A.D. The style of these recent novels is increasingly complex: Punctuation is suppressed, sentences and paragraphs run on for pages, and narration is mixed with introspection, dialogue with reflection and description, to a point where reading is far from a passive and relaxing experience. Goytisolo is a cosmopolite intellectual who has proven his ability as a novelist, and is now attempting something more complex than creating characters and telling stories about them. It is an open question whether this intentional densification of his style, to the sacrifice of clarity in action, statement, and plot, is an esthetic gain.

There is a similarity of stylistic preoccupation in Juan Benet's *Volverás a Región* (*You Will Return to Región*). Benet is a civil engineer by profession, who brings a level-headed cartographer's mind to a treatment of land, rivers, hills, and the passions of the people who inhabit them. Yet his best-known novel is a complex, antilogical treatment of a *pueblo* still mutilated by Civil War factionalism and anxieties. Here too we find the convoluted, endless paragraphs and prose that is dense, yet sinuous, taken in small chunks, reflected on, and slowly digested. There is plot, but the plot is mysterious, often jumbled, and its development is impeded by the author's need to digress and embellish.

Luis Martín-Santos published one novel before his early death in an automobile accident in 1964 which proved to be a landmark in the renovation of Spànish prose style of the mid-sixties. He was a psychiatrist who also possessed a strong background in philosophy, well established in his field with books on existentialist approaches to psychoanalysis. His novel *Tiempo de silencio* (*Time of Silence*) concerns a young medical researcher struggling to complete his work on the formation of cancerous cells in laboratory rats, with inadequate funds and equipment in 1949. He is a pleasant, idealistic loser who becomes involved with Madrid slum dwellers in his search for a special breed of rats to continue his experiments. Arrested and accused of participation in a clumsy and fatal abortion, he is cleared and released, but the unsavory publicity has ended his already dubious research career. This might have been another bleak social novel of postwar Madrid, but the style and language, humor, irony, and pace of the work lift it far above the general current of the period. The novel was an immediate success and was soon translated into English, French, German, and Italian.

The reading public for new Spanish novels, in decline from the twenties through the mid-forties, has steadily increased since that time in Spain, Latin America,

Europe, and the United States. Contributing to this vitality was the establishment of a number of literary prizes, national, regional, and private, and the growth of publishing houses able to sponsor the work of young and unknown authors. The gradual lessening of the stranglehold of political censorship was also a great factor in releasing the spirit and enhancing the quality of the Spanish novel. When Angel María de Lera won the Planeta prize in 1967 for his novel *Las ultimas banderas* (*The Last Flags*) and began signing copies in bookstores in Madrid, it was clear that the iron restraint which had retarded Spanish literary development since 1940 was waning. The novel is not remarkable except in context; it deals with Republican soldiers who make a last stand in Madrid as the Franco forces close in to establish their victory in the Spanish capital. The story is told honestly and objectively, without judgment or propagandistic overtones, but it certainly could not have been published in Spain a decade earlier.

The Spanish novelist today feels that he has a voice and a receptive audience, that he is free to write as he pleases, and that he can project his vision beyond the limitations of the moment and of his own small group to a world of readers of Spanish—and even beyond that, through translation abroad. There is good hope that an increasing stimulus of this sort will give renewed impetus and universality to the language and mentality that has produced enormous monuments in the genre.

Summary

The work of the Generation of 1898 and the derivations from Modernism dominated the first quarter of the twentieth century. A group of university-oriented poets and critics, forming the Generation of 1927, continues the search for "pure" poetry in primarily intellectual directions. Their revival of interest in the baroque poet Luis de Góngora and a reinterpretation of his esthetic open new areas of poetic expression, as do post-World War I movements in the "epoch of the -isms." The outstanding figure in both poetry and theater up to the outbreak of the Civil War is Federico García Lorca. His poetry and plays combine classical, folklore, and surrealist elements to produce tragedy, farce, and a major body of lyric poetry. The Civil War and its aftermath of censorship and repression had a paralyzing effect in all genres. Many intellectuals and creative writers left Spain as a result, and continued to write, lecture, and teach in exile. The theater experienced a severe decline. From the last plays of Lorca in the middle thirties to the present time there have been no significant innovations and no outstanding playwrights have appeared, although a number of competent writers have kept the theaters alight with historical drama, situation pieces, and light farces.

Philosophy, the essay, and literary criticism have flourished. The work of José Ortega y Gasset has been widely translated and is generally familiar to European and American readers. Medieval studies have made important advances through the work of Ramón Menéndez Pidal. The Spanish exiles have played an important role in presenting the culture and literature of Spain abroad—Américo Castro in the United States, Salvador Madariaga in England, and a host of illustrious *émigrés* throughout Europe and the Americas in a twentieth century diaspora of very considerable dimensions. In reciprocity, Hispanic studies abroad have achieved great vitality, with excellent critical studies on all periods and in all genres, and the establishment of innumerable literary and linguistic reviews.

The novel underwent a general decline in the period

from World War I to the middle forties. From that time it has grown very considerably in importance, scope, and originality. One of the foremost figures in this regeneration is Camilo José Cela, whose first novel initiated a school of *tremendismo*, a style of realism with an existentialist cast. While this has been perhaps the most widely discussed movement in recent criticism, more traditional lines have been followed as well, such as the regional, historical, and—especially—the social novel. The latter takes on sombre and realistic tones in the fifties to describe an impoverished and stagnant post war milieu. Spain begins to emerge from its economic depression in the sixties and, in a society becoming gradually more open, the novel assumes more experimental tones, seeking a renovation in individual style and innovative techniques of narration.

SELECTED BIBLIOGRAPHY OF WORKS IN ENGLISH

General Bibliographies

Newmark, Maxim. *Dictionary of Spanish Literature.* New York: 1956.

O'Brien, Robert. *Spanish Plays in English Translation: An Annotated Bibliography.* New York: 1963.

Pane, Remigio U. *English Translations from the Spanish, 1484–1943.* New Brunswick: 1944.

Rudder, Robert S. *The Literature of Spain in English Translation.* New York: 1975.

History of Spain and Spanish Civilization

Adams, Nicholson B. *The Heritage of Spain: An Introduction to Its Civilization.* New York: 1943.

Brenan, Gerald. *The Spanish Labyrinth.* Cambridge: 1950. Repr. 1960.

Castro, Américo. *The Structure of Spanish History.* Trans. Edmund King. Princeton: 1954.

Livermore, Harold. *A History of Spain.* New York: 1960.

Madariaga, Salvador. *Spain: A Modern History.* New York: 1958.

Menéndez Pidal, Ramón. *The Spaniards in Their History.* Trans. Walter Starkie. London: 1950.

Peers, E. Allison, ed. *Spain: A Companion to Spanish Studies.* New York: 1929. Rev. by R. F. Brown, 1956.

Histories of Spanish Literature

Adams, N.B. and Keller, J.E. *A Brief Survey of Spanish Literature.* Paterson: 1960.
Bell, Aubrey F. G. *Castilian Literature.* Oxford: 1938. Repr. 1968.
Brenan, Gerald. *The Literature of the Spanish People.* Cambridge: 1953. Repr. 1957.
Chandler, Richard E. and Schwartz, Kessel. *A New History of Spanish Literature.* Baton Rougue: 1961.
Northup, George T. *An Introduction to Spanish Literature.* Rev. by N. B. Adams. Chicago: 1960. Repr. 1965.
Peers, E. Allison. *A Short History of the Romantic Movement in Spain.* Liverpool: 1949.

Anthologies and Collections

Bentley, Eric, ed. *The Classic Theater,* Vol. III. *Six Spanish Plays.* New York: 1959.
Cohen, J. M., ed. *The Penguin Book of Spanish Verse.* Baltimore: 1962.
Corrigan, R. W., ed. *Masterpieces of the Modern Spanish Theater.* New York: 1967.
Fitzmaurice-Kelly, James and Trend, J. B. *The Oxford Book of Spanish Verse.* Oxford: 1940.
Flores, Angel, ed. *An Anthology of Spanish Poetry from Garcilaso to García Lorca.* New York: 1961.
———. *Great Spanish Stories.* New York: 1956.
———. *Great Spanish Short Stories.* New York: 1962.
———. *Spanish Drama.* New York: 1962.
Jones, Willis Knapp, ed. *Spanish One-Act Plays in English: A Comprehensive Anthology of Spanish Drama from the Twelfth Century to the Present.* Dallas: 1934.
O'Brien, Robert, ed. *Early Spanish Plays.* New York: 1964.
———. *The Genius of the Spanish Theater.* New York: 1964.
———. *Spanish Plays of the Nineteenth Century.* New York: 1964.

Pattison, Walter T. *Representative Spanish Authors.* New York: 1958.
Peers, E. Allison. *A Critical Anthology of Spanish Verse.* London: 1948.
Resnick, Seymour and Parmentier, Jeanne. *An Anthology of Spanish Literature in Translation.* New York: 1958.
Starkie, Walter, ed. and trans. *Eight Spanish Plays of the Golden Age.* New York: 1964.
Turnbull, Eleanor L., ed. and trans. *Contemporary Spanish Poetry: Selections from Ten Poets.* Baltimore: 1945.
———. *Ten Centuries of Spanish Poetry.* Baltimore: 1955.
Walsh, Thomas. *Hispanic Anthology.* Repr. 1969.

Critical Works

Bell, Aubrey F. G. *Luis de León: A Study of the Spanish Renaissance.* Oxford: 1925.
Cook, J. A. *Neo-Classic Drama in Spain.* Dallas: 1959.
Crawford, J. P. W. *Spanish Drama Before Lope de Vega.* Philadelphia: 1937.
———. *The Spanish Pastoral Drama.* Philadelphia: 1938.
Eoff, Sherman. *The Modern Spanish Novel.* New York: 1961.
———. *The Novels of Pérez Galdós.* Saint Louis: 1954.
Ferrater Mora, Jose. *Unamuno: A Philosophy of Tragedy.* Berkeley: 1962.
Gilman, Stephen. *The Art of La Celestina.* Madison: 1956.
———. *The Spain of Fernando de Rojas.* Princeton: 1972.
Green, Otis H. *Spain and the Western Tradition.* Madison: 1963–66.
Holt, Marion P. *The Contemporary Spanish Theater.* Boston: 1975.
Honig, Edwin. *García Lorca.* Connecticut: 1962.
Ilie, Paul. *The Surrealist Mode in Spanish Literature.* Michigan: 1968.
Kane, E. K. *Gongorism and the Golden Age.* Chapel Hill: 1928.
Lida de Malkiel, María Rosa. *Two Spanish Masterpieces: The Book of Good Love and the Celestina.* Urbana: 1961.

Nichols, M. A. *A Study of the Golden Age.* London: 1954.
Parker, A. A. *The Approach to the Spanish Drama of the Golden Age.* London: 1957.
———. *Literature and the Delinquent. The Picaresque Novel in Spain and Europe, 1599–1753.* Edinburgh: 1967.
Peers, E. Allison. *Spirit of Flame. A Study of St. John of the Cross.* London: 1945.
———. *Studies on the Spanish Mystics.* London: 1927–30.
Salinas, Pedro. *Reality and the Poet in Spanish Poetry.* Trans. Edith F. Helman. Baltimore: 1940.
Wellwarth, George E. *Spanish Underground Drama.* Philadelphia: 1972.
———. *The New Wave Spanish Drama.* New York: 1970.
Young, Howard T. *The Victorious Expression: A Study of Four Contemporary Spanish Poets: Unamuno, Machado, Jiménez and Lorca.* Madison: 1965.

Translations of Specific Works and Authors

Alercón, Pedro Antonio de. *The Three-Cornered Hat.* Trans. Harriet de Onís. New York: 1958.
Anonymous:
  Lazarillo de Tormes. Trans. Harriet de Onís. New York: 1959.
  Poem of the Cid. Trans. L. B. Simpson. Berkeley: 1957.
  Poem of the Cid. Trans. W. S. Merwin. New York: 1962.
Barea, Arturo. *The Broken Root.* Trans. Ilsa Barea. New York: 1951.
Baroja, Pio. *The Restlessness of Shanti Andía.* Trans. Anthony Kerrigan. Ann Arbor: 1959.
Blasco Ibañez, Vicente. *Blood and Sand.* Trans. Frances Partridge. New York: 1958.
———. *Reeds and Mud.* Trans. Lester Beberfall. Boston: 1966.
Böhl de Faber, Cecilia ("Fernán Caballero"). *The Sea Gull.* Trans. Joan MacLean. New York: 1965.
Calderón de la Barca, Pedro. *Life Is a Dream.* Trans. William E. Colford. New York: 1958.

———. *The Mayor of Zalamea*. Trans. William E. Colford. New York: 1959.
———. *Four Plays*. Trans. Edwin Honig. New York: 1961.
Cela, Camilo José. *The Family of Pascual Duarte*. Trans. Anthony Kerrigan. Boston: 1964.
———. *The Hive*. Trans. J. M. Cohen, with Arturo Barea. New York: 1953.
———. *Journey to the Alcarria*. Trans. Frances M. López Morillas. Madison: 1964.
Cervantes, Miguel de. *The Deceitful Marriage and Other Exemplary Novels*. Trans. Walter Starkie. Chicago: 1963.
———. *Don Quijote (The Portable Cervantes)*. Trans. Samuel Putnam. New York: 1962.
———. *Interludes*. Trans. Edwin Honig. Chicago: 1964.
———. *Six Exemplary Novels*. Trans. Harriet de Onís. New York: 1961.
Fernández Moratín, Leandro. *The Maiden's Consent*. Trans. Harriet de Onís. New York: 1963.
Ganivet, Angel. *Spain: An Interpretation (Idearium español)*. Trans. J. R. Carey. London: 1964.
García Lorca, Federico. *Selected Poems*. Trans. Francisco García Lorca and Donald M. Allen. Norfolk: 1955. Repr. 1961.
———. *The Poet in New York and Other Poems*. Trans. Ben Belitt. New York: 1955.
———. *Three Tragedies*. Trans. O'Connell and Graham-Luján. New York: 1947.
Gironella, José María. *The Cypresses Believe in God*. Trans. Harriet de Onís. New York: 1955.
———. *The Million Dead*. Trans. Joan MacLean. New York: 1963.
———. *Peace After War (Ha estallado la paz)*. Trans. Joan MacLean. New York: 1969.
Goytisolo, Juan. *Children of Chaos (Duelo en la paraíso)*. Trans. Christine Brook-Rose. London: 1958.
———. *The Young Assassins (Juegos de Manos)*. Trans. John Rust. New York: 1959.
———. *Fiestas*. Trans. Herbert Weinstock. New York: 1960.

———. *Island of Women*. Trans. José Iglesias. New York: 1962.
———. *Marks of Identity*. Trans. Gregory Rabassa. New York: 1969.
Jiménez, Juan Ramón. *Platero and I*. Trans. William H. and Mary M. Roberts. New York: 1960.
———. *Three Hundred Poems*. Trans. Eloise Roach. Austin: 1962.
Laforet, Carmen *Nada*. Trans. Inez Muñoz. London: 1961.
Lera, Angel María de. *The Horns of Fear*. Trans. Ilsa Barea. New York: 1961.
Lope de Vega, Félix. *Five Plays*. Trans. Jill Booty. New York: 1961.
Machado, Antonio. *Eighty Poems*. Trans. W. Barnstone. New York: 1959.
Martín-Santos, Luis. *Time of Silence*. Trans. G. Leeson. New York: 1964.
Matute, Ana María *The Lost Children (Los hijos muertos)*. Trans. Joan MacLean. New York: 1968.
———. *School of Sun (Primera Memoria)*. Trans. E. Kerrigan. New York: 1963.
Ortega y Gasset, José. *The Dehumanization of Art and Notes on the Novel*. Trans. Helen Weyl. Princeton: 1948.
———. *Invertebrate Spain*. Trans. Mildred Adams. New York: 1937.
———. *The Modern Theme (El tema de nuestro tiempo)*. Trans. James Cleugh. New York: 1933. Repr. 1961.
———. *The Revolt of the Masses*. Trans. anonymous. New York: 1932. Repr. 1950.
Palacio Valdés, Armando. *José*. Trans. Harriet de Onís. New York: 1961.
Pérez de Ayala, Ramón. *Tiger Juan*. Trans. Walter Starkie. New York: 1933.
Pérez Galdós, Benito. *Doña Perfecta*. Trans. Harriet de Onís. New York: 1961.
———. *Compassion (Misericordia)*. Trans. Harriet de Onís. New York: 1960.
———. *Miau*. Trans. J. M. Cohen. Philadelphia: 1965. Repr. 1966.

Rojas, Fernando de. *The Celestina.* Trans. L. B. Simpson. Berkeley: 1959.
———. *Celestina.* Trans. Mack Hendricks Singleton. Madison: 1962.
Salinas, Pedro. *Lost Angel and Other Poems.* Trans. Eleanor Turnbull. Baltimore: 1938.
San Juan de la Cruz. *The Poems.* Trans. Willis Barnstone. Bloomington, Indiana: 1968.
Sánchez Ferlosio, Rafael. *The One Day of the Week (El Jamara).* Trans. J. M. Cohen. New York: 1962.
Sender, Ramon. *Dark Wedding (Epitalamio del prieto Trinidad).* Trans. Eleanor Clark. New York: 1943.
———. *Seven Red Sundays.* Trans. Sir Peter Chalmers Mitchell. New York: 1936. Repr. 1968.
———. *Requiem for a Spanish Peasant.* Trans. Elinor Randall. New York: 1960.
Unamuno, Miguel de. *Abel Sánchez and Other Stories.* Trans. Anthony Kerrigan. Chicago: 1956.
———. *The Agony of Christianity.* Trans. Kurt F. Reinhardt.
———. *The Life of Don Quixote and Sancho.* Trans. Homer P. Earle. New York: 1927.
———. *Three Exemplary Novels.* Trans. Angel Flores. New York: 1956.
———. *The Tragic Sense of Life in Men and Peoples.* Trans. J. P. Crawford Flitch. New York: 1921.
Valera, Juan. *Pepita Jiménez.* Trans. Harriet de Onís. New York: 1964.
Valle-Inclán, Ramón del. *The Pleasant Memoirs of the Marquis of Bradomín: Four Sonatas.* Trans. M. H. Broun and Thomas Walsh. New York: 1924.
———. *The Tyrant, A Novel of Warm Lands.* Trans. Margarita Pavitt. New York: 1929.

INDEX

Abel Sánchez, 175, 177
Aben Humeya, 136
Abdu'r-Rahman III, 9, 26
Abuelo, El, 160
Academies, 115, 118, 124, 126, 127
Acción española, 179
Aesop, 46
Agudeza y arte de ingenio, 88
Aguja de navegar cultos, 90
Alarcón, Pedro de, 155–56
Alas, Leopoldo ("Clarín"), 151, 154–55
Alberti, Rafael, 211–12, 221
Alcalá Yáñez, Jerónimo de, 83
Alcalde de Zalamea, El, 111
Al combate de Trafalgar, 129
Alegría del capitán Ribot, La, 151
Aleixandre, Vicente, 206–08, 218
Alemán, Mateo, 81–82
Alfonso X, "the Wise," 27, 39–41, 46, 51
Algo pasa en la calle, 254
Aljamiado, 18
Allegory, 39, 42–43, 46, 55, 61, 67, 68–69
Al margen de los clásicos, 164
Almohades, 12, 29

Almorávides, 11–12
Alonso, Dámaso, 205–06, 210
Altamira, 2
Alvarez Quintero, Serafín and Joaquín, 185
Amadís de Gaula, 63–64, 72
Amantes de Teruel, Los, 137
Amaya, o los vascos en el siglo VIII, 149
A.M.D.G., 242
Amor y pedagogía, 175
Ana Klieber, 231
Andalusia, 5, 6, 7, 9–13, 151, 185, 194, 197–98, 216–17
Andanzas y visiones españolas, 175
Andersen, Hans Christian, 50
Anticlericalism, 43–44, 80
Antonio Azorín, 164
Arabic
  language, 17–18, 19, 21
  literature, 18, 26–29, 30 31, 41, 68, 80, 115
Arbol de la ciencia, El, 169–70
Arcadia, 78
Aristotle, 28, 71
Arjona, Manuel María de, 121
Arniches, Carlos, 185
Arrabal, Fernando, 254

Arte nuevo de hacer comedias, El, 105
Así que pasen cinco años, 217
Authority, Liberty and Function, 180
Auto, 64–66, 92, 103, 108–9, 112, 124
Auto de los Reyes Magos, 64–65
Auto del Repelón, 66
Averroës, 28–29, 30
Avicebrón, 29
"Azorín" (Martínez Ruiz), 164–65, 166, 168, 169, 179, 180, 184, 199
Azul, 188

Baena, Juan Alfonso de, 55, 72
Barea, Arturo, 246
Baroja, Pío, 166, 168–71, 179, 180, 184, 199, 243
Baroque, 87, 89–90, 92, 108
Basques, 2
  language, 13–14
Barraca, La, 157
Baudelaire, 187
Bécquer, Gustavo Adolfo, 144–45, 146
Benavente, Jacinto, 166, 180–84, 199, 222
Benet, Juan, 257–58
Berbers, 8, 9, 11
Berceo, Gonzalo de, 37–39, 40, 41, 45, 46, 50, 138, 187
Biography, 62, 72, 238–39
Blasco Ibáñez, Vicente, 156–57
Bleiberg, Germán, 218

Blood and Sand, 156
Boccaccio, 48, 49, 72
Bodas de sangre, 214, 217
Böhl de Faber, Cecelia ("Fernán Caballero"), 149–50
Boileau-Despréaux, Nicolas, 118
Book of Religious and Philosophical Sects, 28
Boscán, Juan, 75, 78
Bossuet, 96
Bousoño, Carlos, 221
Bretón de los Herreros, Manuel, 130–31
Bride of Lammermoor, 149
Buero Vallejo, Antonio, 226–29, 232, 234
Burlador de Sevilla, El, 106–8
Buscón, El (*Historia de la vida del Buscón...*), 84–85
Byron, 108, 129, 175
Byzantine Empire, 7, 25

Caballero Cifar, El, 63
Caballero de Olmedo, El, 104–5
Cadalso, José, 119
Cádiz, 3, 30
Café-theatre, 233
Cain, 175
Calderón de la Barca, Pedro, 67, 99, 108–12, 113, 137, 242
Calila y Dimna, 41, 49, 51
Calvo Sotelo, Joaquín, 232
Camino, El, 253
Camino de perfección, El, 93
Campoamor, Ramón de, 145–46, 187

INDEX

Camus, Albert, 248
Cañas y barro, 157
Canción de Cuna (Cradle Song), 185–86
Cancionero, 55, 72
Canciones, 213
Canciones de tierras altas, 194
Candide, 114
Cantares de Gesta, 31–37, 38, 41, 50, 52–53, 73
Cántico, 205
Cántico espiritual, 94–95
Cantigas, 27, 39–40, 46, 51
Canto a Teresa, 142–43
Canto errante, El, 192
Cantos de vida y esperanza, 191, 192
Carcel de amor, La, 68–69
Cármenes de Granada, Los, 151
Cartas eruditas y curiosas, 122
Cartas marruecas, 119
Carthage, 3–4, 13, 15, 21, 30
Casa de Bernarda Alba, La, 214–15
Casalduero, Joaquín, 239
Casona, Alejandro, 224–26
Castiglione, 75
Castillo interior o las moradas, El, 93
Castillo Solórzano, 83
Castro, Américo, 239, 260
Cela, Camilo José, 247–50, 251, 261
Celaya, Gabriel, 261
Celestina, La (Tragicomedia de Calisto y Melibea), 69–72, 73, 77, 80, 83 113, 138
Celtiberian culture, 2
Celts, 2, 4, 5, 14–15
Cenicienta, La, 184
Cervantes Saavedra, Miguel de, 48, 64, 77, 78, 97–102, 151, 152, 156, 159, 162, 174, 175
Charlemagne, 53
Cicero, 88
Cigarrales de Toledo, Los, 108
Cinco horas con Mario, 253
Cinco libros de Ariadna, Los, 245
Cipreses creen en Dios, Los, 245
"Clarín" (Leopoldo Alas), 151, 154–55
Clásicos y modernos, 164
Claudel, 205
Colmena, La, 250
Comedia, 97, 98, 99, 112
  See also Theatre
Comedia nueva, La, 125–26
Comedieta de Ponza, 55
Commedia dell'arte, 183
Comedias bárbaras, Las, 223
Conceptismo, 87–88, 90, 112
Concierto de San Ovidio, El 227
Conde Lucanor, El, 49, 51, 240
Condenado por desconfiado, El, 105, 107
Confesiones de un pequeño filósofo, 164
Conjuración de Venecia, La, 136

Coplas del Provinciano, 60–61
Coplas de Mingo Revulgo, 61
Coplas por la muerte de su padre, 56–57
Corbacho (Reproval of Earthly Love), 61
Córdoba, 9–10, 11, 21–22, 23, 26, 28, 30
Corneille, Pierre, 118
Corpus Barga, 166
Costumbrismo, 131–34
    articles, 137
    in the novel, 149–52
Counter Reformation, 81, 93
Courtier, The, 75
Courtly love, 68–70, 71
Covadonga, 10
Creationism, 209
Crémer, Victoriano, 221
Crisis del humanismo, La, 180
Cristo de Velázquez, El, 177–178
Criticism
    Marqués de Santillana, 55, 66–67
    Quevedo, 85–86
    Quintana, 129
    Hartzenbusch, 137
    Valera, 150–51
    Palacio Valdés, 151
    "Clarín," 151, 154
    Pardo Bazán, 152–53
    Benavente, 180–81
    Salinas, 204
    Dámaso Alonso, 205–06
    Mendez Pelayo, 235
    Menéndez Pidal, 236
    Ortega y Gasset, 236–38
    Madariaga, 238
    Marañón, 238
    Castro, 239
    Casalduero, 239
    Valbuena Prat, 240
    Díaz Plaja, 240
    Marías, 240
    Barea, 246
    Pérez de Ayala, 241
    Cela, 250–251
    Goytísolo, 257
Criticón, El, 88–89
Crónica del alba, 245
Crónica general, 40, 41
Crónicas, 48
Cruz, Ramón de la, 126, 127, 146, 156
Cuaderna vía, 37, 42
Cuestión palpitante, La, 152
Culta latiniparla, La, 90
Culteranismo, 86, 89, 112
Curandero de su honra, El, 230

Dama del alba, La, 225
Dama duende, La, 111
Dante, 56, 148
Danza de la muerte, 58–60, 77
Darío, Rubén, 188–93, 195, 200, 204, 224, 241
Decameron, 49
Defensa de la Hispanidad, 180
Defoe, Daniel, 81
Deism, 120–21
Delibes, Miguel, 252

INDEX

Diablo mundo, El, 142–43
Día de difuntos de 1836, 133
Diálogo de la lengua, 77
Dialogue of Bias against Fortune, 55
"Dialogue of Mercury and Charon," 77
Diana, 78
Díaz Plaja, Guillermo, 240
Dickens, Charles, 150–60, 169
Diego, Gerardo, 209–10, 222
Divine Comedy, 56
Divino Orfeo, El, 109
Divinas palabras, 223
Doble historia del Dr. Valmy, La, 229
Doloras, 145
Doña Blanca de Navarra, 149
Donado hablador, El, 83
Don Alvaro, o la fuerza del sino, 134–35, 136
Doña Perfecta, 158, 163
Doña Urraca de Castilla, 149
Don Juan Tenorio, 138–40
Don Juan theme, 106–8, 138–40, 141, 154, 177, 180, 186, 203
Don Quijote de la Mancha, 64, 77–78, 98, 100–02, 112, 113, 162, 174, 180, 240
Dorotea, La, 105
Dove's Necklace, The, 28
Duelo en el paraiso, 256
Duque de Viseo, El, 129

Echegaray, José, 146–48, 182
Eclogue, 66, 74–75

Edipo, 136
Egloga de Antonio Bienvenida, 210
Either/Or, 173
Elena, 131
Encina, Juan del, 66, 77, 78
En Flandes se ha puesto el sol, 185
English (language) influence in Spanish literature, 20, 127
En la ardiente oscuridad, 227
Enlightenment (Neoclassicism), 87, 113, 114, 128, 148, 161, 180
Entremés. See Theater
Epic poetry, 24–25, 31–37, 38, 41–42, 50, 51, 52–53
Episodios nacionales, 157, 159, 240
"Epoch of the -isms" (Creationism, Expressionism, Futurism, Surrealism, Ultraism, Vanguardism), 208, 210, 211, 218, 220, 233, 240, 260
Erasmus, 76–77, 92
Eruditos a la violeta, Los, 119
Escenas matritenses, 132
Escuadra hacia la muerte, 230
España de Mio Cid, La, 236
Espejo de la muerte, El, 175
Esperpento, 167, 223–25, 234
Espinel, Vicente, 83
Espronceda, José de, 140–43, 145
Essay, 235–38, 260–61

Estebanillo González, Life of, 83
Estudiante de Salamanca, El, 141
Etymologies, 25
Euripides, 211
Existentialism, 206, 218, 230, 231, 236, 251, 258

Fable, 49, 123–24, 137
Fábulas morales, 124
Falla, Manuel de, 155
Familia de Pascual Duarte, La, 247–48, 251
Feijóo, Fray Benito Jerónimo, 121–23
Fielding, 81
Fiesta al noroeste, 253
Fiesta de toros en Madrid, 124
Fiestas, 256
Figuras de la pasión del Señor, Las, 244
Fileno, Zambardo y Cardonio, Egloga de, 66
Flor de mayo, 157
Forja de un rebelde, La, 246
Forza del destino, La, 136
Four Horsemen of the Apocalypse, 156
Fray Gerundio de Campazas, 117
French influence in Spanish literature, 20, 55, 67, 72, 77, 84, 124, 127, 187, 205, 212
Fronterizo ballads, 53

Fuente de la mora encantada, La, 129–30
Fuente Ovejuna, 103–4, 231
Furgón de cola, 257

Galatea, 78, 98, 99
Galdós, Benito Pérez, 157–60, 162–63, 169, 199, 240–41
Gallego (Galician Portuguese), 27, 39, 50–51
Gallo de Sócrates, El, 155
Ganivet, Angel, 165–66
Gaos, Vicente, 221
García Gutiérrez, Antonio, 136–37
García Lorca, Federico, 211–18, 222, 233, 260
Garcilaso de la Vega, 73–75, 78, 90, 94, 120, 187, 192, 218, 220
Garduña de Sevilla, La, 83
Gargantua and Pantagruel, 42
Gaviota, La, 150
Generaciones y semblanzas, 62
Generation of 1898, 132, 133, 162–87, 201–3, 236, 240–241, 259
Generation of 1927, 202, 207, 221, 246, 259
Generation of 1936, 218
Gil Blas de Santillana, 117
   Spanish version, 117
Gil y Carrasco, Enrique, 149
Gironella, José María, 246–47
Gloria, 158, 163
Goethe, 87, 129, 142
Golding, Lawrence, 256

INDEX

Goliardic tradition, 47
Gómez de la Serna, Ramón, 239
Góngora, Luis de (gongorismo), 89–90, 112, 187, 202, 205, 210, 211, 218, 260
González, Fray Diego, 118–19
Goytisolo, Juan, 255–57
Gracián, Baltasar, 87–88
Gramática castellana, 76
Gran Galeota, El, 148, 182
Gran teatro del mundo, El, 108
Grau, Jacinto, 186
Greguerías (Gómez de la Serna), 239
Guía espiritual, 96
Guillén, Jorge, 204–6, 210, 222
Gutiérrez Nájera, 187
Guzmán de Alfarache, 81–82, 83
Guzmán el Bueno, 124

Hacia otra España, 179
Hadrian, 16
Ha estellado la paz, 247
Hamlet, 110, 125
Harpías en Madrid, Las, 83
Hartzenbusch, Juan Eugenio, 137
Haz de leña, El, 148
Hercules Mad, 23
Hermana San Sulpicio, La, 151–52
Hermano Juan, El, 177
Hernández, Miguel, 218–20

Herrera, Fernando de, 90–91, 118
Hierro, José, 221
Hija de Celestina, La, 83–84
Hijas del Cid, Las, 185
Hijos de la ira, 206
Hijos muertos, Los, 253
Historia de una escalera, 226
History of Aestheic Ideas in Spain, 160
History of Spanish Heterodoxists, 160
Hombre imperfecto a su perfectísimo Autor, El, 120
Hombre y Dios, 206
Homer, 56
Horace, 121
Hormesinda, 124
Huerto de Melibea, El, 205
Huidobro, Vicente, 209
Humanism, 55, 62, 76–77, 180
Humoradas, 145

Iberian peoples, 1–2, 5–6, 13, 14
Ibn Hazm, 28
Idearium español, 165
Idilio de un enfermo, El, 151
Inquietudes de Shanti Andía, Las, 170
Intereses creados, Los, 183–84
Invertebrate Spain, 236
Iriarte, Tomás de, 123–24
Isla, La, 243
Isla, Padre José Francisco de, 117

Isla y los demonios, La, 252
Isla, La, 256
Italian influence in Spanish literature, 20, 55–56, 66–68, 71, 72, 73–77, 89, 91, 94, 102, 183, 192

Jarama, El, 255
Jarchya, 18–19, 27
Jiménez, Juan Ramón, 195–98, 200, 202, 203, 221
Journals and periodicals, 115–16, 119, 127, 151, 236–37, 245, 250
Jovellanos, Gaspar Melchor de, 119–20, 129
Joyce, James, 254
Juan de Mairena, 195
Juan Manuel, Don, 49–50, 51, 240
Juegos de manos, 256

Kierkegaard, Søren, 173
King Lear, 160

Laberinto de Fortuna (Las Trescientas), 56
Laberinto del mundo, El, 109
La Fontaine, 123
Laforet, Carmen, 251–52
Larra, Mariano José de, 132–34
Latin literature, 22–24, 55, 66, 71, 89
Lazarillo de Tormes, 79–80, 81, 82, 83, 84, 113, 240
Lecciones de literatura, 153

Leconte de Lisle, 187
Lecturas españolas, 164
Lengua poética de Góngora, La, 205
León, Fray Luis de, 90, 91–92, 118, 120
Lera, Angel María, de, 259
Lesage, Alain René, 117
L'Etranger, 248
Leyendas
  of Zorrilla, 138
  of Bécquer, 144
Libro de Buen Amor (Book of Good Love), 27, 42–48, 51, 58, 61, 66, 71, 73, 80, 113, 139
Libro de su vida, El, 93
Life of Don Quijote and Sancho, 194–95
Literatura en 1881, La, 151
Literatura francesa moderna, La, 153
Llama de amor viva, 94
Lope de Vega, Félix, 67, 78, 97, 99, 102–5, 112, 113, 137, 186, 232
López de Ayala, Adelardo, 146, 147
López de Ayala, Pero, 48–49, 51, 52
Lord of the Flies, 256
Lucan, Marcus Anneus, 22–23, 30, 56
Luces de Bohemia, 224
Lucha por la vida, La, 170
Lucrecia, 124
Luther, Martin, 92
Luzán, Ignacio, 118, 123

INDEX

Lyric poetry, 38–40, 43, 46, 49, 53, 55, 73–75, 78, 86, 91, 112, 119, 120–21, 124, 202–21
Arabic, 26–28

Machado, Antonio, 186, 193–95, 197, 200
Machado, Manuel, 195
Madariaga, Salvador de, 238, 260
Madre naturaleza, La, 153, 167
Maeztu, Ramiro de, 166, 179–80, 199
Magic Mountain, The, 248
Maimonides, 29, 30
Majos de Cádiz, Los, 151
Malquerida, La, 183
Mann, Thomas, 248
Manrique, Jorge, 56–58, 204
Marañón, Gregorio, 238
Marcela, o ¿cuál de los tres?, 130
Marcos de Obregón, 83
Marianela, 158
Marías, Julian, 240
Marquina, Eduardo, 185
Marta y María, 151
Martí José, 187
Martial, Marcus Valerius, 24, 30
Martín, Recuerda, José, 234
Martín-Santos, Luis, 258
Martínez Ballesteros, 234
Martínez de la Rosa, Francisco, 136
Martínez de Toledo, Alfonso (Archpriest of Talavera), 61
Martínez Ruiz, José ("Azorín"), 164–65, 166, 168, 169, 179, 180, 184, 199
Martínez Sierra, Gregorio, 185
Marxism, 203, 230
Máscaras, Las, 241
Materia, 207–8
Matute, Ana Maria, 253–54
Maugham, W. Somerset, 248
Maximinia, 151
Medea, 23
Médico de su honra, El, 111, 230
Meléndez Valdés, Juan, 120–21, 129
Memorias para la historia de la poesía . . . , 122–23
Mena, Juan de, 56, 71, 72, 73, 89
Menéndez Pidal, Ramón, 236, 260
Menéndez y Pelayo, Marcelino, 160–61, 235
Meninas, Las, 227
Mercederes, Los, 254
Mesonero y Romanos, Ramón de, 132
Mester de clerecía, 37–39, 41–42, 48, 50, 51, 52–53, 72, 138
Mezclilla, 154
Miau, 163
Milagros de nuestra señora, 37–39, 40
Miró, Gabriel, 243

Misericordia, 158–59, 163
Mocedades de Rodrigo, 41
Modernismo, 187–200, 202, 212, 240, 259
Modern Theme, 236
Molière, 108, 125
Molinos, Miguel de, 96
Montalvo, Garci Ordóñez de, 63
Montemayor, Jorge de, 78
Morah Nebukin, 29
Moraima, 136
Moratín, Leandro Fernández de, 124–27, 130, 131, 146, 148, 181
Moratín, Nicolás Fernández de, 125
Mordaza, La, 231
Moro expósito, El, 134
Mozárabes, 18
Mr. Witt en el Cantón, 244
¡Muera Don Quijote!, 174
Muérete y verás, 130–31
Mujer nueva, La, 252
Muñoz, Carlos, 234
Muratori, Ludovico, 118
Muwashshah, 26–27
Mysticism, 92–97

Nada, 251–52
National Library, 115, 160
Naturalism, 83–84, 152–54, 157, 159
Navarro Villoslada, Francisco, 149
Nebrija, Antonio, 76
Nero, 22–23
Neruda, Carlos, 234
Nido ajeno, El, 182, 183

Niebla, 175
Nietzsche, Friedrich Wilhelm, 87, 170, 179
Nivola, 178, 240
Nobel prize
 Echegaray, 147
 Benavente, 184
 Jiménez, 195
 Aleixandre, 207
Noche oscura del alma, 94
Noches lugubres, 119
Nora, Eugenio de, 221
Novel, 43, 51, 67, 100–2, 112, 161
 contemporary, 240–59
 of chivalry, 62–64, 69, 72, 78, 79, 112
 sentimental, 68–69, 71
 Byzantine, 69
 pastoral, 78–79, 102, 112
 picaresque, 79–85, 99, 102, 112, 116–17, 148, 159, 170
 romantic, 148–49
 regional, 149–52, 157–58
 naturalistic, 152–61
Novelas contemporáneas, 159
Novelas ejemplares, 99, 175
Nuestro padre San Daniel, 244
Nuevas andanzas . . . de Lazarillo de Tormes, 248–49
Núñez de Arce, Gaspar, 148

Obispo leproso, El, 244
Obras espirituales, 94
Ocho comedias y ocho entremeses, 97, 99

INDEX

Odyssey, 241
Olmo, Lauro, 234
Oráculo manual, El, 88
Origen del pensamiento, El, 151
Origins of the Novel, 160
Ortega y Gasset, José, 235–37, 243, 249, 260
Ortero, Blas de, 221
Otro, El, 177
Ovid, 46, 71

Pabellón de reposo, 248
Paisaje de España visto por los españoles, El, 164
Palacio Valdés, Armando, 151–52
Palique, 154
Panchatantra, 41
Panero, Luis, 218
Papeles de son Armadáns, 250
Pardo Bazán, Countess Emilia, 152–54, 167, 183, 240–41
Parnassianism, 187
Pasión de la tierra, 206
Paso, Alfonso, 232
Pata de la raposa, La, 242
Pazos de Ulloa, Los, 153–54, 167
Pelayo, 129
Peñas arriba, 156
Pepita Jiménez, 150–51
Pequeño teatro, 253
Pereda, José María, 156
Pérez de Ayala, Ramón, 241–43
Pérez de Guzmán, Fernán, 62

Pérez Galdós, Benito, 157–60, 162–63, 169, 199
Persiles y Sigismunda, 99
Petrarch, 48, 55, 72
Phaedra, 23
Pharsalia, 22, 23
Pícara Justina, La, 83
Picaresque novel, 43, 79–85
Pipá, 155
Pirandello, Luigi, 175
Platero y yo, 197
Plato, 110
Plautus, 71, 105
Plutarch, 62
Poe, Edgar Allen, 248
Poema de Fernán González, 37
Poema del cante jondo, 212
Poema (or Cantar) de mío Cid, 17, 21, 32–36, 37, 48, 50, 57, 113, 205, 236
Poeta en Nueva York, 214
Poética
 of Luzán, 118, 123
 of Campoamor, 145–46
Polifemo, 89
Por tierras de Portugal y España, 175–76
Prímera memoria, 253, 256
Príncipe que todo lo aprendió en los libros, El, 184
Prohibido suicidarse en primavera, 225
Prometeo, 241
Propalladia, 66–67
Prosas profanas, 188
Proverbios del sabio Salomón, 41
Punic Wars, 4–5, 30

Quevedo, Francisco de, 84–87, 90, 92, 114, 133
Quietism, 96
Quintana, Manuel José, 129–30
Quintillian, Marcus Fabius, 23–24, 30
Quiroga, Elena, 253

Rabelais, 42
Raíz rota, La, 246
Rayo que no cesa, El, 219–20,
Razón de Amor, 204
Reality and the Poet in Spanish Poetry, 204
Regenta, La, 154–55
Reivindicación del conde don Julián, 257
Renaissance, 20, 24, 48, 55, 61, 67–68, 72, 73–75, 82, 89, 91, 92, 104–5, 114, 120, 187
Requiem por un campesino español, 245
Revista de Occidente, 237
Revolt of the Masses, The, 236
Revolución y la novela en Rusia, La, 153
Rimado de Palacio, 48, 51
Rimas, 144–45
Rinconete y Cortadillo, 99–100
Rivas, Duke of (Don Angel de Saavedra), 132, 134–36, 145
Riverita, 151
Rodríguez, Claudio, 221
Rodrigo, *romance de Don*, 54–55
Rojas, Fernando de, 70, 71–72, 83, 205
Roland (*Song of*), 32, 35
Romance languages, 15–17, 18–19, 21
  Latin, 15–16, 18
  Vulgar Latin, 15–17

Salas Barbadillo, Geronimo de, 83
San Pedro, Diego de, 68
Santiago de Compostela, 6
Santillana, Marqués de, 55–56, 66, 71, 72, 73, 89, 187
Sarmiento, Fray Martin, 122–23
Sartre, Jean-Paul, 231, 251
Sastre Alfonso, 230–32
Satire, 42–45, 49, 58–61, 67, 72, 80, 84, 90, 120, 125–26, 131–34
School of Salamanca, 91, 118–21
School of Seville, 90–91, 118, 121
Schopenhauer, 87
Scott, Sir Walter, 129, 134, 149
Semblanzas literarias, 151
Señas de identidad, 257
Sendebar, 49
Sender, Ramón, 244–46
Seneca, Lucius Annaeus, 22–23, 30, 71, 85, 88, 169
Señor de Bembibre, El, 149
Señorita malcriada, La, 123

INDEX

Señorito mimado, El, 123-24
Shakespeare, William, 50, 81, 108, 146, 160
Shelley, 129, 224-25
Sí de las niñas, El, 125
Siete domingos rojos, 245
Siete partidas, 40
Silva, José Asunción, 187
Simón Bocanegra, 137
Sirena varada, La, 225
Sobre los ángeles, 211-12
Soldados lloran de noche, Los, 254
Soledades, 89, 90, 205
Solos de "Clarín," 154
Sombra del ciprés es alargada, La, 252-53
Sombrero del señor cura, El, 155
Sombrero de tres picos, El, 155-56
Sonatas: Estío, Otoño, 167
Soneto a Cristo crucificado, 96-97
Song of Solomon, 94
Sonnets in the Italian Style, 55
Sophocles, 110, 211
Sorpresa, 213
Sotileza, 156
Spain
    Phoenician contact, 1, 3, 5, 13, 15, 30
    Greek contact, 1, 3-4, 13, 15, 30
    geography and pre-history, 1-5, 13
    Iberian settlement, 2, 5, 13
    Celtic migrations into, 2, 5, 14-15
    Roman Spain, 4-6, 15, 21-24, 30
    Christianity in, 6, 8
    Gothic and Visigothic, 6-8, 17, 21, 24-26, 30, 31, 92
    Byzantine, 7, 25
    reconquest, 9-13, 20, 92
    Mohammedan and Moorish, 26-29, 30, 32
    Hebraic culture, 29, 30
Spain: A Modern History, 238
Spanish Science, 160
Stuñiga, Lope de, 55, 72
Subida al Monte Carmelo, 94
Sueños, Los, 85, 133
Sueños hay que verdades son, 108
Surrealism, 203, 206, 207, 209, 211, 212, 218, 220, 240
Symbolism, 187

Taifas, 11-12
Tamayo y Baus, Manuel, 146, 147
Taming of the Shrew, The, 50
Tanto por ciento, El, 146
Teatro crítico universal, 121-22
Tell-Tale Heart, The, 248
Terence, 71, 105
Teresa de Manzanares, 83
Tertullian, 6
Theater
    liturgical drama, 64

early Spanish, 65–67, 78
Golden Age, 97, 98, 99–
  100, 102–12
Enlightenment, 120, 124–
  29, 135–36
pre-romantic, 130–31
romantic, 134–40
entremeses, 97–99
sainete, 126–27, 131, 156,
  185
twentieth century, 222–34
zarzuela, 126
costumbrista, 185–86
*Thousand and One Nights,
  The*, 110
Three Exemplary Novels, 176
Tiempo di Silencio, 258
Tierra roja, 231
Tigre Juan, 242
Tinieblas en las cumbres, 242
Tirso de Molina (Fray Gabriel Téllez), 67, 105–8, 112, 137, 138
Tolstoy, 169
To Roosevelt, 191
Torquemada series (of Galdós), 158
Torre, Guillermo de, 209
Torres Naharro, Bartolomé, 66–67, 77
Torres Villaroel, Diego, 116
Tragicomedia de Calisto y Melibea, 69–72, 73, 113
Tragic Sense of Life in Men and Nations, The, 173–74
Tragaluz, El, 228–29
Trampa, La, 254
Tremendismo, 247–48, 249, 251, 256, 257, 261

Trovador, El, 136

Unamuno, Miguel de, 166, 171–79, 184, 194–95, 199, 237–38, 240, 246
Un drama nuevo, 146, 182
Un hombre, 246
Un millón de muertos, 247
Ultimas banderas, Las, 259

VABUMB, 166, 180, 190
Valbuena Prat, Angel, 240
Valdés, Alfonso de, 77
Valdés, Juan de, 62, 77
Valera, Juan, 150, 188
Valéry, 205
Valle-Inclán, Ramón del, 166–68, 169, 179, 183, 186–87, 199, 222-24, 233, 234, 240
Vandals, 7
Verdi, Giuseppe, 136, 137
Verdugo, El, 141
Verlaine, 169, 187
Viaje a la Alcarria, 250
Vida de don Diego de Torres Villaroel, 116
Vida de San Ildefonso, 41
Vida es sueño, La, 109–11
Viento del norte, 254
Villon, François, 56
Virgil, 56, 66, 71
Visigoths, 7–8, 11, 17–18, 21, 24–26, 30, 31, 37
Vivanco, Luis Felipe, 218
Voltaire, 114
Voluntad, La, 164
Volverás a Región, 257–58
Voz de Madrid, La, 224

Yerma, 214, 216

Zalacaín el aventurero, 170
Zapatera prodigiosa, La, 217
Zéjel, 26–28
Zola, 83, 152, 157
Zorrilla, José, 108, 137–40